C Student Solutions Manual
to Accompany
C How To Program, Fourth Edition

Deitel® Books, Cyber Classrooms, Complete Tra
published by

HOW TO PROGRAM Series
Advanced Java™ 2 Platform How to Program
C How to Program, 4/E
C++ How to Program, 4/E
C#® How to Program
e-Business and e-Commerce How to Program
Internet and World Wide Web How to Program, 2/E
Java™ How to Program, 5/E
Perl How to Program
Python How to Program
Visual Basic® 6 How to Program
Visual Basic® .NET How to Program, 2/E
Visual C++® .NET How to Program
Wireless Internet & Mobile Business How to Program
XML How to Program

.NET How to Program Series
C# How to Program
Visual Basic® .NET How to Program, 2/E
Visual C++® .NET How to Program

Visual Studio® Series
C# How to Program
Getting Started with Microsoft® Visual C++®
*   6 with an Introduction to MFC*
Simply C#: An Application-Driven Tutorial
*   Approach*
Simply Visual Basic® .NET: An Application-
*   Driven Tutorial Approach*
*   (Visual Studio .NET 2002 Edition)*
Simply Visual Basic® .NET: An Application-
*   Driven Tutorial Approach*
*   (Visual Studio .NET 2003 Edition)*
Visual Basic® 6 How to Program
Visual Basic® .NET How to Program, 2/E
Visual C++® .NET How to Program

CS1 Programming Series
Java™ Software Design

Simply Series
Simply C#: An Application-Driven Tutorial
*   Approach*
Simply Java™ Programming: An Application-
*   Driven Tutorial Approach*
Simply Visual Basic® .NET: An Application
*   Driven Tutorial Approach*
*   (Visual Studio .NET 2002 Edition)*
Simply Visual Basic® .NET: An Application
*   Driven Tutorial Approach*
*   (Visual Studio .NET 2003 Edition)*

DEITEL® Developer Series
Java™ Web Services for Experienced
*   Programmers*
Web Services A Technical Introduction

Computer Science Series
Operating Systems, 3/E

For Managers Series
e-Business and e-Commerce for Managers

ining Courses and Web-Based Training Courses
Prentice Hall

The Complete Training Course Series

The Complete C++
Training Course, 4/E
The Complete C#
Training Course
The Complete e-Business and
e-Commerce Programming
Training Course
The Complete Internet and
World Wide Web Programming Training
Course, 2/E
The Complete Java™ 2
Training Course, 5/E
The Complete Perl
Training Course
The Complete Python
Training Course
The Complete Visual Basic® 6
Training Course
The Complete Visual Basic® .NET
Training Course, 2/E
The Complete Wireless Internet &
Mobile Business Programming Training
Course
The Complete XML Programming
Training Course

Interactive *Multimedia Cyber Classroom* Series

C++ Multimedia Cyber Classroom, 4/E
C# Multimedia Cyber Classroom
e-Business and e-Commerce Multimedia
Cyber Classroom
Internet and World Wide Web Multimedia
Cyber Classroom, 2/E
Java™ 2 Multimedia Cyber Classroom, 5/E
Perl Multimedia Cyber Classroom
Python Multimedia Cyber Classroom
Visual Basic® 6 Multimedia Cyber Classroom
Visual Basic® .NET Multimedia Cyber
Classroom, 2/E
Wireless Internet & Mobile Business
Programming Multimedia Cyber
Classroom
XML Multimedia Cyber Classroom

Interactive *Web-Based Training* Series

Premium CourseCompass Version of Visual
Basic® .NET Multimedia Cyber
Classroom, 2/E
Premium CourseCompass Version of Java 2
Multimedia Cyber Classroom, 5/E
Premium CourseCompass Version of C++
Multimedia Cyber Classroom, 4/E

To follow the Deitel publishing program, please register at:

www.deitel.com/newsletter/subscribe.html

for the *DEITEL® BUZZ ONLINE* e-mail newsletter.

To communicate with the authors, send e-mail to:

deitel@deitel.com

For information on corporate on-site seminars offered by Deitel & Associates, Inc. worldwide, visit:

www.deitel.com

For continuing updates on Prentice Hall and Deitel publications visit:

www.deitel.com,
www.prenhall.com/deitel or
www.InformIT.com/deitel

C Student Solutions Manual

to Accompany

C How To Program, Fourth Edition

H. M. Deitel
Deitel & Associates, Inc.

P. J. Deitel
Deitel & Associates, Inc.

PEARSON EDUCATION, INC., Upper Saddle River, New Jersey 07458

Library of Congress Cataloging-in-Publication Data

On file

Vice President and Editorial Director, ECS: *Marcia J. Horton*
Senior Acquisitions Editor: *Kate Hargett*
Assistant Editor: *Sarah Parker*
Editorial Assistant: *Michael Giacobbe*
Associate Editor: *Carole Snyder*
Vice President and Director of Production and Manufacturing, ESM: *David W. Riccardi*
Executive Managing Editor: *Vince O'Brien*
Managing Editor: *Tom Manshreck*
Production Editor: *John F. Lovell*
Production Editor, Media: *Bob Engelhardt*
Director of Creative Services: *Paul Belfanti*
Creative Director: *Carole Anson*
Cover Designer: *Geoffrey Cassar*
Manufacturing Manager: *Trudy Pisciotti*
Manufacturing Buyer: *Ilene Kahn*
Marketing Manager: *Pamela Shaffer*
Marketing Assistant: *Barrie Reinhold*

10 9 8 7 6 5 4 3 2 1

ISBN 0-13-145245-2

Pearson Education Ltd., *London*
Pearson Education Australia Pty. Ltd., *Sydney*
Pearson Education Singapore, Pte. Ltd.
Pearson Education North Asia Ltd., *Hong Kong*
Pearson Education Canada, Inc., *Toronto*
Pearson Educacion de Mexico, S.A. de C.V.
Pearson Education–Japan, *Tokyo*
Pearson Education Malaysia, Pte. Ltd.
Pearson Education, Inc., *Upper Saddle River, New Jersey*

Trademarks

Contents

1   Introduction to Computers, the Internet and the
World Wide Web   1

2   Introduction to C Programming   3

3   Structured Program Development in C   11

4   C Program Control   30

5   C Functions   50

6   C Arrays   73

7   C Pointers   97

8   C Characters and Strings   118

9   C Formatted Input/Output   140

10   C Structures, Unions, Bit Manipulations and
Enumerations   146

11   C File Processing   154

12   C Data Structures   159

13 The Preprocessor   180

14 Other C Topics   184

15 C++ as a "Better C"   187

16 C++ Classes and Data Abstraction   190

17 C++ Classes: Part II   204

18 C++ Operator Overloading   213

19 C++ Inheritance   220

20 C++ Virtual Functions and Polymorphism   229

21 C++ Stream Input/Output   231

22 C++ Templates   239

23 C++ Exception Handling   244

24 Introduction to Java Applications and Applets   246

25 Beyond C and C++: Operators, Methods
and Arrays in Java   249

26 Java Object-Based Programming   262

27 Java Object-Oriented Programming   281

28 Java Graphics and Java 2D   290

29 Java Graphical User Interface Components   296

30 Java Multimedia: Images, Animation and Audio   311

1

Introduction to Computers, the Internet and the World Wide Web

Solutions to Selected Exercises

1.3 Categorize each of the following items as either hardware or software:
  a) CPU

  ANS: *hardware.*

  b) C compiler

  ANS: *software.*

  c) ALU

  ANS: *hardware.*

  d) C preprocessor

  ANS: *software.*

  e) input unit

  ANS: *hardware.*

  f) a word processor program

  ANS: *software.*

1.4 Why might you want to write a program in a machine-independent language instead of a machine-dependent language? Why might a machine-dependent language be more appropriate for writing certain types of programs?

  ANS: *Machine-independent languages are useful for writing programs to be executed on multiple computer platforms. Machine-dependent languages are appropriate for writing programs to be executed on a single platform. Machine-dependent languages tend to exploit the efficiencies of a particular machine.*

1.8 Discuss the meaning of each of the following names:
  a) `stdin`

  ANS: *This refers to the standard input device. The standard input device is normally connected to the keyboard*

  b) `stdout`

ANS: *This refers to the standard output device. The standard output device is normally connected to the computer screen.*

c) `stderr`

ANS: *This refers to the standard error device. Error messages are normally sent to this device which is typically connected to the computer screen.*

Introduction to
C Programming

Solutions to Selected Exercises

2.9 Write a single C statement or line that accomplishes each of the following:
  a) Print the message "Enter two numbers."
  ANS: `printf( "Enter two numbers\n" );`

  b) Assign the product of variables b and c to variable a.
  ANS: `a = b * c;`

  c) State that a program performs a sample payroll calculation (i.e., use text that helps to document a program).
  ANS: `/* Sample payroll calculation program */`

  d) Input three integer values from the keyboard and place these values in integer variables a, b and c.
  ANS: `scanf( "%d%d%d", &a, &b, &c );`

2.12 What, if anything, prints when each of the following C statements is performed? If nothing prints, then answer "nothing." Assume x = 2 and y = 3.
  a) `printf( "%d", x );`
  ANS: 2

  b) `printf( "%d", x + x );`
  ANS: 4

  c) `printf( "x=" );`
  ANS: x=

  d) `printf( "x=%d", x );`
  ANS: x=2

  e) `printf( "%d = %d", x + y, y + x );`
  ANS: 5 = 5

  f) `z = x + y;`

ANS: *Nothing. Value of* x + y *is assigned to* z.

g) scanf("%d%d", &x, &y);

ANS: *Nothing. Two integer values are read into the location of* x *and the location of* y.

h) /* printf("x + y = %d", x + y); */

ANS: *Nothing. This is a comment.*

i) printf("\n");

ANS: *A newline character is printed, and the cursor is positioned at the beginning of the next line on the screen.*

2.14   Given the equation $y = ax^3 + 7$, which of the following, if any, are correct C statements for this equation?

```
a) y = a * x * x * x + 7;
b) y = a * x * x * ( x + 7 );
c) y = ( a * x ) * x * ( x + 7 );
d) y = ( a * x ) * x * x + 7;
e) y = a * ( x * x * x ) + 7;
f) y = a * x * ( x * x + 7 );
```

ANS: *(a), (d), and (e).*

2.17   Write a program that prints the numbers 1 to 4 on the same line. Write the program using the following methods.

a) Using one printf statement with no conversion specifiers.
b) Using one printf statement with four conversion specifiers.
c) Using four printf statements.

ANS:

```
1   /* Exercise 2.17 Solution */
2   #include <stdio.h>
3
4   int main()
5   {
6      printf( "1 2 3 4\n\n" ); /* part a */
7
8      printf( "%d %d %d %d\n\n", 1, 2, 3, 4 ); /* part b */
9
10     printf( "1 " ); /* part c */
11     printf( "2 " );
12     printf( "3 " );
13     printf( "4\n" );
14
15     return 0; /* indicates successful termination */
16
17  } /* end main */
```

Fig. S2.1   Solution to Exercise 2.17. (Part 1 of 2.)

```
1 2 3 4

1 2 3 4

1 2 3 4
```

Fig. S2.1   Solution to Exercise 2.17. (Part 2 of 2.)

2.18   Write a program that asks the user to enter two integers, obtains the numbers from the user, then prints the larger number followed by the words "is larger." If the numbers are equal, print the message "These numbers are equal." Use only the single-selection form of the if statement you learned in this chapter.

    ANS:

```
 1   /* Exercise 2.18 Solution */
 2   #include <stdio.h>
 3
 4   int main()
 5   {
 6      int x; /* define first number */
 7      int y; /* define second number */
 8
 9      printf( "Enter two numbers: " ); /* prompt */
10      scanf( "%d%d", &x, &y );          /* read two integers */
11
12      /* compare the two numbers */
13      if ( x > y ) {
14         printf( "%d is larger\n", x );
15      } /* end if */
16
17      if ( x < y ) {
18         printf( "%d is larger\n", y );
19      } /* end if */
20
21      if ( x == y ) {
22         printf( "These numbers are equal\n" );
23      } /* end if */
24
25      return 0; /* indicate successful termination */
26
27   } /* end main */
```

```
Enter two numbers: 5 20
20 is larger
```

Fig. S2.2   Solution to Exercise 2.18.

```
Enter two numbers: 239 92
239 is larger
```

```
Enter two numbers: 17 17
These numbers are equal
```

2.23   Write a program that reads in five integers and then determines and prints the largest and the smallest integers in the group. Use only the programming techniques you have learned in this chapter.

ANS:

```
1   /* Exercise 2.23 Solution */
2   #include <stdio.h>
3
4   int main()
5   {
6      int largest;   /* largest integer */
7      int smallest;  /* smallest integer */
8      int int1;       /* define int1 for user input */
9      int int2;       /* define int2 for user input */
10     int int3;       /* define int3 for user input */
11     int temp;       /* temporary integer for swapping */
12
13     printf( "Input 5 integers: " ); /* prompt user and read 5 ints */
14     scanf( "%d%d%d%d%d", &largest, &smallest, &int1, &int2, &int3 );
15
16     if ( smallest > largest ) { /* make comparisons */
17        temp = largest;
18        largest = smallest;
19        smallest = temp;
20     } /* end if */
21
22     if ( int1 > largest ) {
23        largest = int1;
24     } /* end if */
25
26     if ( int1 < smallest ) {
27        smallest = int1;
28     } /* end if */
29
30     if ( int2 > largest ) {
31        largest = int2;
32     } /* end if */
33
```

Fig. S2.3   Solution to Exercise 2.23. (Part 1 of 2.)

```
34        if ( int2 < smallest ) {
35           smallest = int2;
36        } /* end if */
37
38        if ( int3 > largest ) {
39           largest = int3;
40        } /* end if */
41
42        if ( int3 < smallest ) {
43           smallest = int3;
44        } /* end if */
45
46        printf( "The largest value is %d\n", largest );
47        printf( "The smallest value is %d\n", smallest );
48
49        return 0; /* indicate successful termination */
50
51   } /* end main */
```

```
Input 5 integers: 9 4 5 8 7
The largest value is 9
The smallest value is 4
```

Fig. S2.3   Solution to Exercise 2.23. (Part 2 of 2.)

2.24   Write a program that reads an integer and determines and prints whether it is odd or even. [*Hint*: Use the remainder operator. An even number is a multiple of two. Any multiple of two leaves a remainder of zero when divided by 2.]

    ANS:

```
1    /* Exercise 2.24 Solution */
2    #include <stdio.h>
3
4    int main()
5    {
6       int integer; /* integer input by user */
7
8       printf( "Input an integer: " ); /* prompt */
9       scanf( "%d", &integer );          /* read integer */
10
11      /* test if integer is even */
12      if ( integer % 2 == 0 ) {
13         printf( "%d is an even integer\n", integer );
14      } /* end if */
15
16      /* test if integer is odd */
17      if ( integer % 2 != 0 ) {
18         printf( "%d is an odd integer\n", integer );
```

Fig. S2.4   Solution to Exercise 2.24.   (Part 1 of 2.)

```
19        } /* end if */
20
21        return 0; /* indicate successful termination */
22
23   } /* end main */
```

```
Input an integer: 78
78 is an even integer
```

Fig. S2.4   Solution to Exercise 2.24.   (Part 2 of 2.)

```
Input an integer: 79
79 is an odd integer
```

2.28   Distinguish between the terms fatal error and non-fatal error. Why might you prefer to experience a fatal error rather than a non-fatal error?

> **ANS:** *A fatal error causes the program to terminate prematurely. A nonfatal error occurs when the logic of the program is incorrect, and the program does not work properly. A fatal error is preferred for debugging purposes. A fatal error immediately lets you know there is a problem with the program, whereas a nonfatal error can be subtle and possibly go undetected.*

2.31   Using only the techniques you learned in this chapter, write a program that calculates the squares and cubes of the numbers from 0 to 10 and uses tabs to print the following table of values:

number	square	cube
0	0	0
1	1	1
2	4	8
3	9	27
4	16	64
5	25	125
6	36	216
7	49	343
8	64	512
9	81	729
10	100	1000

ANS:

```
1    /* Exercise 2.31 Solution */
2    #include <stdio.h>
3
4    int main()
5    {
6       int count = 0; /* initialize count to zero */
7
8       /* calculate the square and cube for the numbers 0 to 10 */
9       printf( "\nnumber\tsquare\tcube\n" );
10      printf( "%d\t%d\t%d\n", count, count * count,
11         count * count * count );
12
13      count = count + 1; /* increment count by 1 */
14      printf( "%d\t%d\t%d\n", count, count * count,
15         count * count * count );
16
17      count = count + 1;
18      printf( "%d\t%d\t%d\n", count, count * count,
19         count * count * count );
20
21      count = count + 1;
22      printf( "%d\t%d\t%d\n", count, count * count,
23         count * count * count );
24
25      count = count + 1;
26      printf( "%d\t%d\t%d\n", count, count * count,
27         count * count * count );
28
29      count = count + 1;
30      printf( "%d\t%d\t%d\n", count, count * count,
31         count * count * count );
32
33      count = count + 1;
34      printf( "%d\t%d\t%d\n", count, count * count,
35         count * count * count );
36
37      count = count + 1;
38      printf( "%d\t%d\t%d\n", count, count * count,
39         count * count * count );
40
41      count = count + 1;
42      printf( "%d\t%d\t%d\n", count, count * count,
43         count * count * count );
44
45      count = count + 1;
46      printf( "%d\t%d\t%d\n", count, count * count,
47         count * count * count );
48
49      count = count + 1;
```

Fig. S2.5   Solution to Exercise 2.31.   (Part 1 of 2.)

```
50       printf( "%d\t%d\t%d\n", count, count * count,
51          count * count * count );
52
53       return 0; /* indicate successful termination */
54
55    } /* end main */
```

Fig. S2.5   Solution to Exercise 2.31.   (Part 2 of 2.)

Structured Program Development in C

Solutions to Selected Exercises

3.11 Identify and correct the errors in each of the following [*Note*: There may be more than one error in each piece of code]:

```
a) if ( age >= 65 );
      printf( "Age is greater than or equal to 65\n" );
   else
      printf( "Age is less than 65\n" );
```
ANS:
```
if ( age >= 65 ) /* ; removed */
   printf( "Age is greater than or equal to 65\n" );
else
   printf( "Age is less than 65\n" );
```

```
b) int x = 1, total;

   while ( x <= 10 ) {
      total += x;
      ++x;
   }
```
ANS:
```
int x = 1, total = 0;
while ( x <= 10 ) {
   total += x;
   ++x;
}
```

```
c) While ( x <= 100 )
      total += x;
      ++x;
```
ANS:
```
while ( x <= 100 ) {
   total += x;
   ++x;
}
```

```
d) while ( y > 0 ) {
       printf( "%d\n", y );
       ++y;
   }
```
ANS:
```
while ( y > 0 ) {
   printf( "%d\n", y );
   --y;
}
```

3.13   What does the following program print?

```
1   #include <stdio.h>
2
3   int main()
4   {
5      int x = 1, total = 0, y;
6
7      while ( x <= 10 ) {
8         y = x * x;
9         printf( "%d\n", y );
10        total += y;
11        ++x;
12     }
13
14     printf("Total is %d\n", total);
15
16     return 0;
17  }
```

Fig. S3.1   Exercise 3.13: What does this program print?

ANS:

```
1
4
9
16
25
36
49
64
81
100
Total is 385
```

Fig. S3.2   Solution for Exercise 3.13.

3.14   Write a single pseudocode statement that indicates each of the following:
a) Display the message "Enter two numbers".
ANS: *print "enter two numbers"*

b) Assign the sum of variables x, y, and z to variable p.
ANS: $p = x + y + z$

c) The following condition is to be tested in an if...else selection statement: The current value of variable m is greater than twice the current value of variable v.

ANS: *if m is greater than twice v*
      do this ...
   else
      do this ...

d) Obtain values for variables s, r, and t from the keyboard.

ANS: *input s, input r, input t*

3.16 State which of the following are *true* and which are *false*. If a statement is *false*, explain why.

a) Experience has shown that the most difficult part of solving a problem on a computer is producing a working C program.

ANS: *False. The algorithm is the hardest part of solving a problem.*

b) A sentinel value must be a value that cannot be confused with a legitimate data value.

ANS: *True.*

c) Flowlines indicate the actions to be performed.

ANS: *False. Flowlines indicate the order in which steps are performed.*

d) Conditions written inside decision symbols always contain arithmetic operators (i.e., +, -, *, /, and %).

ANS: *False. They normally contain conditional operators.*

e) In top-down, stepwise refinement, each refinement is a complete representation of the algorithm.

ANS: *True.*

3.17 Drivers are concerned with the mileage obtained by their automobiles. One driver has kept track of several tankfuls of gasoline by recording miles driven and gallons used for each tankful. Develop a program that will input the miles driven and gallons used for each tankful. The program should calculate and display the miles per gallon obtained for each tankful. After processing all input information, the program should calculate and print the combined miles per gallon obtained for all tankfuls. Here is a sample input/output dialog:

```
Enter the gallons used (-1 to end): 12.8
Enter the miles driven: 287
The miles / gallon for this tank was 22.421875

Enter the gallons used (-1 to end): 10.3
Enter the miles driven: 200
The miles / gallon for this tank was 19.417475

Enter the gallons used (-1 to end): 5
Enter the miles driven: 120
The miles / gallon for this tank was 24.000000

Enter the gallons used (-1 to end): -1

The overall average miles/gallon was 21.601423
```

ANS:

2)   *Top:*
      Determine the average miles/gallon for each tank of gas, and the overall miles/gallon for
      an arbitrary number of tanks of gas

      First refinement:
      Initialize variables

      Input the gallons used and the miles driven, and calculate and print the miles/gallon for
      each tank of gas. Keep track of the total miles and the total gallons.

      Calculate and print the overall average miles/gallon.

      Second refinement*:*
      Initialize totalGallons to zero.
      Initialize totalMiles to zero.

      Input the gallons used for the first tank.
      While the sentinel value (-1) has not been entered for the gallons
          Add gallons to the running total in totalGallons
          Input the miles driven for the current tank
          Add miles to the running total in totalMiles
          Calculate and print the miles/gallon
          Input the gallons used for the next tank

3)   *Set totalAverage to totalMiles divided by totalGallons.*
      print the average miles/gallon

```
1   /* Exercise 3.17 Solution */
2   #include <stdio.h>
3
4   int main()
5   {
6       double gallons;            /* gallons used for current tank*/
7       double miles;              /* miles driven for current tank*/
8       double totalGallons = 0.0; /* total gallons used */
9       double totalMiles = 0.0;   /* total miles driven */
10      double totalAverage;       /* average miles/gallon */
11
12      /* get gallons used for first tank */
13      printf( "Enter the gallons used ( -1 to end): " );
14      scanf( "%lf", &gallons );
15
16      /* loop until sentinel value read from user */
17      while ( gallons != -1.0 ) {
18          totalGallons += gallons; /* add current tank gallons to total */
```

Fig. S3.3   Solution for Exercise 3.17. (Part 1 of 2.)

```
19
20          printf( "Enter the miles driven: " ); /* get miles driven */
21          scanf( "%lf", &miles );
22          totalMiles += miles; /* add current tank miles to total */
23
24          /* display miles per gallon for current tank */
25          printf( "The Miles / Gallon for this tank was %f\n\n",
26             miles / gallons );
27
28          /* get next tank's gallons */
29          printf( "Enter the gallons used ( -1 to end ): " );
30          scanf( "%lf", &gallons );
31       } /* end while */
32
33       /* calculate average miles per gallon over all tanks */
34       totalAverage = totalMiles / totalGallons;
35       printf( "\nThe overall average Miles/Gallon was %f\n", totalAverage );
36
37       return 0; /* indicate successful termination */
38
39    } /* end main */
```

Fig. S3.3   Solution for Exercise 3.17. (Part 2 of 2.)

3.19   One large chemical company pays its salespeople on a commission basis. The salespeople receive $200 per week plus 9% of their gross sales for that week. For example, a salesperson who sells $5000 worth of chemicals in a week receives $200 plus 9% of $5000, or a total of $650. Develop a program that will input each salesperson's gross sales for last week and will calculate and display that salesperson's earnings. Process one salesperson's figures at a time. Here is a sample input/output dialog:

```
Enter sales in dollars ( -1 to end): 5000.00
Salary is: $650.00

Enter sales in dollars ( -1 to end ): 1234.56
Salary is: $311.11

Enter sales in dollars ( -1 to end ): 1088.89
Salary is: $298.00

Enter sales in dollars ( -1 to end ): -1
```

ANS:
2)   *Top:*
     For an arbitrary number of salespeople, determine each salesperson's earnings for the last week.

     First refinement:
     Input the salesperson's sales for the week, calculate and print the salesperson's wages for the week, then process the next salesperson.

Second refinement:
Input the first salesperson's sales in dollars.
While the sentinel value (-1) has not been entered for the sales
       Calculate the salesperson's wages for the week
       Print the salesperson's wages for the week
       Input the next salesperson's sales in dollars

3)

```
1    /* Exercise 3.19 Solution */
2    #include <stdio.h>
3
4    int main()
5    {
6       double sales; /* gross weekly sales */
7       double wage;  /* commissioned earnings */
8
9       /* get first sales */
10      printf( "Enter sales in dollars ( -1 to end): " );
11      scanf( "%lf", &sales );
12
13      /* loop until sentinel value read from user */
14      while ( sales != -1.0 ) {
15         wage = 200.0 + 0.09 * sales; /* calculate wage */
16
17         /* display salary */
18         printf( "Salary is: $%.2f\n\n", wage );
19
20         /* prompt for next sales */
21         printf( "Enter sales in dollars ( -1 to end ): " );
22         scanf( "%lf", &sales );
23      } /* end while */
24
25      return 0; /* indicate successful termination */
26
27   } /* end main */
```

Fig. S3.4   Solution for Exercise 3.19.

3.22   Write a program that demonstrates the difference between predecrementing and postdecrementing using the decrement operator `--`.

       ANS:

```
1    /* Exercise 3.22 Solution */
2    #include <stdio.h>
3
4    int main()
5    {
6       int c; /* define c to use decrement operator */
```

Fig. S3.5   Solution for Exercise 3.22.   (Part 1 of 2.)

```
 7
 8        c = 5;
 9        printf( "%d\n", c );
10        printf( "%d\n", --c ); /* predecrement */
11        printf( "%d\n\n", c );
12
13        c = 5;
14        printf( "%d\n", c );
15        printf( "%d\n", c-- ); /* postdecrement */
16        printf( "%d\n\n", c );
17
18        return 0; /* indicate successful termination */
19
20    } /* end main */
```

```
5
4
4

5
5
4
```

Fig. S3.5   Solution for Exercise 3.22.   (Part 2 of 2.)

3.24   The process of finding the largest number (i.e., the maximum of a group of numbers) is used frequently in computer applications. For example, a program that determines the winner of a sales contest
would input the number of units sold by each salesperson. The salesperson who sells the most units wins
the contest. Write a pseudocode program and then a program that inputs a series of 10 numbers, and determines and prints the largest of the numbers. [*Hint*: Your program should use three variables as follows]:

counter: A counter to count to 10 (i.e., to keep track of how many numbers have
        been input and to determine when all 10 numbers have been processed)
number: The current number input to the program
largest: The largest number found so far

   ANS:
            Input the first number directly into the variable largest
            Increment counter *to* 10
            While counter *is less than or equal to* 10
                input a new variable into the variable number
                If number is greater than largest
                    replace largest *with number*
                Increment counter
            *Print the value of the largest (*while *condition false when* counter *is 11)*

```
1    /* Exercise 3.24 Solution */
2    #include <stdio.h>
3
4    int main()
5    {
6       int counter; /* counter for 10 repetitions */
7       int number;  /* current number input */
8       int largest; /* largest number found so far */
9
10       /* get first number */
11       printf( "Enter the first number: " );
12       scanf( "%d", &largest );
13       counter = 2;
14
15       /* loop 9 more times */
16       while ( counter <= 10 ) {
17          printf( "Enter next number: " ); /* get next number */
18          scanf( "%d", &number );
19
20          /* if current number input is greater than largest number,
21             update largest */
22          if ( number > largest ) {
23             largest = number;
24          } /* end if */
25
26          counter++;
27       } /* end while */
28
29       printf( "Largest is %d\n", largest ); /* display largest number */
30
31       return 0; /* indicate successful termination */
32
33    } /* end main */
```

```
Enter the first number: 7
Enter next number: 37
Enter next number: 78
Enter next number: 2
Enter next number: 437
Enter next number: 72
Enter next number: 1
Enter next number: 4
Enter next number: 36
Enter next number: 100
Largest is 437
```

Fig. S3.6   Solution for Exercise 3.24.

3.26 Write a program that utilizes looping to produce the following table of values:

A	A+2	A+4	A+6
3	5	7	9
6	8	10	12
9	11	13	15
12	14	16	18
15	17	19	21

ANS:

```
1   /* Exercise 3.26 Solution */
2   #include <stdio.h>
3
4   int main()
5   {
6      int a = 3; /* counter */
7
8      /* display table headers */
9      printf( "A\tA+2\tA+4\tA+6\n\n" );
10
11     /* loop 5 times */
12     while ( a <= 15 ) {
13
14        /* calculate and display table values */
15        printf( "%d\t%d\t%d\t%d\n", a, a + 2, a + 4, a + 6 );
16        a += 3;
17     } /* end while */
18
19     return 0; /* indicate successful termination */
20
21  } /* end main */
```

Fig. S3.7   Solution for Exercise 3.26.

3.29 What does the following program print?

```
1   #include <stdio.h>
2
3   /* function main begins program execution */
4   int main()
5   {
6      int count = 1; /* initialize count */
7
8      while ( count <= 10 ) { /* loop 10 times */
9
10        /* output line of text */
11        printf( "%s\n", count % 2 ? "****" : "++++++++" );
```

Fig. S3.8   Exercise 3.29: What does this program print?   (Part 1 of 2.)

```
12              count++; /* increment count */
13        } /* end while */
14
15        return 0; /* indicate program ended successfully */
16
17    } /* end function main */
```

Fig. S3.8   Exercise 3.29: What does this program print?   (Part 2 of 2.)

ANS:

```
****
++++++++
****
++++++++
****
++++++++
****
++++++++
****
++++++++
****
++++++++
```

Fig. S3.9   Solution for Exercise 3.29.

3.30   What does the following program print?

```
1    #include <stdio.h>
2
3    /* function main begins program execution */
4    int main()
5    {
6        int row = 10; /* initialize row */
7        int column;    /* define column */
8
9        while ( row >= 1 ) { /* loop until row < 1 */
10           column = 1;         /* set column to 1 as iteration begins */
11
12           while ( column <= 10 ) {              /* loop 10 times */
13              printf( "%s", row % 2 ? "<": ">" ); /* output */
14              column++;                          /* increment column */
15           } /* end inner while */
16
17           row--;              /* decrement row */
18           printf( "\n" ); /* begin new output line */
19        } /* end outer while */
20
21        return 0; /* indicate program ended successfully */
22
23    } /* end function main */
```

Fig. S3.10   Exercise 3.30: What does this program print?

ANS:

```
>>>>>>>>>
<<<<<<<<<
>>>>>>>>>
<<<<<<<<<
>>>>>>>>>
<<<<<<<<<
>>>>>>>>>
<<<<<<<<<
>>>>>>>>>
<<<<<<<<<
```

Fig. S3.11   Solution for Exercise 3.30.

3.31   *(Dangling Else Problem)* Determine the output for each of the following when x is 9 and y is 11 and when x is 11 and y is 9. Note that the compiler ignores the indentation in a C program. Also, the compiler always associates an e1se with the previous if unless told to do otherwise by the placement of braces {}. Because, on first glance, the programmer may not be sure which if an e1se matches, this is referred to as the "dangling else" problem. We have eliminated the indentation from the following code to make the problem more challenging. [*Hint:* Apply indentation conventions you have learned.]

a)
```
if ( x < 10 )
if ( y > 10 )
printf( "*****\n" );
else
printf( "#####\n" );
printf( "$$$$$\n" );
```

ANS:

x = 9, y = 11

```
*****
$$$$$
```

x = 11, y = 9

```
$$$$$
```

b)
```
if ( x < 10 ) {
if ( y > 10 )
printf( "*****\n" );
}
else {
```

```
      printf( "#####\n" );
      printf( "$$$$$\n" );
      }
```
ANS:

x = 9, y = 11

```
*****
```

x = 11, y = 9

```
#####
$$$$$
```

3.35 A palindrome is a number or a text phrase that reads the same backwards as forwards. For example, each of the following five-digit integers are palindromes: 12321, 55555, 45554 and 11611. Write a program that reads in a five-digit integer and determines whether or not it is a palindrome. [*Hint:* Use the division and remainder operators to separate the number into its individual digits.]

ANS:

```
1    /* Exercise 3.35 Solution */
2    #include<stdio.h>
3
4    int main()
5    {
6       int number;       /* input number */
7       int temp1;        /* first temporary integer */
8       int temp2;        /* second temporary integer */
9       int firstDigit;   /* first digit of input */
10      int secondDigit;  /* second digit of input */
11      int fourthDigit;  /* fourth digit of input */
12      int fifthDigit;   /* fifth digit of input */
13
14      printf( "Enter a five-digit number: " ); /* get number */
15      scanf( "%d", &number );
16
17      temp1 = number;
18
19      /* determine first digit by integer division by 10000 */
20      firstDigit = temp1 / 10000;
21      temp2 = temp1 % 10000;
22
```

Fig. S3.12 Solution for Exercise 3.35 (Part 1 of 2.)

```
23      /* determine second digit by integer division by 1000 */
24      secondDigit = temp2 / 1000;
25      temp1 = temp2 % 1000;
26
27      temp2 = temp1 % 100;
28
29      /* determine fourth digit by integer division by 10 */
30      fourthDigit = temp2 / 10;
31      temp1 = temp2 % 10;
32
33      fifthDigit = temp1;
34
35      /* if first and fifth digits are equal */
36      if ( firstDigit == fifthDigit ) {
37
38         /* if second and fourth digits are equal */
39         if ( secondDigit == fourthDigit ) {
40
41            /* number is a palindrome */
42            printf( "%d is a palindrome\n", number );
43         } /* end if */
44         else { /* number is not a palindrome */
45            printf( "%d is not a palindrome\n", number );
46         } /* end else */
47
48      } /* end if */
49      else { /* number is not a palindrome */
50         printf( "%d is not a palindrome\n", number );
51      } /* end else */
52
53      return 0; /* indicate successful termination */
54
55   } /* end main */
```

```
Enter a five-digit number: 18181
18181 is a palindrome
```

Fig. S3.12   Solution for Exercise 3.35   (Part 2 of 2.)

```
Enter a five-digit number: 16738
16738 is not a palindrome
```

3.39   Write a program that reads an integer and determines and prints how many digits in the integer are 7s.

ANS:

```
1   /* Exercise 3.39 Solution */
2   #include <stdio.h>
3
4   int main()
5   {
6      int number;           /* user input */
7      int numCopy;          /* copy of number */
8      int factor = 10000;   /* set factor to pick off digits */
9      int digit;            /* individual digit of number */
10     int sevens = 0;       /* sevens counter */
11
12     printf( "Enter a 5-digit number: " ); /* get number from user */
13     scanf( "%d", &number );
14
15     numCopy = number;
16
17     /* loop through each of the 5 digits */
18     while ( factor >= 1 ) {
19        digit = numCopy / factor; /* pick off next digit */
20
21        if ( digit == 7 ) { /* if digit equals 7, increment sevens */
22           ++sevens;
23        } /* end if */
24
25        numCopy %= factor;
26        factor /= 10;
27     } /* end while */
28
29     /* output number of sevens */
30     printf( "The number %ld has %d seven(s) in it\n", number, sevens );
31
32     return 0; /* indicate successful termination */
33
34  } /* end main */
```

```
Enter a 5-digit number: 17737
The number 17737 has 3 seven(s) in it
```

Fig. S3.13 Solution for Exercise 3.39.

```
Enter a 5-digit number: 11727
The number 11727 has 2 seven(s) in it
```

3.40   Write a program that displays the following checkerboard pattern.

```
* * * * * * * *
 * * * * * * * *
* * * * * * * *
 * * * * * * * *
* * * * * * * *
 * * * * * * * *
* * * * * * * *
 * * * * * * * *
```

Your program must use only three output statements, one of each of the following forms:

```
printf( "* " );
printf( " " );
printf( "\n" );
```

   ANS:

```
1   /* Exercise 3.40 Solution */
2   #include <stdio.h>
3
4   int main()
5   {
6      int side = 8; /* side counter */
7      int row;       /* row counter */
8      int mod;       /* remainder */
9
10     /* loop 8 times */
11     while ( side >= 1 ) {
12        row = 8; /* reset row counter */
13        mod = side % 2;
14
15        /* loop 8 times */
16        while ( row >= 1 ) {
17
18           /* if odd row, begin with a space */
19           if ( mod != 0 ) {
20              printf( " " );
21              mod = 0;
22           } /* end if */
23
24           printf( "* " );
25           --row;
26        } /* end while */
27
28        printf( "\n" ); /* go to next line */
```

Fig. S3.14   Solution for Exercise 3.40   (Part 1 of 2.)

```
29          --side;
30      } /* end while */
31
32      return 0; /* indicate successful termination */
33
34  } /* end main */
```

Fig. S3.14   Solution for Exercise 3.40   (Part 2 of 2.)

3.42   Write a program that reads the radius of a circle (as a float value) and computes and prints the diameter, the circumference and the area. Use the value 3.14159 for π.

    ANS:

```
1   /* Exercise 3.42 Solution */
2   #include<stdio.h>
3
4   int main()
5   {
6      float radius;        /* input radius */
7      float pi = 3.14159; /* value for pi */
8
9      printf( "Enter the radius: "); /* get radius value */
10     scanf( "%f", &radius );
11
12     /* compute and display diameter */
13     printf( "The diameter is %.2f\n", radius * 2 );
14
15     /* compute and display circumference */
16     printf( "The circumference is %.2f\n", 2 * pi * radius );
17
18     /* compute and display area */
19     printf( "The area is %.2f\n", pi * radius * radius );
20
21     return 0; /* indicate successful termination */
22
23  } /* end main */
```

```
Enter the radius: 4.7
The diameter is 9.40
The circumference is 29.53
The area is 69.40
```

Fig. S3.15   Solution for Exercise 3.42

3.46   A company wants to transmit data over the telephone, but they are concerned that their phones may be tapped. All of their data is transmitted as four-digit integers. They have asked you to write a program that will encrypt their data so that it may be transmitted more securely. Your program should read a four-digit integer and encrypt it as follows: Replace each digit by the remainder after *(the sum of that digit plus 7)* is divided by *10*. Then, swap the first digit with the third, and swap the second digit with the fourth. Then print the encrypted integer. Write a separate program that inputs an encrypted four-digit integer and decrypts it to form the original number.

ANS:

```
1    /* Exercise 3.46 Part A solution */
2    #include <stdio.h>
3
4    int main()
5    {
6       int first;  /* first digit replacement */
7       int second; /* second digit replacement */
8       int third;  /* third digit replacement */
9       int fourth; /* fourth digit replacement */
10      int digit;  /* input number */
11      int temp1;  /* temporarily hold digit */
12      int temp2;  /* temporarily hold digit */
13      int encryptedNumber; /* resulting encrypted number */
14
15      /* prompt for input */
16      printf( "Enter a four digit number to be encrypted: " );
17      scanf( "%d", &digit );
18
19      temp1 = digit;
20
21      /* retrieve each digit and replace with
22         (sum of digit and 7) mod 10 */
23      first = ( temp1 / 1000 + 7 ) % 10;
24      temp2 = temp1 % 1000;
25
26      second = ( temp2 / 100 + 7 ) % 10;
27      temp1 = temp2 % 100;
28
29      third = ( temp1 / 10 + 7 ) % 10;
30      temp2 = temp1 % 10;
31
32      fourth = ( temp2 + 7 ) % 10;
33
34      /* swap first and third */
35      temp1 = first;
36      first = third * 1000; /* multiply by 1000 for 1st digit component */
37      third = temp1 * 10; /* multiply by 10 for 3rd digit component */
38
39      /* swap second and fourth */
40      temp1 = second;
41      second = fourth * 100; /* multiply by 100 for 2nd digit component */
42      fourth = temp1 * 1;
43
44      /* add components to obtain encrypted number */
45      encryptedNumber = first + second + third + fourth;
46
47      /* display encrypted number */
48      printf( "Encrypted number is %d\n", encryptedNumber );
```

Fig. S3.16   Solution for Exercise 3.46, Part A.   (Part 1 of 2.)

```
49
50      return 0; /* indicate successful termination */
51
52  } /* end main */
```

```
Enter a four digit number to be encrypted: 5678
Encrypted number is 4523
```

Fig. S3.16   Solution for Exercise 3.46, Part A.   (Part 2 of 2.)

```
1   /* Exercise 3.46 Part B Solution */
2   #include <stdio.h>
3
4   int main()
5   {
6       int first;      /* first decrypted digit */
7       int second;     /* second decrypted digit */
8       int third;      /* third decrypted digit */
9       int fourth;     /* fourth decrypted digit */
10      int decrypted; /* decrypted number */
11      int temp1;      /* temporarily hold digit */
12      int temp2;      /* temporarily hold digit */
13      int encryptedNumber; /* input number */
14
15      /* prompt for input */
16      printf( "Enter a four digit encrypted number: " );
17      scanf( "%d", &encryptedNumber );
18
19      temp1 = encryptedNumber;
20
21      /* retrieve each digit and decrypt by
22         (sum of digit and 3) mod 10 */
23      first = ( temp1 / 1000 );
24      temp2 = temp1 % 1000;
25
26      second = ( temp2 / 100 );
27      temp1 = temp2 % 100;
28
29      third = ( temp1 / 10 );
30      temp2 = temp1 % 10;
31
32      fourth = temp2;
33
34      temp1 = ( first + 3 ) % 10;
35      first = ( third + 3 ) % 10;
36      third = temp1;
37
38      temp1 = ( second + 3 ) % 10;
39      second = ( fourth + 3 ) % 10;
```

Fig. S3.17   Solution for Exercise 3.46, Part B.   (Part 1 of 2.)

```
40        fourth = temp1;
41
42        /* add components to obtain decrypted number */
43        decrypted = ( first * 1000 ) + ( second * 100 ) +
44                    ( third * 10 ) + fourth;
45
46        /* display decrypted number */
47        printf( "Decrypted number is %d\n", decrypted );
48
49        return 0; /* indicate successful termination */
50
51    } /* end main */
```

```
Enter a four digit encrypted number: 4523
Decrypted number is 5678
```

Fig. S3.17   Solution for Exercise 3.46, Part B.   (Part 2 of 2.)

C Program Control

Solutions to Selected Exercises

4.6 State which values of the control variable x are printed by each of the following for statements:

a) **for** (x = 2; x <= 13; x += 2)
      printf("%d\n", x);

ANS: 2, 4, 6, 8, 10, 12

b) **for** (x = 5; x <= 22; x += 7)
      printf("%d\n", x);

ANS: 5, 12, 19

c) **for** (x = 3; x <= 15; x += 3)
      printf("%d\n", x);

ANS: 3, 6, 9, 12, 15

d) **for** (x = 1; x <= 5; x += 7)
      printf("%d\n", x);

ANS: 1

e) **for** (x = 12; x >= 2; x -= 3)
      printf("%d\n", x);

ANS: 12, 9, 6, 3

4.7 Write for statements that print the following sequences of values:

a) 1, 2, 3, 4, 5, 6, 7

ANS:
for (i = 1; i <= 7; i++)
      printf("%d ", i);

b) 3, 8, 13, 18, 23

ANS:
/* increments of 5 */
for (i = 3; i <= 23; i += 5)
      printf("%d ", i);

c) 20, 14, 8, 2, -4, -10

ANS:

```
/* decrements of 6 */
for ( i = 20; i >= -10; i -= 6 )
        printf( "%d ", i );
```

d) 19, 27, 35, 43, 51

ANS:

```
/* increments of 8 */
for ( i = 19; i <= 51; i += 8 )
      printf( "%d ", i );
```

4.9   Write a program that sums a sequence of integers. Assume that the first integer read with `scanf` specifies the number of values remaining to be entered. Your program should read only one value each time `scanf` is executed. A typical input sequence might be

5 100 200 300 400 500

where the 5 indicates that the subsequent five values are to be summed.

ANS:

```
1    /* Exercise 4.9 Solution */
2    #include <stdio.h>
3
4    int main( void )
5    {
6       int sum = 0; /* current sum */
7       int number;   /* number of values */
8       int value;    /* current value */
9       int i;        /* counter */
10
11      /* display prompt */
12      printf( "Enter the number of values"
13            " to be processed: " );
14      scanf( "%d", &number ); /* input number of values */
15
16      /* loop number times */
17      for ( i = 1; i <= number; i++ ) {
18         printf( "Enter a value: " );
19         scanf( "%d", &value );
20         sum += value; /* add to sum */
21      } /* end for */
22
23      /* display sum */
24      printf( "Sum of the %d values is %d\n", number, sum );
25
26      return 0; /* indicate successful termination */
27
28   } /* end main */
```

Fig. S4.1   Solution for Exercise 4.9.   (Part 1 of 2.)

```
Enter the number of values to be processed: 5
Enter a value: 10
Enter a value: 15
Enter a value: 20
Enter a value: 25
Enter a value: 30
Sum of the 5 values is 100
```

Fig. S4.1   Solution for Exercise 4.9.   (Part 2 of 2.)

4.11   Write a program that finds the smallest of several integers. Assume that the first value read specifies the number of values remaining.

ANS:

```
1   /* Exercise 4.11 Solution */
2   #include <stdio.h>
3
4   int main( void )
5   {
6      int number;    /* number of integers */
7      int value;     /* value input by user */
8      int smallest;  /* smallest number */
9      int i;         /* counter */
10
11     /* prompt user for number of integers */
12     printf( "Enter the number of integers to be processed: " );
13     scanf( "%d", &number );
14
15     /* prompt user for an integer */
16     printf( "Enter an integer: " );
17     scanf( "%d", &smallest );
18
19     /* loop until user has entered all integers */
20     for ( i = 2; i <= number; i++ ) {
21        printf( "Enter next integer: " ); /* get next integer */
22        scanf( "%d", &value );
23
24        /* if value is smaller than smallest */
25        if ( value < smallest ) {
26           smallest = value;
27        } /* end if */
28
29     } /* end for */
30
31     printf( "\nThe smallest integer is: %d\n", smallest );
32
33     return 0; /* indicate successful termination */
34
35  } /* end main */
```

Fig. S4.2   Solution for Exercise 4.11.   (Part 1 of 2.)

```
Enter the number of integers to be processed: 5
Enter an integer: 372
Enter next integer: 920
Enter next integer: 73
Enter next integer: 8
Enter next integer: 3433

The smallest integer is: 8
```

Fig. S4.2   Solution for Exercise 4.11.   (Part 2 of 2.)

4.12   Write a program that calculates and prints the sum of the even integers from 2 to 30.
     ANS:

```
1    /* Exercise 4.12 Solution */
2    #include <stdio.h>
3
4    int main( void )
5    {
6       int i;         /* counter */
7       int sum = 0; /* current sum of integers */
8
9       /* loop through even integers up to 30 */
10      for ( i = 2; i <= 30; i += 2 ) {
11         sum += i; /* add i to sum */
12      } /* end for */
13
14      printf( "Sum of the even integers from 2 to 30 is: %d\n", sum );
15
16      return 0; /* indicate successful termination */
17
18   } /* end main */
```

```
Sum of the even integers from 2 to 30 is: 240
```

Fig. S4.3   Solution for Exercise 4.12.

4.14   The *factorial* function is used frequently in probability problems. The factorial of a positive inte-
ger n (written $n!$ and pronounced "n factorial") is equal to the product of the positive integers from 1 to n.
Write a program that evaluates the factorials of the integers from 1 to 5. Print the results in tabular format.
What difficulty might prevent you from calculating the factorial of 20?
     ANS:

```
1    /* Exercise 4.14 Solution */
2    #include <stdio.h>
3
```

Fig. S4.4   Solution for Exercise 4.14.   (Part 1 of 2.)

```
4   int main( void )
5   {
6      int i;          /* outer counter */
7      int j;          /* inner counter */
8      int factorial; /* current factorial value */
9
10     printf( "X\tFactorial of X\n" ); /* display table headers */
11
12     /* compute the factorial for 1 to 5 */
13     for ( i = 1; i <= 5; i++ ) {
14        factorial = 1;
15
16        /* calculate factorial of current number */
17        for ( j = 1; j <= i; j++ ) {
18           factorial *= j;
19        } /* end inner for */
20
21        printf( "%d\t%d\n", i, factorial );
22     } /* end outer for */
23
24     return 0; /* indicate successful termination */
25
26  } /* end main */
```

```
X       Factorial of X
1       1
2       2
3       6
4       24
5       120
```

Fig. S4.4   Solution for Exercise 4.14.   (Part 2 of 2.)

4.18   One interesting application of computers is drawing graphs and bar charts (sometimes called "histograms"). Write a program that reads five numbers (each between 1 and 30). For each number read, your program should print a line containing that number of adjacent asterisks. For example, if your program reads the number seven, it should print *******.

    ANS:

```
1   /* Exercise 4.18 Solution */
2   #include <stdio.h>
3
4   int main( void )
5   {
6      int i;          /* outer counter */
7      int j;          /* inner counter */
8      int number; /* current number */
9
```

Fig. S4.5   Solution for Exercise 4.18.   (Part 1 of 2.)

```
10        printf( "Enter 5 numbers between 1 and 30: " );
11
12        /* loop 5 times */
13        for ( i = 1; i <= 5; i++ ) {
14           scanf( "%d", &number );
15
16           /* print asterisks corresponding to current input */
17           for ( j = 1; j <= number; j++ ) {
18              printf( "*" );
19           } /* end for */
20
21           printf( "\n" );
22        } /* end for */
23
24        return 0; /* indicate successful termination */
25
26     } /* end main */
```

```
Enter 5 numbers between 1 and 30: 28 5 13 24 7
****************************
*****
*************
*************************
*******
```

Fig. S4.5   Solution for Exercise 4.18. (Part 2 of 2.)

4.19   A mail order house sells five different products whose retail prices are shown in the following table:

Product number	Retail price
1	$ 2.98
2	$ 4.50
3	$ 9.98
4	$ 4.49
5	$ 6.87

Write a program that reads a series of pairs of numbers as follows:
   a) Product number
   b) Quantity sold for one day

Your program should use a switch statement to help determine the retail price for each product. Your program should calculate and display the total retail value of all products sold last week.

ANS:

```
1    /* Exercise 4.19 Solution */
2    #include <stdio.h>
3
4    int main( void )
5    {
6       int product;        /* current product number */
7       int quantity;       /* quantity of current product sold */
8       double total = 0.0; /* current total retail value */
9
10      /* prompt for input */
11      printf( "Enter pairs of item numbers and quantities.\n");
12      printf( "Enter -1 for the item number to end input.\n" );
13      scanf( "%d", &product );
14
15      /* loop while sentinel value not read from user */
16      while ( product != -1 ) {
17         scanf( "%d", &quantity );
18
19         /* determine product number and corresponding retail price */
20         switch ( product ) {
21
22            case 1:
23               total += quantity * 2.98; /* update total */
24               break;
25
26            case 2:
27               total += quantity * 4.50; /* update total */
28               break;
29
30            case 3:
31               total += quantity * 9.98; /* update total */
32               break;
33
34            case 4:
35               total += quantity * 4.49; /* update total */
36               break;
37
38            case 5:
39               total += quantity * 6.87; /* update total */
40               break;
41
42            default:
43               printf( "Invalid product code:  %d\n", product );
44               printf( "              Quantity:  %d\n", quantity );
45         } /* end switch */
46
47         scanf( "%d", &product ); /* get next input */
48      } /* end while */
49
```

Fig. S4.6   Solution for Exercise 4.19.   (Part 1 of 2.)

```
50        /* display total retail value */
51        printf( "The total retail value was:  %.2f\n", total );
52
53        return 0; /* indicate successful termination */
54
55   } /* end main */
```

```
Enter pairs of item numbers and quantities.
Enter -1 for the item number to end input.
1 1
2 1
3 1
4 1
5 1
6 1
Invalid product code:   6
          Quantity:   1
1 1
-1
The total retail value was:   31.80
```

Fig. S4.6   Solution for Exercise 4.19.   (Part 2 of 2.)

4.21   Rewrite the program of Fig. 4.2 so that the initialization of the variable counter is done in the definition instead of the for statement.

ANS:

```
1   /* Exercise 4.21 Solution */
2   #include <stdio.h>
3
4   int main( void )
5   {
6      int counter = 1; /* initialize counter */
7
8      /* leave first statement empty */
9      for (  ; counter <= 10; counter++ ) {
10        printf( "%d\n", counter );
11     } /* end for */
12
13     return 0; /* indicate successful termination */
14
15  } /* end main */
```

Fig. S4.7   Solution for Exercise 4.21.   (Part 1 of 2.)

```
 1
 2
 3
 4
 5
 6
 7
 8
 9
10
```

Fig. S4.7   Solution for Exercise 4.21. (Part 2 of 2.)

4.26   Calculate the value of π from the infinite series

$$\pi = 4 - \frac{4}{3} + \frac{4}{5} - \frac{4}{7} + \frac{4}{9} - \frac{4}{11} + \cdots$$

Print a table that shows the value of π approximated by one term of this series, by two terms, by three terms, etc. How many terms of this series do you have to use before you first get 3.14? 3.141? 3.1415? 3.14159?

> **ANS:** *3.14 occurs at an accuracy of 627, 3.141 occurs at an accuracy of 2458, 3.1415 occurs at an accuracy around 147,000, and 3.14159 occurs at an accuracy around 319,000.*

```c
 1    /* Exercise 4.26 Solution */
 2    #include<stdio.h>
 3
 4    int main( void )
 5    {
 6       long double pi = 0.0;      /* approximated value for pi */
 7       long double num = 4.0;     /* numerator */
 8       long double denom = 1.0; /* denominator of current term */
 9       long int loop;             /* loop counter */
10       long int accuracy;         /* number of terms */
11
12       accuracy = 400000; /* set decimal accuracy */
13
14       /* display table headers */
15       printf( "Accuracy set at: %ld\n", accuracy );
16       printf( "term\t\t  pi\n" );
17
18       /* loop through each term */
19       for ( loop = 1; loop <= accuracy; loop++ ) {
20
21          /* if odd-numbered term, add current term */
22          if ( loop % 2 != 0 ) {
23             pi += num / denom;
24          } /* end if */
```

Fig. S4.8   Solution for Exercise 4.26. (Part 1 of 2.)

```
25          else { /* if even-numbered term, subtract current term */
26              pi -= num / denom;
27          } /* end else */
28
29          /* display number of terms and approximated
30              value for pi with 8 digits of precision */
31          printf( "%ld\t\t%Lf\n", loop, pi );
32
33          denom += 2.0; /* update denominator */
34
35      } /* end for */
36
37      return 0; /* indicate successful termination */
38
39  } /* end main */
```

```
Accuracy set at: 400000
term                pi
1                   4.000000
2                   2.666667
3                   3.466667
4                   2.895238
5                   3.339683
6                   2.976046

...

995                 3.142598
996                 3.140589
997                 3.142596
998                 3.140591
999                 3.142594

...

399998              3.141590
399999              3.141595
400000              3.141590
```

Fig. S4.8   Solution for Exercise 4.26. (Part 2 of 2.)

4.30   Rewrite the program of Fig. 4.7 by replacing the switch statement with a nested if...else statement; be careful to deal with the default case properly. Then rewrite this new version by replacing the nested if...else statement with a series of if statements; here, too, be careful to deal with the default case properly (this is more difficult than in the nested if...else version). This exercise demonstrates that switch is a convenience and that any switch statement can be written with only single-selection statements.

```
1   /* Exercise 4.30 Part A Solution */
2   #include <stdio.h>
3
4   int main( void )
5   {
6      int grade;        /* current grade */
7      int aCount = 0; /* total A grades */
8      int bCount = 0; /* total B grades */
9      int cCount = 0; /* total C grades */
10     int dCount = 0; /* total D grades */
11     int fCount = 0; /* total F grades */
12
13     /* prompt user for grades */
14     printf( "Enter the letter grades." );
15     printf( " Enter the EOF character to end input:\n" );
16
17     /* while EOF not entered by user */
18     while ( ( grade = getchar() ) != EOF ) {
19
20        /* Update count for appropriate grade */
21        if ( grade == 'A' || grade == 'a' ) {
22           ++aCount;
23        } /* end if */
24        else if ( grade == 'B' || grade == 'b' ) {
25           ++bCount;
26        } /* end else if */
27        else if ( grade == 'C' || grade == 'c' ) {
28           ++cCount;
29        } /* end else if */
30        else if ( grade == 'D' || grade == 'd' ) {
31           ++dCount;
32        } /* end else if */
33        else if ( grade == 'F' || grade == 'f' ) {
34           ++fCount;
35        } /* end else if */
36        else if ( grade == '\n' || grade == ' ' ) {
37           ;        /* empty body */
38        } /* end else if */
39        else {
40           printf( "Incorrect letter grade entered." );
41           printf( " Enter a new grade.\n" );
42        } /* end else */
43
44     } /* end while */
45
46     /* display totals for each grade */
47     printf( "\nTotals for each letter grade were:\n" );
48     printf( "A: %d\n", aCount );
49     printf( "B: %d\n", bCount );
50     printf( "C: %d\n", cCount );
```

Fig. S4.9   Solution for Exercise 4.30, Part A.   (Part 1 of 2.)

```
51        printf( "D: %d\n", dCount );
52        printf( "F: %d\n", fCount );
53
54        return 0; /* indicate successful termination */
55
56   } /* end main */
```

```
Enter the letter grades. Enter the EOF character to end input:
A
c
b
d
e
Incorrect letter grade entered. Enter a new grade.
f
^Z

Totals for each letter grade were:
A: 1
B: 1
C: 1
D: 1
F: 1
```

Fig. S4.9   Solution for Exercise 4.30, Part A.   (Part 2 of 2.)

```
1    /* Exercise 4.30 Part B Solution */
2    #include <stdio.h>
3
4    int main( void )
5    {
6       int grade;        /* current grade */
7       int aCount = 0;  /* total A grades */
8       int bCount = 0;  /* total B grades */
9       int cCount = 0;  /* total C grades */
10      int dCount = 0;  /* total D grades */
11      int fCount = 0;  /* total F grades */
12
13      /* prompt user for grades */
14      printf( "Enter the letter grades." );
15      printf( " Enter the EOF character to end input:\n" );
16
17      /* while EOF not entered by user */
18      while ( ( grade = getchar() ) != EOF ) {
19
20         /* update count for appropriate grade */
21         if ( grade == 'A' || grade == 'a' ) {
22            ++aCount;
```

Fig. S4.10   Solution for Exercise 4.30, Part B.   (Part 1 of 3.)

```
23          } /* end if */
24
25          if ( grade == 'B' || grade == 'b' ) {
26              ++bCount;
27          } /* end if */
28
29          if ( grade == 'C' || grade == 'c' ) {
30              ++cCount;
31          } /* end if */
32
33          if ( grade == 'D' || grade == 'd' ) {
34              ++dCount;
35          } /* end if */
36
37          if ( grade == 'F' || grade == 'f' ) {
38              ++fCount;
39          } /* end if */
40
41          if ( grade == '\n' || grade == ' ' ) {
42              ;   /* empty body */
43          } /* end if */
44
45          /* default */
46          if ( grade != 'a' && grade != 'A' &&
47              grade != 'B' && grade != 'b' &&
48              grade != 'c' && grade != 'C' &&
49              grade != 'd' && grade != 'd' &&
50              grade != 'f' && grade != 'F' &&
51              grade != '\n'&& grade != ' ' ) {
52
53              printf( "Incorrect letter grade entered." );
54              printf( " Enter a new grade.\n" );
55          } /* end if */
56
57      } /* end while */
58
59      /* display totals for each grade */
60      printf( "\nTotals for each letter grade were:\n" );
61      printf( "A: %d\n", aCount );
62      printf( "B: %d\n", bCount );
63      printf( "C: %d\n", cCount );
64      printf( "D: %d\n", dCount );
65      printf( "F: %d\n", fCount );
66
67      return 0; /* indicate successful termination */
68
69  } /* end main */
```

Fig. S4.10   Solution for Exercise 4.30, Part B.   (Part 2 of 3.)

```
Enter the letter grades. Enter the EOF character to end input:
A
b
c
s
Incorrect letter grade entered. Enter a new grade.
d
f
^Z

Totals for each letter grade were:
A: 1
B: 1
C: 1
D: 1
F: 1
```

Fig. S4.10   Solution for Exercise 4.30, Part B.   (Part 3 of 3.)

4.31   Write a program that prints the following diamond shape. You may use `printf` statements that print either a single asterisk (*) or a single blank. Maximize your use of repetition (with nested `for` statements) and minimize the number of `printf` statements.

```
    *
   ***
  *****
 *******
*********
 *******
  *****
   ***
    *
```

ANS:

```
1   /* Exercise 4.31 Solution */
2   #include <stdio.h>
3
4   int main( void )
5   {
6      int line;    /* line counter */
7      int space;   /* space counter */
8      int asterisk; /* asterisk counter */
9
10     /* top half */
```

Fig. S4.11   Solution for Exercise 4.31.   (Part 1 of 2.)

```
11     for ( line = 1; line <= 9; line += 2 ) {
12
13         /* print preceding spaces */
14         for ( space = ( 9 - line ) / 2; space > 0; space-- ) {
15            printf( " " );
16         } /* end for */
17
18         /* print asterisks */
19         for ( asterisk = 1; asterisk <= line; asterisk++ ) {
20            printf( "*" );
21         } /* end for */
22
23         printf( "\n" );
24     } /* end for */
25
26     /* bottom half */
27     for ( line = 7; line >= 0; line -= 2 ) {
28
29         /* print preceding spaces */
30         for ( space = ( 9 - line ) / 2; space > 0; space-- ) {
31            printf( " " );
32         } /* end for */
33
34         /* print asterisks */
35         for ( asterisk = 1; asterisk <= line; asterisk++ ) {
36            printf( "*" );
37         } /* end for */
38
39         printf( "\n" );
40     } /* end for */
41
42     return 0; /* indicate successful termination */
43
44  } /* end main */
```

Fig. S4.11   Solution for Exercise 4.31.   (Part 2 of 2.)

4.36   Write a program that inputs the year in the range 1994 through 1999 and uses for-loop repetition to produce a condensed, neatly printed calendar. Watch out for leap years.

ANS:

```
1   /* Exercise 4.36 Solution */
2   /* This is a simple calender solution, that does */
3   /* not account for the shifting of dates from    */
4   /* year to year.                                  */
5
6   #include<stdio.h>
7
8   int main( void )
9   {
```

Fig. S4.12   Solution for Exercise 4.36.   (Part 1 of 5.)

```
10      int year;           /* current year */
11      int leapYear;       /* leap year, 1 = yes, 0 = no */
12      int days;           /* total days in current month */
13      int month;          /* current month */
14      int space;          /* space counter */
15      int dayPosition;    /* starting day position of year */
16      int dayNum;         /* counter for days of the month */
17
18      /* loop until input is valid */
19      do {
20         printf( "Enter a calendar year between 1994 and 1999: " );
21         scanf( "%d", &year );
22      } while ( year < 1994 || year > 1999 ); /* end do...while */
23
24      /* determine starting day position */
25      switch ( year ) {
26
27         case 1994:
28            dayPosition = 7;
29            break; /* exit switch */
30
31         case 1995:
32            dayPosition = 1;
33            break; /* exit switch */
34
35         case 1996:
36            dayPosition = 2;
37            break; /* exit switch */
38
39         case 1997:
40            dayPosition = 4;
41            break; /* exit switch */
42
43         case 1998:
44            dayPosition = 5;
45            break; /* exit switch */
46
47         case 1999:
48            dayPosition = 6;
49            break; /* exit switch */
50      } /* end switch */
51
52      /* check for leap years */
53      if ( year % 400 == 0 ) {
54         leapYear = 1;
55      } /* end if */
56      else if ( year % 4 == 0 && year % 100 != 0 ) {
57         leapYear = 1;
58      } /* end else if */
59      else {
```

Fig. S4.12   Solution for Exercise 4.36.   (Part 2 of 5.)

```
60          leapYear = 0;
61       } /* end else */
62
63       /* loop through months and print calendar */
64       for ( month = 1; month <= 12; month++ ) {
65
66          /* begin with the month */
67          switch ( month ) {
68
69             case 1:
70                printf( "\n\nJanuary %d\n", year );
71                days = 31;
72                break; /* exit switch */
73
74             case 2:
75                printf( "\n\nFebruary %d\n", year );
76                days = leapYear == 1 ? 29 : 28;
77                break; /* exit switch */
78
79             case 3:
80                printf( "\n\nMarch %d\n", year );
81                days = 31;
82                break; /* exit switch */
83
84             case 4:
85                printf( "\n\nApril %d\n", year );
86                days = 30;
87                break; /* exit switch */
88
89             case 5:
90                printf( "\n\nMay %d\n", year );
91                days = 31;
92                break; /* exit switch */
93
94             case 6:
95                printf( "\n\nJune %d\n", year );
96                days = 30;
97                break; /* exit switch */
98
99             case 7:
100               printf( "\n\nJuly %d\n", year );
101               days = 31;
102               break; /* exit switch */
103
104            case 8:
105               printf( "\n\nAugust %d\n", year );
106               days = 31;
107               break; /* exit switch */
108
109            case 9:
```

Fig. S4.12   Solution for Exercise 4.36.   (Part 3 of 5.)

```
110                 printf( "\n\nSeptember %d\n", year );
111                 days = 30;
112                 break; /* exit switch */
113
114            case 10:
115                 printf( "\n\nOctober %d\n", year );
116                 days = 31;
117                 break; /* exit switch */
118
119            case 11:
120                 printf( "\n\nNovember %d\n", year );
121                 days = 30;
122                 break; /* exit switch */
123
124            case 12:
125                 printf( "\n\nDecember %d\n", year );
126                 days = 31;
127                 break; /* exit switch */
128         } /* end switch */
129
130         printf( " S  M  T  W  R  F  S\n" ); /* print heads */
131
132         /* move to proper space to begin printing month */
133         for ( space = 1; space < dayPosition; space++ ) {
134            printf( "   " );
135         } /* end for */
136
137         /* print days of the month */
138         for ( dayNum = 1; dayNum <= days; dayNum++ ) {
139            printf( "%2d ", dayNum );
140
141            /* if end of the week, start a new line */
142            if ( dayPosition % 7 == 0 ) {
143               printf( "\n" );
144               dayPosition = 1; /* reset dayPosition */
145            } /* end if */
146            else {
147               ++dayPosition;
148            } /* end else */
149
150         } /* end for */
151
152      } /* end for */
153
154      return 0; /* indicate successful termination */
155
156 } /* end main */
```

Fig. S4.12   Solution for Exercise 4.36.   (Part 4 of 5.)

```
Enter a calendar year between 1994 and 1999: 1999


January 1999
 S  M  T  W  R  F  S
                1  2
 3  4  5  6  7  8  9
10 11 12 13 14 15 16
17 18 19 20 21 22 23
24 25 26 27 28 29 30
31

February 1999
 S  M  T  W  R  F  S
    1  2  3  4  5  6
 7  8  9 10 11 12 13
14 15 16 17 18 19 20
21 22 23 24 25 26 27
28

March 1999
 S  M  T  W  R  F  S
    1  2  3  4  5  6
 7  8  9 10 11 12 13
14 15 16 17 18 19 20
21 22 23 24 25 26 27
28 29 30 31
 .
 .
 .
```

Fig. S4.12   Solution for Exercise 4.36.   (Part 5 of 5.)

4.37   A criticism of the break statement and the continue statement is that each is unstructured. Actually, break statements and continue statements can always be replaced by structured statements, although doing so can be awkward. Describe in general how you would remove any break statement from a loop in a program and replace that statement with some structured equivalent. [*Hint*: The break statement leaves a loop from within the body of the loop. The other way to leave is by failing the loop-continuation test. Consider using in the loop-continuation test a second test that indicates "early exit because of a 'break' condition."] Use the technique you developed here to remove the break statement from the program of Fig. 4.11.

ANS:

```
1   /* Exercise 4.37 Solution */
2   #include <stdio.h>
3
4   int main( void )
5   {
```

Fig. S4.13   Solution for Exercise 4.37.   (Part 1 of 2.)

```
6      int x;              /* loop counter */
7      int breakOut = 1; /* breakout condition */
8
9      /* test for breakout condition */
10     for ( x = 1; x <= 10 && breakOut == 1; x++ ) {
11
12        /* break out of loop after x = 4 */
13        if ( x == 4 ) {
14           breakOut = -1;
15        } /* end if */
16
17        printf( "%d ", x );
18     } /* end for */
19
20     printf( "\nBroke out of loop at x = %d\n", x );
21
22     return 0; /* indicate successful termination */
23
24  } /* end main */
```

```
1 2 3 4
Broke out of loop at x = 5
```

Fig. S4.13   Solution for Exercise 4.37.   (Part 2 of 2.)

C Functions

Solutions to Selected Exercises

5.9 A parking garage charges a $2.00 minimum fee to park for up to three hours. The garage charges an additional $0.50 per hour for each hour *or part thereof* in excess of three hours. The maximum charge for any given 24-hour period is $10.00. Assume that no car parks for longer than 24 hours at a time. Write a program that will calculate and print the parking charges for each of 3 customers who parked their cars in this garage yesterday. You should enter the hours parked for each customer. Your program should print the results in a neat tabular format, and should calculate and print the total of yesterday's receipts. The program should use the function `calculateCharges` to determine the charge for each customer. Your outputs should appear in the following format:

```
Enter the hours parked for 3 cars: 1.5 4.0 24.0
   Car          Hours          Charge
    1             1.5            2.00
    2             4.0            2.50
    3            24.0           10.00
TOTAL            29.5           14.50
```

ANS:

```
1   /* Exercise 5.9 Solution */
2   #include <stdio.h>
3   #include <math.h>
4
5   double calculateCharges( double hours ); /* function prototype */
6
7   int main()
8   {
9      double h;                   /* number of hours for current car */
10     double currentCharge;       /* parking charge for current car */
```

Fig. S5.1   Solution for Exercise 5.9.   (Part 1 of 3.)

```
11      double totalCharges = 0.0; /* total charges */
12      double totalHours = 0.0;   /* total number of hours */
13      int i;                     /* loop counter */
14      int first = 1;             /* flag for printing table headers */
15
16      printf( "Enter the hours parked for 3 cars: " );
17
18      /* loop 3 times for 3 cars */
19      for ( i = 1; i <= 3; i++ ) {
20         scanf( "%lf", &h );
21         totalHours += h; /* add current hours to total hours */
22
23         /* if first time through loop, display headers */
24         if ( first ) {
25            printf( "%5s%15s%15s\n", "Car", "Hours", "Charge" );
26
27            /* set flag to false to prevent from printing again */
28            first = 0;
29         } /* end if */
30
31         /* calculate current car's charge and update total */
32         totalCharges += ( currentCharge =  calculateCharges( h ) );
33
34         /* display row data for current car */
35         printf( "%5d%15.1f%15.2f\n", i, h, currentCharge );
36      } /* end for */
37
38      /* display row data for totals */
39      printf( "%5s%15.1f%15.2f\n", "TOTAL", totalHours, totalCharges );
40
41      return 0; /* indicate successful termination */
42
43   } /* end main */
44
45   /* calculateCharges returns charge according to number of hours */
46   double calculateCharges( double hours )
47   {
48      double charge; /* calculated charge */
49
50      /* $2 for up to 3 hours */
51      if ( hours < 3.0 ) {
52         charge = 2.0;
53      } /* end if */
54
55      /* $.50 for each hour or part thereof in excess of 3 hours */
56      else if ( hours < 19.0 ) {
57         charge = 2.0 + .5 * ceil( hours - 3.0 );
58      } /* end else if */
59      else { /* maximum charge $10 */
60         charge = 10.0;
```

Fig. S5.1   Solution for Exercise 5.9.   (Part 2 of 3.)

```
61      } /* end else */
62
63      return charge; /* return calculated charge */
64
65  } /* end function calculateCharges */
```

Fig. S5.1   Solution for Exercise 5.9.   (Part 3 of 3.)

5.10   An application of function `floor` is rounding a value to the nearest integer. The statement

```
y = floor( x + .5 );
```

will round the number x to the nearest integer, and assign the result to y. Write a program that reads several numbers and uses the preceding statement to round each of these numbers to the nearest integer. For each number processed, print both the original number and the rounded number.

ANS:

```
1   /* Exercise 5.10 Solution */
2   #include <stdio.h>
3   #include <math.h>
4
5   void calculateFloor( void ); /* function prototype */
6
7   int main()
8   {
9      calculateFloor(); /* call function calculateFloor */
10
11     return 0; /* indicate successful termination */
12
13  } /* end main */
14
15  /* calculateFloor rounds 5 inputs */
16  void calculateFloor( void )
17  {
18     double x; /* current input */
19     double y; /* current input rounded */
20     int loop; /* loop counter */
21
22     /* loop for 5 inputs */
23     for ( loop = 1; loop <= 5; loop++ ) {
24        printf( "Enter a floating point value: " );
25        scanf( "%lf", &x );
26
27        /* y holds rounded input */
28        y = floor( x + .5 );
29        printf( "%f rounded is %.1f\n\n", x, y );
30     } /* end for */
31
32  } /* end function calculateFloor */
```

Fig. S5.2   Solution for Exercise 5.10.   (Part 1 of 2.)

```
Enter a floating point value: 1.5
1.500000 rounded is 2.0

Enter a floating point value: 5.55
5.550000 rounded is 6.0

Enter a floating point value: 73.2341231432
73.234123 rounded is 73.0

Enter a floating point value: 9.0
9.000000 rounded is 9.0

Enter a floating point value: 4
4.000000 rounded is 4.0
```

Fig. S5.2   Solution for Exercise 5.10.   (Part 2 of 2.)

5.13   Write statements that assign random integers to the variable n in the following ranges:

a) $1 \leq n \leq 2$
ANS: n = 1 + rand() % 2;

b) $1 \leq n \leq 100$
ANS: n = 1 + rand() % 100;

c) $0 \leq n \leq 9$
ANS: n = rand() % 10;

d) $1000 \leq n \leq 1112$
ANS: n = 1000 + rand() % 113;

e) $-1 \leq n \leq 1$
ANS: n = -1 + rand() % 3;

f) $-3 \leq n \leq 11$
ANS: n = -3 + rand() % 15;

5.16   Write a function integerPower(base, exponent) that returns the value of

base^exponent

For example, integerPower(3, 4) = 3 * 3 * 3 * 3. Assume that exponent is a positive, nonzero integer, and base is an integer. Function integerPower should use for to control the calculation. Do not use any math library functions.

ANS:

```
1   /* Exercise 5.16 Solution */
2   #include <stdio.h>
3
```

Fig. S5.3   Solution for Exercise 5.16.   (Part 1 of 2.)

```
 4   int integerPower( int b, int e );
 5
 6   int main()
 7   {
 8      int exp;  /* integer exponent */
 9      int base; /* integer base */
10
11      printf( "Enter integer base and exponent: " );
12      scanf( "%d%d", &base, &exp );
13
14      printf( "%d to the power %d is: %d\n",
15             base, exp, integerPower( base, exp ) );
16
17      return 0; /* indicate successful termination */
18
19   } /* end main */
20
21   /* integerPower calculates and returns b raised to the e power */
22   int integerPower( int b, int e )
23   {
24      int product = 1; /* resulting product */
25      int i;           /* loop counter */
26
27      /* multiply product times b (e repetitions) */
28      for ( i = 1; i <= e; i++ ) {
29         product *= b;
30      } /* end for */
31
32      return product; /* return resulting product */
33
34   } /* end function integerPower */
```

```
Enter integer base and exponent: 5 3
5 to the power 3 is: 125
```

Fig. S5.3   Solution for Exercise 5.16. (Part 2 of 2.)

5.17   Write a function `multiple` that determines for a pair of integers whether the second integer is a multiple of the first. The function should take two integer arguments and return 1 (true) if the second is a multiple of the first, and 0 (false) otherwise. Use this function in a program that inputs a series of pairs of integers.

        ANS:

```
1   /* Exercise 5.17 Solution */
2   #include <stdio.h>
3
4   int multiple( int a, int b ); /* function prototype */
5
```

Fig. S5.4   Solution for Exercise 5.17. (Part 1 of 2.)

```
 6   int main()
 7   {
 8      int x; /* first integer */
 9      int y; /* second integer */
10      int i; /* loop counter */
11
12      /* loop 3 times */
13      for ( i = 1; i <= 3; i++ ) {
14         printf( "Enter two integers: " );
15         scanf( "%d%d", &x, &y );
16
17         /* determine if second is multiple of first */
18         if ( multiple( x, y ) ) {
19            printf( "%d is a multiple of %d\n\n", y, x );
20         } /* end if */
21         else {
22            printf( "%d is not a multiple of %d\n\n", y, x );
23         } /* end else */
24
25      } /* end for */
26
27      return 0; /* indicate successful termination */
28
29   } /* end main */
30
31   /* multiple determines if b is multiple of a */
32   int multiple( int a, int b )
33   {
34      return !( b % a );
35
36   } /* end function multiple */
```

```
Enter two integers: 2 10
10 is a multiple of 2

Enter two integers: 5 17
17 is not a multiple of 5

Enter two integers: 3 696
696 is a multiple of 3
```

Fig. S5.4   Solution for Exercise 5.17. (Part 2 of 2.)

5.19   Write a function that displays at the left margin of the screen a solid square of asterisks whose side is specified in integer parameter side. For example, if side is 4, the function displays:

```
Enter side: 4
****
****
****
****
```

ANS:

```
1   /* Exercise 5.19 Solution */
2   #include <stdio.h>
3
4   void square( int s ); /* function prototype */
5
6   int main()
7   {
8      int side; /* input side length */
9
10     printf( "Enter side: " );
11     scanf( "%d", &side );
12
13     square( side ); /* display solid square of asterisks */
14
15     return 0; /* indicate successful termination */
16
17  } /* end main */
18
19  /* square displays solid square of asterisks with specified side */
20  void square( int s )
21  {
22     int i; /* outer loop counter */
23     int j; /* inner loop counter */
24
25     /* loop side times for number of rows */
26     for ( i = 1; i <= s; i++ ) {
27
28        /* loop side times for number of columns */
29        for ( j = 1; j <= s; j++ ) {
30           printf( "*" );
31        } /* end for */
32
33        printf( "\n" );
34     } /* end for */
35
36  } /* end function square */
```

Fig. S5.5   Solution for Exercise 5.19.

5.24   Implement the following integer functions:
   a) Function celsius returns the Celsius equivalent of a Fahrenheit temperature.
   b) Function fahrenheit returns the Fahrenheit equivalent of a Celsius temperature.
   c) Use these functions to write a program that prints charts showing the Fahrenheit equivalents of all Celsius temperatures from 0 to 100 degrees, and the Celsius equivalents of all Fahrenheit temperatures from 32 to 212 degrees. Print the outputs in a neat tabular format that minimizes the number of lines of output while remaining readable.

ANS:

```
1   /* Exercise 5.24 Solution */
2   #include <stdio.h>
3
4   int celcius( int fTemp );     /* function prototype */
5   int fahrenheit( int cTemp ); /* function prototype */
6
7   int main()
8   {
9      int i; /* loop counter */
10
11     /* display table of Fahrenheit equivalents of Celsius temperature */
12     printf( "Fahrenheit equivalents of Celcius temperatures:\n" );
13     printf( "Celcius\t\tFahrenheit\n" );
14
15     /* display Fahrenheit equivalents of Celsius 0 to 100 */
16     for ( i = 0; i <= 100; i++ ) {
17        printf( "%d\t\t%d\n", i, fahrenheit( i ) );
18     } /* end for */
19
20     /* display table of Celsius equivalents of Fahrenheit temperature */
21     printf( "\nCelcius equivalents of Fahrenheit temperatures:\n" );
22     printf( "Fahrenheit\tCelcius\n" );
23
24     /* display Celsius equivalents of Fahrenheit 32 to 212 */
25     for ( i = 32; i <= 212; i++ ) {
26        printf( "%d\t\t%d\n", i, celcius( i ) );
27     } /* end for */
28
29     return 0; /* indicate successful termination */
30
31  } /* end main */
32
33  /* celsius returns Celsius equivalent of fTemp,
34     given in Fahrenheit */
35  int celcius( int fTemp )
36  {
37     return ( int ) ( 5.0 / 9.0 * ( fTemp - 32 ) );
38
39  } /* end function celsius */
40
41  /* fahrenheit returns Fahrenheit equivalent of cTemp,
42     given in Celsius */
43  int fahrenheit( int cTemp )
44  {
45     return ( int ) ( 9.0 / 5.0 * cTemp + 32 );
46
47  } /* end function fahrenheit */
```

Fig. S5.6   Solution for Exercise 5.24.   (Part 1 of 2.)

```
Fahrenheit equivalents of Celcius temperatures:
Celcius          Fahrenheit
0                32
1                33
2                35
3                37
4                39
5                41
6                42
7                44
8                46
9                48
.
.
.
Celcius equivalents of Fahrenheit temperatures:
Fahrenheit       Celcius
32               0
33               0
34               1
35               1
36               2
37               2
38               3
39               3
40               4
41               5
.
.
.
```

Fig. S5.6   Solution for Exercise 5.24.   (Part 2 of 2.)

5.26   An integer number is said to be a *perfect number* if its factors, including 1 (but not the number itself), sum to the number. For example, 6 is a perfect number because 6 = 1 + 2 + 3. Write a function perfect that determines if parameter number is a perfect number. Use this function in a program that determines and prints all the perfect numbers between 1 and 1000. Print the factors of each perfect number to confirm that the number is indeed perfect. Challenge the power of your computer by testing numbers much larger than 1000.

ANS:

```
1    /* Exercise 5.26 Solution */
2    #include <stdio.h>
3
4    int perfect( int value ); /* function prototype */
5
6    int main()
7    {
```

Fig. S5.7   Solution for Exercise 5.26.   (Part 1 of 2.)

```
 8      int j; /* loop counter */
 9
10      printf( "For the integers from 1 to 1000:\n" );
11
12      /* loop from 2 to 1000 */
13      for ( j = 2; j <= 1000; j++ ) {
14
15         /* if current integer is perfect */
16         if ( perfect( j ) ) {
17            printf( "%d is perfect\n", j );
18         } /* end if */
19
20      } /* end for */
21
22      return 0; /* indicate successful termination */
23
24   } /* end main */
25
26   /* perfect returns true if value is perfect integer,
27      i.e., if value is equal to sum of its factors */
28   int perfect( int value )
29   {
30      int factorSum = 1; /* current sum of factors */
31      int i;             /* loop counter */
32
33      /* loop through possible factor values */
34      for ( i = 2; i <= value / 2; i++ ) {
35
36         /* if i is factor */
37         if ( value % i == 0 ) {
38            factorSum += i; /* add to sum */
39         } /* end if */
40
41      } /* end for */
42
43      /* return true if value is equal to sum of factors */
44      if ( factorSum == value ) {
45         return 1;
46      } /* end if */
47      else {
48         return 0;
49      } /* end else */
50
51   } /* end function perfect */
```

```
For the integers from 1 to 1000:
6 is perfect
28 is perfect
496 is perfect
```

Fig. S5.7　　Solution for Exercise 5.26.　(Part 2 of 2.)

5.30   Write a function `qualityPoints` that inputs a student's average and returns 4 if a student's average is 90–100, 3 if the average is 80–89, 2 if the average is 70–79, 1 if the average is 60-69, and 0 if the average is lower than 60.

   ANS:

```
1    /* Exercise 5.30 Solution */
2    #include <stdio.h>
3
4    int qualityPoints( int average ); /* function prototype */
5
6    int main()
7    {
8       int average; /* current average */
9       int loop;    /* loop counter */
10
11      /* loop for 5 inputs */
12      for ( loop = 1; loop <= 5; loop++ ) {
13         printf( "\nEnter the student's average: " );
14         scanf( "%d", &average );
15
16         /* determine and display corresponding quality points */
17         printf( "%d on a 4 point scale is %d\n",
18            average, qualityPoints( average ) );
19      } /* end for */
20
21      return 0; /* indicate successful termination */
22
23   } /* end main */
24
25   /* qualityPoints takes average in range 0 to 100 and
26      returns corresponding quality points on 0 to 4 scale */
27   int qualityPoints( int average )
28   {
29
30      /* 90 <= average <= 100 */
31      if ( average >= 90 ) {
32         return 4;
33      } /* end if */
34      else if ( average >= 80 ) { /* 80 <= average <= 89 */
35         return 3;
36      } /* end else if */
37      else if ( average >= 70 ) { /* 70 <= average <= 79 */
38         return 2;
39      } /* end else if */
40      else if ( average >= 60 ) { /* 60 <= average <= 69 */
41         return 1;
42      } /* end else if */
43      else { /* 0 <= average < 60 */
44         return 0;
45      } /* end else */
46
```

Fig. S5.8   Solution for Exercise 5.30.   (Part 1 of 2.)

```
47    } /* end function qualityPoints */
```

```
Enter the student's average: 92
92 on a 4 point scale is 4

Enter the student's average: 87
87 on a 4 point scale is 3

Enter the student's average: 75
75 on a 4 point scale is 2

Enter the student's average: 63
63 on a 4 point scale is 1

Enter the student's average: 22
22 on a 4 point scale is 0
```

Fig. S5.8   Solution for Exercise 5.30.   (Part 2 of 2.)

5.32   Computers are playing an increasing role in education. Write a program that will help an elementary school student learn multiplication. Use `rand` to produce two positive one-digit integers. It should then type a question such as:

    How much is 6 times 7?

The student then types the answer. Your program checks the student's answer. If it is correct, print "Very good!" and then ask another multiplication question. If the answer is wrong, print "No. Please try again." and then let the student try the same question again repeatedly until the student finally gets it right.

   ANS:

```
1    /* Exercise 5.32 solution */
2    #include <stdio.h>
3    #include <stdlib.h>
4    #include <time.h>
5
6    void multiplication( void ); /* function prototype */
7
8    int main( void )
9    {
10       srand( time( NULL ) ); /* seed random number generator */
11       multiplication(); /* begin multiplication practice */
12
13       return 0; /* indicate successful termination */
14
15    } /* end main */
16
17    /* multiplication produces pairs of random numbers and
18       prompts user for product */
19    void multiplication( void )
20    {
21       int x;               /* first factor */
22       int y;               /* second factor */
```

Fig. S5.9   Solution for Exercise 5.32.   (Part 1 of 2.)

```
23      int response = 0; /* user response for product */
24
25      /* use sentinel-controlled repetition */
26      printf( "Enter -1 to end.\n" );
27
28      /* loop while sentinel value not read from user */
29      while ( response != -1 ) {
30         x = rand() % 10; /* generate 1-digit random number */
31         y = rand() % 10; /* generate another 1-digit random number */
32
33         printf( "How much is %d times %d? ", x, y );
34         scanf( "%d", &response );
35
36         /* loop while not sentinel value or correct response */
37         while ( response != -1 && response != x * y ) {
38            printf( "No. Please try again.\n? " );
39            scanf( "%d", &response );
40         } /* end while */
41
42         /* correct response */
43         if ( response != -1 ) {
44            printf( "Very good!\n\n" );
45         } /* end if */
46
47      } /* end while */
48
49      printf( "That's all for now. Bye.\n" );
50
51   } /* end function multiplication */
```

```
Enter -1 to end.
How much is 0 times 7? 0
Very good!

How much is 0 times 0? 0
Very good!

How much is 2 times 6? 18
No. Please try again.
? 12
Very good!

How much is 5 times 0? 0
Very good!

How much is 9 times 2? 18
Very good!

How much is 6 times 1? -1
That's all for now. Bye.
```

Fig. S5.9   Solution for Exercise 5.32.   (Part 2 of 2.)

5.35   Write a C program that plays the game of "guess the number" as follows: Your program chooses the number to be guessed by selecting an integer at random in the range 1 to 1000. The program then types:

```
I have a number between 1 and 1000.
Can you guess my number?
Please type your first guess.
```

The player then types a first guess. The program responds with one of the following:

```
1. Excellent! You guessed the number!
   Would you like to play again (y or n)?
2. Too low. Try again.
3. Too high. Try again.
```

If the player's guess is incorrect, your program should loop until the player finally gets the number right. Your program should keep telling the player Too high or Too low to help the player "zero in" on the correct answer. [*Note:* The searching technique employed in this problem is called *binary search*. We will say more about this in the next problem.]

ANS:

```
1   /* Exercise 5.35 solution */
2   #include <stdio.h>
3   #include <stdlib.h>
4   #include <time.h>
5
6   void guessGame( void ); /* function prototype */
7
8   int main()
9   {
10     srand( time( NULL ) ); /* seed random number generator */
11     guessGame();
12
13     return 0; /* indicate successful termination */
14
15  } /* end main */
16
17  /* guessGame generates numbers between 1 and 1000
18     and checks user's guess */
19  void guessGame( void )
```

Fig. S5.10   Solution for Exercise 5.35.   (Part 1 of 3.)

```
20  {
21     int x;        /* randomly generated number */
22     int guess;    /* user's guess */
23     int response; /* response to continue game, 1=yes, 2=no */
24
25     /* loop until user types 2 to quit game */
26     do {
27
28        /* generate random number between 1 and 1000
29           1 is shift, 1000 is scaling factor */
30        x = 1 + rand() % 1000;
31
32        /* prompt for guess */
33        printf( "\nI have a number between 1 and 1000.\n" );
34        printf( "Can you guess my number?\n" );
35        printf( "Please type your first guess.\n? " );
36        scanf( "%d", &guess );
37
38        /* loop until correct number */
39        while ( guess != x ) {
40
41           /* if guess is too low */
42           if ( guess < x ) {
43              printf( "Too low. Try again.\n? " );
44           } /* end if */
45           else { /* guess is too high */
46              printf( "Too high. Try again.\n? " );
47           } /* end else */
48
49           scanf( "%d", &guess );
50        } /* end while */
51
52        /* prompt for another game */
53        printf( "\nExcellent! You guessed the number!\n" );
54        printf( "Would you like to play again?\n" );
55        printf( "Please type ( 1=yes, 2=no )? " );
56        scanf( "%d", &response );
57     } while ( response == 1 ); /* end do...while */
58
59  } /* end function guessGame */
```

Fig. S5.10   Solution for Exercise 5.35.   (Part 2 of 3.)

```
I have a number between 1 and 1000.
Can you guess my number?
Please type your first guess.
? 500
Too low. Try again.
? 750
Too high. Try again.
? 625
Too low. Try again.
? 687
Too high. Try again.
? 656
Too low. Try again.
? 671
Too low. Try again.
? 678
Too high. Try again.
? 675
Too high. Try again.
? 673
Too high. Try again.
? 672

Excellent! You guessed the number!
Would you like to play again?
Please type ( 1=yes, 2=no )? 2
```

Fig. S5.10   Solution for Exercise 5.35.   (Part 3 of 3.)

5.37   Write a recursive function power(base, exponent) that when invoked returns

base^{exponent}

For example, power(3, 4) = 3 * 3 * 3 * 3. Assume that exponent is an integer greater than or equal to 1. *Hint:* The recursion step would use the relationship

base^{exponent} = base * base$^{exponent - 1}$

and the terminating condition occurs when exponent is equal to 1 because

base^1 = base

ANS:

```
1   /* Exercise 5.37 Solution */
2   #include <stdio.h>
3
4   long power( long base, long exponent ); /* function prototype */
5
6   int main()
```

Fig. S5.11   Solution for Exercise 5.37.   (Part 1 of 2.)

```
 7   {
 8       long b; /* base */
 9       long e; /* exponent */
10
11       printf( "Enter a base and an exponent: " );
12       scanf( "%ld%ld", &b, &e );
13
14       /* calculate and display b raised to the e power */
15       printf( "%ld raised to the %ld is %ld\n", b, e, power( b, e ) );
16
17       return 0; /* indicate successful termination */
18
19   } /* end main */
20
21   /* power recursively calculates base raised to the exponent
22      assume exponent >= 1 */
23   long power( long base, long exponent )
24   {
25
26       /* base case: exponent equals 1, return base */
27       if ( exponent == 1 ) {
28           return base;
29       } /* end if */
30       else { /* recursive step */
31           return base * power( base, exponent - 1 );
32       } /* end else */
33
34   } /* end function power */
```

```
Enter a base and an exponent: 5 10
5 raised to the 10 is 9765625
```

Fig. S5.11   Solution for Exercise 5.37. (Part 2 of 2.)

5.41   (*Visualizing Recursion*) It is interesting to watch recursion "in action." Modify the factorial function of Fig. 5.14 to print its local variable and recursive call parameter. For each recursive call, display the outputs on a separate line and add a level of indentation. Do your utmost to make the outputs clear, interesting, and meaningful. Your goal here is to design and implement an output format that helps a person understand recursion better. You may want to add such display capabilities to the many other recursion examples and exercises throughout the text.

> **ANS:** [*Note:* The printf in function printRecursion uses the conversion specification %*d. The * enables the programmer to specify the field width as a variable argument in the printf. In this case variable n is used as the field width, and its value is output.]

```
1    /* Exercise 5.41 Solution */
2    #include <stdio.h>
3
4    long factorial( long number ); /* function prototype */
5    void printRecursion( int n );   /* function prototype */
6
7    int main()
8    {
9       int i; /* loop counter */
10
11      /* calculate factorial( i ) and display result */
12      for ( i = 0; i <= 10; i++ ) {
13         printf( "%2d! = %ld\n", i, factorial( i ) );
14      } /* end for */
15
16      return 0; /* indicate successful termination */
17
18   } /* end main */
19
20   /* recursive definition of function factorial */
21   long factorial( long number )
22   {
23
24      /* base case */
25      if ( number <= 1 ) {
26         return 1;
27      } /* end if */
28      else { /* recursive step */
29         printRecursion( number ); /* add outputs and indentation */
30         return ( number * factorial( number - 1 ) );
31      } /* end else */
32
33   } /* end function factorial */
34
35   /* printRecursion adds outputs and indentation to help
36      visualize recursion */
37   void printRecursion( int n )
38   {
39      printf( "number = %*d\n", n, n );
40   } /* end function printRecursion */
```

Fig. S5.12   Solution for Exercise 5.41. (Part 1 of 2.)

```
 0! = 1
 1! = 1
number =  2
 2! = 2
number =   3
number = 2
 3! = 6
number =    4
number =   3
number = 2
 4! = 24
number =     5
number =    4
number =   3
number = 2
 5! = 120
 .
 .
 .
number =          9
number =         8
number =        7
number =       6
number =      5
number =     4
number =   3
number = 2
 9! = 362880
number =           10
number =          9
number =         8
number =        7
number =       6
number =      5
number =     4
number =   3
number = 2
10! = 3628800
```

Fig. S5.12   Solution for Exercise 5.41. (Part 2 of 2.)

5.45   Write function `distance` that calculates the distance between two points *(x1, y1)* and *(x2, y2)*. All numbers and return values should be of type `double`.

     ANS:

```
1   /* Exercise 5.45 Solution */
2   #include <stdio.h>
3   #include <math.h>
```

Fig. S5.13   Solution for Exercise 5.45. (Part 1 of 2.)

```
4
5    /* function prototype */
6    double distance( double xOne, double yOne, double xTwo, double yTwo );
7
8    int main()
9    {
10      double x1;   /* x coordinate of first point */
11      double y1;   /* y coordinate of first point */
12      double x2;   /* x coordinate of second point */
13      double y2;   /* y coordinate of second point */
14      double dist; /* distance between two points */
15
16      /* prompt for first point coordinates */
17      printf( "Enter the first point: " );
18      scanf( "%lf%lf", &x1, &y1 );
19
20      /* prompt for second point coordinates */
21      printf( "Enter the second point: " );
22      scanf( "%lf%lf", &x2, &y2 );
23
24      dist = distance( x1, y1, x2, y2 ); /* calculate distance */
25
26      printf( "Distance between ( %.2f, %.2f )"
27              " and ( %.2f, %.2f ) is %.2f\n",
28              x1, y1, x2, y2, dist );
29
30      return 0; /* indicate successful termination */
31
32   } /* end main */
33
34   /* distance calculates distance between 2 points
35      given by (xOne, yOne) and (xTwo, yTwo) */
36   double distance( double xOne, double yOne, double xTwo, double yTwo )
37   {
38      double distance; /* distance between two points */
39
40      distance = sqrt( pow( xOne - xTwo, 2 ) + pow( yOne - yTwo, 2 ) );
41
42      return distance;
43
44   } /* end function distance */
```

```
Enter the first point: 3 4
Enter the second point: 0 0
Distance between ( 3.00, 4.00 ) and ( 0.00, 0.00 ) is 5.00
```

Fig. S5.13   Solution for Exercise 5.45. (Part 2 of 2.)

5.46   What does the following program do?

```c
1   #include <stdio.h>
2
3   /* function main begins program execution */
4   int main()
5   {
6      int c; /* variable to hold character input by user */
7
8      if ( ( c = getchar() ) != EOF ) {
9         main();
10        printf( "%c", c );
11     } /* end if */
12
13     return 0; /* indicates successful termination */
14
15   } /* end main */
```

Fig. S5.14   Exercise 5.46: What does this program do?

ANS: *Inputs a character and recursively calls* main() *until the* EOF *character is entered. Every character entered is then output in reverse order.*

```
a b c

c b a
```

Fig. S5.15   Solution for Exercise 5.46.

5.47   What does the following program do?

```c
1   #include <stdio.h>
2
3   int mystery( int a, int b ); /* function prototype */
4
5   /* function main begins program execution */
6   int main()
7   {
8      int x; /* first integer */
9      int y; /* second integer */
10
11     printf( "Enter two integers: " );
12     scanf( "%d%d", &x, &y );
13
14     printf( "The result is %d\n", mystery( x, y ) );
15
```

Fig. S5.16   Exercise 5.47: What does this program do? (Part 1 of 2.)

```
16        return 0; /* indicates successful termination */
17
18   } /* end main */
19
20   /* Parameter b must be a positive integer
21      to prevent infinite recursion */
22   int mystery( int a, int b )
23   {
24      /* base case */
25      if ( b == 1 ) {
26         return a;
27      } /* end if */
28      else { /* recursive step */
29         return a + mystery( a, b - 1 );
30      } /* end else */
31
32   } /* end function mystery */
```

Fig. S5.16   Exercise 5.47: What does this program do? (Part 2 of 2.)

ANS: *The problem mimics multiplication by adding up* a, b *times.*

```
Enter two integers: 87 6
The result is 522
```

Fig. S5.17 Solution for Exercise 5.47.

5.50   Find the error in each of the following program segments and explain how to correct it:

a) **double** cube(**float**);   /* function prototype */
```
        ...
        cube( float number )   /* function definition */
        {
           return number * number * number;
        }
```
ANS: *Function definition is missing return type.*
```
double cube( float );  /* function prototype */
...
double cube( float number )  /* function definition */
{
   return number * number * number;
}
```

b) **register auto int** x = 7;

ANS: *Too many storage class definitions. Auto class definition is not necessary.*
```
register int x = 7;  /* auto removed */
```

c) **int** randomNumber = srand();

ANS: `srand()` *seeds the random number generator, and has a void return type. Function* `rand()` *produces random numbers.*
```
int randomNumber = rand();
```

d) **double** y = 123.45678;
   int x;
   x = y;
   printf("%f\n", (**double**) x);

ANS: *Decimal value is lost when a* `double` *is assigned to an integer. Type-casting the* `int` *to* `double` *cannot bring back the original decimal value. Only* 123.000000 *can be printed.*
```
double y = 123.45678;
double x;

x = y;
printf( "%f\n", x );
```

e) **double** square(**double** number)
   {
       double number;

       return number * number;
   }

ANS: `number` *is defined twice.*
```
double square( double number )
{
   return number * number;
}
```

f) **int** sum(**int** n)
   {
       if (n == 0)
           return 0;
       else
           return n + sum(n);
   }

ANS: *Infinite recursion.*
```
int sum( int n )
{
   if ( n == 0 )
      return 0;
   else
      return n + sum( n - 1 );
}
```

C Arrays

Solutions to Selected Exercises

6.10 Use a single-subscripted array to solve the following problem. A company pays its salespeople on a commission basis. The salespeople receive $200 per week plus 9 percent of their gross sales for that week. For example, a salesperson who grosses $3000 in sales in a week receives $200 plus 9 percent of $3000, or a total of $470. Write a C program (using an array of counters) that determines how many of the salespeople earned salaries in each of the following ranges (assume that each salesperson's salary is truncated to an integer amount):

    a) $200–299
    b) $300–399
    c) $400–499
    d) $500–599
    e) $600–699
    f) $700–799
    g) $800–899
    h) $900–999
    i) $1000 and over

    ANS:

```
1   /* Exercise 6.10 Solution */
2   #include <stdio.h>
3
4   int main()
5   {
6      int salaries[ 11 ] = { 0 };  /* array to hold salary counts */
7      int sales;                   /* current employee's sales */
8      double salary;               /* current employee's salary */
9      double i = 0.09;             /* commission percentage */
10
```

Fig. S6.1   Solution for Exercise 6.10.   (Part 1 of 3.)

```
11      /* prompt user for gross sales */
12      printf( "Enter employee gross sales ( -1 to end ): " );
13      scanf( "%d", &sales );
14
15      /* while sentinel value not read from user */
16      while ( sales != -1 ) {
17
18         /* calculate salary based on sales */
19         salary = 200.0 + sales * i;
20         printf( "Employee Commission is $%.2f\n", salary );
21
22         /* update appropriate salary range */
23         if ( salary >= 200 && salary < 1000 ) {
24            ++salaries[ ( int ) salary / 100 ];
25         } /* end if */
26         else if ( salary >= 1000 ) {
27            ++salaries[ 10 ];
28         } /* end else if */
29
30         /* prompt user for another employee sales amount */
31         printf( "\nEnter employee gross sales ( -1 to end ): " );
32         scanf( "%d", &sales );
33      } /* end while */
34
35      /* display table of ranges and employees in each range */
36      printf( "\nEmployees in the range:\n" );
37      printf( "$200-$299 : %d\n", salaries[ 2 ] );
38      printf( "$300-$399 : %d\n", salaries[ 3 ] );
39      printf( "$400-$499 : %d\n", salaries[ 4 ] );
40      printf( "$500-$599 : %d\n", salaries[ 5 ] );
41      printf( "$600-$699 : %d\n", salaries[ 6 ] );
42      printf( "$700-$799 : %d\n", salaries[ 7 ] );
43      printf( "$800-$899 : %d\n", salaries[ 8 ] );
44      printf( "$900-$999 : %d\n", salaries[ 9 ] );
45      printf( "Over $1000: %d\n", salaries[ 10 ] );
46
47      return 0; /* indicate successful termination */
48
49   } /* end main */
```

Fig. S6.1   Solution for Exercise 6.10.   (Part 2 of 3.)

```
Enter employee gross sales ( -1 to end ): 3000
Employee Commission is $470.00

Enter employee gross sales ( -1 to end ): 1000
Employee Commission is $290.00

Enter employee gross sales ( -1 to end ): 10000
Employee Commission is $1100.00

Enter employee gross sales ( -1 to end ): 8000
Employee Commission is $920.00

Enter employee gross sales ( -1 to end ): 200
Employee Commission is $218.00

Enter employee gross sales ( -1 to end ): 7000
Employee Commission is $830.00

Enter employee gross sales ( -1 to end ): -1

Employees in the range:
$200-$299 : 2
$300-$399 : 0
$400-$499 : 1
$500-$599 : 0
$600-$699 : 0
$700-$799 : 0
$800-$899 : 1
$900-$999 : 1
Over $1000: 1
```

Fig. S6.1   Solution for Exercise 6.10.   (Part 3 of 3.)

6.12   Write single statements that perform each of the following single-subscripted array operations:
   a) Initialize the 10 elements of integer array counts to zeros.
   ANS:
   ```
   for ( i = 0; i <= 9; i++ )
      counts[ i ] = 0;
   ```

   b) Add 1 to each of the 15 elements of integer array bonus.
   ANS:
   ```
   for ( i = 0; i <= 14; i++ )
      ++bonus[ i ];
   ```

   c) Read the 12 values of floating-point array monthlyTemperatures from the keyboard.
   ANS:
   ```
   for ( i = 0; i <= 11; i++ ) {
      printf( "Enter a temperature: " );
      scanf( "%f", &monthlyTemperatures[ i ] );
   }
   ```

d) Print the 5 values of integer array `bestScores` in column format.

ANS:
```
for ( i = 0; i <= 4; i++ ) {
    printf( "%d\t", bestScores[ i ] );
```

6.15   Use a single-subscripted array to solve the following problem. Read in 20 numbers, each of which is between 10 and 100, inclusive. As each number is read, print it only if it is not a duplicate of a number already read. Provide for the "worst case" in which all 20 numbers are different. Use the smallest possible array to solve this problem.

ANS:

```
1   /* Exercise 6.15 Solution */
2   #include <stdio.h>
3   #define MAX 20
4
5   int main()
6   {
7       int a[ MAX ] = { 0 }; /* array for user input */
8       int i;                /* loop counter */
9       int j;                /* loop counter */
10      int k = 0;            /* number of values currently entered */
11      int duplicate;        /* flag for duplicate values */
12      int value;            /* current value */
13
14      printf( "Enter 20 integers between 10 and 100:\n" );
15
16      /* get 20 integers from user */
17      for ( i = 0; i <= MAX - 1; i++ ) {
18          duplicate = 0;
19          scanf( "%d", &value );
20
21          /* test if integer is a duplicate */
22          for ( j = 0; j < k; j++ ) {
23
24              /* if duplicate, raise flag and break loop */
25              if ( value == a[ j ] ) {
26                  duplicate = 1;
27                  break;
28              } /* end if */
29
30          } /* end for */
31
32          /* if number is not a duplicate enter it in array */
33          if ( !duplicate ) {
34              a[ k++ ] = value;
35          } /* end if */
36
37      } /* end for */
38
```

Fig. S6.2   Solution for Exercise 6.15.   (Part 1 of 2.)

```
39        printf( "\nThe nonduplicate values are:\n" );
40
41        /* display array of nonduplicates */
42        for ( i = 0; a[ i ] != 0; i++ ) {
43           printf( "%d   ", a[ i ] );
44        } /* end for */
45
46        printf( "\n" );
47
48        return 0; /* indicate successful termination */
49
50    } /* end main */
```

```
Enter 20 integers between 10 and 100:
10 11 12 13 14 15 16 17 18 19 20 21 10 11 12 13 14 15 16 17

The nonduplicate values are:
10   11   12   13   14   15   16   17   18   19   20   21
```

Fig. S6.2   Solution for Exercise 6.15.   (Part 2 of 2.)

6.21   (*Airline Reservations System*) A small airline has just purchased a computer for its new automated reservations system. The president has asked you to program the new system. You are to write a program to assign seats on each flight of the airline's only plane (capacity: 10 seats).

Your program should display the following menu of alternatives:

```
Please type 1 for "first class"
Please type 2 for "economy"
```

If the person types 1, then your program should assign a seat in the first class section (seats 1-5). If the person types 2, then your program should assign a seat in the economy section (seats 6-10). Your program should then print a boarding pass indicating the person's seat number and whether it is in the first class or economy section of the plane.

Use a single-subscripted array to represent the seating chart of the plane. Initialize all the elements of the array to 0 to indicate that all seats are empty. As each seat is assigned, set the corresponding elements of the array to 1 to indicate that the seat is no longer available.

Your program should, of course, never assign a seat that has already been assigned. When the first class section is full, your program should ask the person if it is acceptable to be placed in the economy section (and vice versa). If yes, then make the appropriate seat assignment. If no, then print the message "Next flight leaves in 3 hours."

ANS:

```
1    /* Exercise 6.21 Solution */
2    #include <stdio.h>
3    #include <ctype.h>
4
```

Fig. S6.3   Solution for Exercise 6.21.   (Part 1 of 4.)

```
 5   int main()
 6   {
 7      int plane[ 11 ] = { 0 }; /* seats on the plane */
 8      int i = 0;                /* counter */
 9      int firstClass= 1;        /* first class seats start at 1 */
10      int economy = 6;          /* economy seats start at 6 */
11      int choice;               /* user's choice */
12      char response[ 2 ];       /* user's response */
13
14      /* loop 10 times */
15      while ( i < 10 ) {
16         printf( "\n%s\n%s\n? ", "Please type 1 for \"first class\"",
17                "Please type 2 for \"economy\"" );
18         scanf( "%d", &choice );
19
20         /* if user selects first class */
21         if ( choice == 1 ) {
22
23            /* if seat are available in first class */
24            if ( !plane[ firstClass ] && firstClass <= 5 ) {
25               printf( "Your seat assignment is %d\n", firstClass );
26               plane[ firstClass++ ] = 1;
27               i++;
28            } /* end if */
29            /* if no first class seats, but economy seats available */
30            else if ( firstClass > 5 && economy <= 10 ) {
31
32               /* ask if passenger would like to sit in economy */
33               printf( "The first class section is full.\n" );
34               printf( "Would you like to sit in the economy" );
35               printf( " section ( Y or N )? " );
36               scanf( "%s", response );
37
38               /* if response is yes, then assign seat */
39               if ( toupper( response[ 0 ] ) == 'Y' ) {
40                  printf( "Your seat assignment is %d\n", economy );
41                  plane[ economy++ ] = 1;
42                  i++;
43               } /* end if */
44               else { /* print next departure */
45                  printf( "Next flight leaves in 3 hours.\n" );
46               } /* end else */
47
48            } /* end else if */
49            else { /* print next departure */
50               printf( "Next flight leaves in 3 hours.\n" );
51            } /* end else */
52
53         } /* end if */
54         else { /* if user selects economy */
```

Fig. S6.3   Solution for Exercise 6.21. (Part 2 of 4.)

```
55
56              /* if seats available, assign seat */
57              if ( !plane[ economy ] && economy <= 10 ) {
58                 printf( "Your seat assignment is %d\n", economy );
59                 plane[ economy++ ] = 1;
60                 i++;
61              } /* end if */
62              /* if only first class seats are available */
63              else if ( economy > 10 && firstClass <= 5 ) {
64
65                 /* ask if first class is suitable */
66                 printf( "The economy section is full.\n" );
67                 printf( "Would you like to sit in first class" );
68                 printf( " section ( Y or N )? " );
69                 scanf( "%s", response );
70
71                 /* if response is yes, assign seat */
72                 if ( toupper( response[ 0 ] ) == 'Y' ) {
73                    printf( "Your seat assignment is %d\n", firstClass );
74                    plane[ firstClass++ ] = 1;
75                    i++;
76                 } /* end if */
77                 else { /* print next departure */
78                    printf( "Next flight leaves in 3 hours.\n" );
79                 } /* end else */
80
81              } /* end else if */
82              else { /* print next departure */
83                 printf( "Next flight leaves in 3 hours.\n" );
84              } /* end else */
85
86           } /* end else */
87
88        } /* end while */
89
90        printf( "\nAll seats for this flight are sold.\n" );
91
92        return 0; /* indicate successful termination */
93
94  } /* end main */
```

Fig. S6.3   Solution for Exercise 6.21.   (Part 3 of 4.)

```
Please type 1 for "first class"
Please type 2 for "economy"
? 2
Your seat assignment is 6

Please type 1 for "first class"
Please type 2 for "economy"
? 1
Your seat assignment is 1

Please type 1 for "first class"
Please type 2 for "economy"
? 2
Your seat assignment is 7
.
.
.
Please type 1 for "first class"
Please type 2 for "economy"
? 1
The first class section is full.
Would you like to sit in the economy section ( Y or N )? n
Next flight leaves in 3 hours.

Please type 1 for "first class"
Please type 2 for "economy"
? 1
The first class section is full.
Would you like to sit in the economy section ( Y or N )? y
Your seat assignment is 9

Please type 1 for "first class"
Please type 2 for "economy"
? 2
Your seat assignment is 10

All seats for this flight are sold.
```

Fig. S6.3   Solution for Exercise 6.21.   (Part 4 of 4.)

6.23   (*Turtle Graphics*) The Logo language, which is particularly popular among personal computer users, made the concept of *turtle graphics* famous. Imagine a mechanical turtle that walks around the room under the control of a C program. The turtle holds a pen in one of two positions, up or down. While the pen is down, the turtle traces out shapes as it moves; while the pen is up, the turtle moves about freely without writing anything. In this problem you will simulate the operation of the turtle and create a computerized sketchpad as well.

Use a 50-by-50 array `floor` which is initialized to zeros. Read commands from an array that contains them. Keep track of the current position of the turtle at all times and whether the pen is currently up or down. Assume that the turtle always starts at position 0,0 of the floor with its pen up. The set of turtle commands your program must process are shown in the following table:

Command	Meaning
1	Pen up
2	Pen down
3	Turn right
4	Turn left
5,10	Move forward 10 spaces (or a number other than 10)
6	Print the 20-by-20 array
9	End of data (sentinel)

Suppose that the turtle is somewhere near the center of the floor. The following "program" would draw and print a 12-by 12-square:

```
2
5,12
3
5,12
3
5,12
3
5,12
1
6
9
```

As the turtle moves with the pen down, set the appropriate elements of array floor to 1s. When the 6 command (print) is given, wherever there is a 1 in the array, display an asterisk, or some other character you choose. Wherever there is a zero, display a blank. Write a program to implement the turtle graphics capabilities discussed here. Write several turtle graphics programs to draw interesting shapes. Add other commands to increase the power of your turtle graphics language.

ANS:

```
1   /* Exercise 6.23 Solution */
2   #include <stdio.h>
3
4   #define TRUE 1
5   #define FALSE 0
6   #define MAX 100 /* the maximum number of commands */
7
8   /* function prototypes */
9   void getCommands( int commands[][ 2 ] );
10  int turnRight( int d );
11  int turnLeft( int d );
12  void movePen( int down, int a[][ 50 ], int dir, int dist );
13  void printArray( int a[][ 50 ] );
```

Fig. S6.4   Solution for Exercise 6.23.   (Part 1 of 6.)

```
14
15    int main()
16    {
17       int floor[ 50 ][ 50 ] = { 0 };      /* floor grid */
18       int penDown = FALSE;                /* pen down flag */
19       int command;                        /* current command */
20       int direction = 0;                  /* direction indicator */
21       int commandArray[ MAX ][ 2 ] = { 0 }; /* array of commands */
22       int distance;                       /* distance to move */
23       int count = 0;                      /* command counter */
24
25       getCommands( commandArray );
26       command = commandArray[ count ][ 0 ];
27
28       /* continue receiving input while -9 is not entered */
29       while ( command != 9 ) {
30
31          /* determine what command was entered and perform action */
32          switch ( command ) {
33
34             case 1:
35                penDown = FALSE;
36                break; /* exit switch */
37
38             case 2:
39                penDown = TRUE;
40                break; /* exit switch */
41
42             case 3:
43                direction = turnRight( direction );
44                break; /* exit switch */
45
46             case 4:
47                direction = turnLeft( direction );
48                break; /* exit switch */
49
50             case 5:
51                distance = commandArray[ count ][ 1 ];
52                movePen( penDown, floor, direction, distance );
53                break; /* exit switch */
54
55             case 6:
56                printf( "\nThe drawing is:\n\n" );
57                printArray( floor );
58                break; /* exit switch */
59          } /* end switch */
60
61          command = commandArray[ ++count ][ 0 ];
62       } /* end while */
63
```

Fig. S6.4   Solution for Exercise 6.23.   (Part 2 of 6.)

```
64     return 0; /* indicate successful termination */
65
66  } /* end main */
67
68  /* getCommands prompts user for commands */
69  void getCommands( int commands[][ 2 ] )
70  {
71     int i;            /* counter */
72     int tempCommand; /* temporary command holder */
73
74     printf( "Enter command ( 9 to end input ): " );
75     scanf( "%d", &tempCommand );
76
77     /* recieve commands until -9 or 100 commands are entered */
78     for ( i = 0; tempCommand != 9 && i < MAX; i++ ) {
79        commands[ i ][ 0 ] = tempCommand;
80
81        /* ignore comma after 5 is entered */
82        if ( tempCommand == 5 ) {
83           scanf( ",%d", &commands[ i ][ 1 ] );
84        } /* end if */
85
86        printf( "Enter command ( 9 to end input ): " );
87        scanf( "%d", &tempCommand );
88     } /* end for */
89
90     commands[ i ][ 0 ] = 9; /* last command */
91  } /* end function getCommands */
92
93  /* turnRight turns turtle to the right */
94  int turnRight( int d )
95  {
96     return ++d > 3 ? 0 : d;
97
98  } /* end function turnRight */
99
100 /* turnLeft turns turtle to the left */
101 int turnLeft( int d )
102 {
103    return --d < 0 ? 3 : d;
104
105 } /* end function turnLeft */
106
107 /* movePen moves the pen */
108 void movePen( int down, int a[][ 50 ], int dir, int dist )
109 {
110    int i;               /* loop counter */
111    int j;               /* loop counter */
112    static int xPos = 0; /* x coordinate */
113    static int yPos = 0; /* y coordinate */
```

Fig. S6.4   Solution for Exercise 6.23.   (Part 3 of 6.)

```
114
115      /* determine which way to move pen */
116      switch ( dir ) {
117
118         case 0: /* move to the right */
119
120            /* move dist spaces or until edge of floor */
121            for ( j = 1; j <= dist && yPos + j < 50; j++ ) {
122
123               /* draw 1 if pen is down */
124               if ( down ) {
125                  a[ xPos ][ yPos + j ] = 1;
126               } /* end if */
127
128            } /* end for */
129
130            yPos += j - 1;
131            break; /* exit switch */
132
133         case 1: /* move down */
134
135            /* move dist spaces or until edge of floor */
136            for ( i = 1; i <= dist && xPos + i < 50; i++ ) {
137
138               /* draw 1 if pen is down */
139               if ( down ) {
140                  a[ xPos + i ][ yPos ] = 1;
141               } /* end if */
142
143            } /* end for */
144
145            xPos += i - 1;
146            break; /* exit switch */
147
148         case 2: /* move to the left */
149
150            /* move dist spaces or until edge of floor */
151            for ( j = 1; j <= dist && yPos - j >= 0; j++ ) {
152
153               /* draw 1 if pen is down */
154               if ( down ) {
155                  a[ xPos ][ yPos - j ] = 1;
156               } /* end if */
157
158            } /* end for */
159
160            yPos -= j - 1;
161            break; /* exit switch */
162
163         case 3: /* move up */
```

Fig. S6.4   Solution for Exercise 6.23.   (Part 4 of 6.)

```
164
165              /* move dist spaces or until edge of floor */
166              for ( i = 1; i <= dist && xPos - i >= 0; i++ ) {
167
168                 /* draw 1 if pen is down */
169                 if ( down ) {
170                    a[ xPos - i ][ yPos ] = 1;
171                 } /* end if */
172
173              } /* end for */
174
175              xPos -= i - 1;
176              break; /* exit switch */
177        } /* end switch */
178
179 } /* end function movePen */
180
181 /* printArray prints array drawing */
182 void printArray( int a[][ 50 ] )
183 {
184    int i; /* counter */
185    int j; /* counter */
186
187    /* loop through array */
188    for ( i = 0; i < 50; i++ ) {
189
190       /* loop through array */
191       for ( j = 0; j < 50; j++ ) {
192          putchar( a[ i ][ j ] ? '*' : ' ' );
193       } /* end for */
194
195       putchar( '\n' );
196    } /* end for */
197
198 } /* end function printArray */
```

Fig. S6.4   Solution for Exercise 6.23.   (Part 5 of 6.)

```
Enter command ( 9 to end input ): 2
Enter command ( 9 to end input ): 5,12
Enter command ( 9 to end input ): 3
Enter command ( 9 to end input ): 5,12
Enter command ( 9 to end input ): 3
Enter command ( 9 to end input ): 5,12
Enter command ( 9 to end input ): 3
Enter command ( 9 to end input ): 5,12
Enter command ( 9 to end input ): 1
Enter command ( 9 to end input ): 6
Enter command ( 9 to end input ): 9

The drawing is:

*************
*           *
*           *
*           *
*           *
*           *
*           *
*           *
*           *
*           *
*           *
*           *
*************
```

Fig. S6.4   Solution for Exercise 6.23.   (Part 6 of 6.)

6.30   (*The Sieve of Eratosthenes*) A prime integer is any integer that can be divided evenly only by itself and 1. The Sieve of Eratosthenes is a method of finding prime numbers. It works as follows:

1) Create an array with all elements initialized to 1 (true). Array elements with prime subscripts will remain 1. All other array elements will eventually be set to zero.

2) Starting with array subscript 2 (subscript 1 must be prime), every time an array element is found whose value is 1, loop through the remainder of the array and set to zero every element whose subscript is a multiple of the subscript for the element with value 1. For array subscript 2, all elements beyond 2 in the array that are multiples of 2 will be set to zero (subscripts 4, 6, 8, 10, etc.). For array subscript 3, all elements beyond 3 in the array that are multiples of 3 will be set to zero (subscripts 6, 9, 12, 15, etc.).

When this process is complete, the array elements that are still set to one indicate that the subscript is a prime number. These subscripts can then be printed. Write a program that uses an array of 1000 elements to determine and print the prime numbers between 1 and 999. Ignore element 0 of the array.

ANS:

```
1   /* Exercise 6.30 Solution */
2   #include <stdio.h>
```

Fig. S6.5   Solution for Exercise 6.30.   (Part 1 of 3.)

```
 3    #define SIZE 1000
 4
 5    int main()
 6    {
 7       int array[ SIZE ]; /* array to indicate prime numbers */
 8       int loop;            /* loop counter */
 9       int loop2;           /* loop counter */
10       int count = 0;       /* total prime numbers */
11
12       /* set all array elements to 1 */
13       for ( loop = 0; loop < SIZE; loop++ ) {
14          array[ loop ] = 1;
15       } /* end for */
16
17       /* test for multiples of current subscript */
18       for ( loop = 1; loop < SIZE; loop++ ) {
19
20          /* start with array subscript two */
21          if ( array[ loop ] == 1 && loop != 1 ) {
22
23             /* loop through remainder of array */
24             for ( loop2 = loop; loop2 <= SIZE; loop2++ ) {
25
26                /* set to zero all multiples of loop */
27                if ( loop2 % loop == 0 && loop2 != loop ) {
28                   array[ loop2 ] = 0;
29                } /* end if */
30
31             } /* end for */
32
33          } /* end if */
34
35       } /* end for */
36
37       /* display prime numbers in the range 2 - 197 */
38       for ( loop = 2; loop < SIZE; loop++ ) {
39
40          if ( array[ loop ] == 1 ) {
41             printf( "%3d is a prime number.\n", loop );
42             ++count;
43          } /* end if */
44
45       } /* end for */
46
47       printf( "A total of %d prime numbers were found.\n", count );
48
49       return 0; /* indicate successful termination */
50
51    } /* end main */
```

Fig. S6.5   Solution for Exercise 6.30.   (Part 2 of 3.)

```
 2 is a prime number.
 3 is a prime number.
 5 is a prime number.
 7 is a prime number.
11 is a prime number.
13 is a prime number.
17 is a prime number.
19 is a prime number.
 .
 .
 .
971 is a prime number.
977 is a prime number.
983 is a prime number.
991 is a prime number.
997 is a prime number.
A total of 168 prime numbers were found.
```

Fig. S6.5   Solution for Exercise 6.30.   (Part 3 of 3.)

6.31   (*Bucket Sort*) A bucket sort begins with an single-subscripted array of positive integers to be sorted, and a double-subscripted array of integers with rows subscripted from 0 to 9 and columns subscripted from 0 to n - 1 where n is the number of values in the array to be sorted. Each row of the double-subscripted array is referred to as a bucket. Write a function `bucketSort` that takes an integer array and the array size as arguments.

The algorithm is as follows:

1)   Loop through the single-subscripted array and place each of its values in a row of the bucket array based on its ones digit. For example, 97 is placed in row 7, 3 is placed in row 3 and 100 is placed in row 0.

2)   Loop through the bucket array and copy the values back to the original array. The new order of the above values in the single-subscripted array is 100, 3 and 97.

3)   Repeat this process for each subsequent digit position (tens, hundreds, thousands, etc.) and stop when the leftmost digit of the largest number has be processed.

On the second pass of the array, 100 is placed in row 0, 3 is placed in row 0 (it had only one digit) and 97 is placed in row 9. The order of the values in the single-subscripted array is 100, 3 and 97. On the third pass, 100 is placed in row 1, 3 is placed in row zero and 97 is placed in row zero (after 3). The bucket sort is guaranteed to have all the values properly sorted after processing the leftmost digit of the largest number. The bucket sort knows it is done when all the values are copied into row zero of the double-subscripted array.

Note that the double-subscripted array of buckets is ten times the size of the integer array being sorted. This sorting technique provides better performance than a bubble sort, but requires much larger storage capacity. Bubble sort requires only one additional memory location for the type of data being sorted. Bucket sort is an example of a space-time trade-off. It uses more memory, but performs better. This version of the bucket sort requires copying all the data back to the original array on each pass. Another possibility is to create a second double-subscripted bucket array and repeatedly move the data between the two bucket arrays until all the data is copied into row zero of one of the arrays. Row zero then contains the sorted array.

ANS:

```
1   /* Exercise 6.31 Solution */
2   #include <stdio.h>
3
4   /* symbolic constant SIZE must be defined as the array size
5      for bucketSort to work */
6   #define SIZE 12
7
8   /* function prototypes */
9   void bucketSort( int a[] );
10  void distributeElements( int a[], int buckets[][ SIZE ], int digit );
11  void collectElements( int a[], int buckets[][ SIZE ] );
12  int numberOfDigits( int b[], int arraySize );
13  void zeroBucket( int buckets[][ SIZE ] );
14
15  int main()
16  {
17
18     /* array to be sorted */
19     int array[ SIZE ] = { 19, 13, 5, 27, 1, 26, 31, 16, 2, 9, 11, 21 };
20     int i; /* loop counter */
21
22     printf( "Array elements in original order:\n" );
23
24     /* display the unsorted array */
25     for ( i = 0; i < SIZE; i++ ) {
26        printf( "%3d", array[ i ] );
27     } /* end for */
28
29     putchar( '\n' );
30     bucketSort( array ); /* sort the array */
31
32     printf( "\nArray elements in sorted order:\n" );
33
34     /* display sorted array */
35     for ( i = 0; i < SIZE; i++ ) {
36        printf( "%3d", array[ i ] );
37     } /* end for */
38
39     putchar( '\n' );
40
41     return 0; /* indicate successful termination */
42
43  } /* end main */
44
45  /* Perform the bucket sort algorithm */
46  void bucketSort( int a[] )
47  {
48     int totalDigits;                 /* largest # of digits in array */
49     int i;                           /* loop counter */
```

Fig. S6.6   Solution for Exercise 6.31.   (Part 1 of 4.)

```
50     int bucket[ 10 ][ SIZE ] = { 0 }; /* initialize bucket array */
51
52     totalDigits = numberOfDigits( a, SIZE );
53
54     /* put elements in buckets for sorting
55        one sorted, get elements from buckets */
56     for ( i = 1; i <= totalDigits; i++ ) {
57        distributeElements( a, bucket, i );
58        collectElements( a, bucket );
59
60        /* set all bucket contents to zero */
61        if ( i != totalDigits ) {
62           zeroBucket( bucket );
63        } /* end if */
64
65     } /* end for */
66
67  } /* end function bucketSort */
68
69  /* Determine the number of digits in the largest number */
70  int numberOfDigits( int b[], int arraySize )
71  {
72     int largest = b[ 0 ]; /* assume first element is largest */
73     int i;                /* loop counter */
74     int digits = 0;       /* total number of digits */
75
76     /* find largest array element */
77     for ( i = 1; i < arraySize; i++ ) {
78
79        if ( b[ i ] > largest ) {
80           largest = b[ i ];
81        } /* end if */
82
83     } /* end for */
84
85     /* find number of digits of largest element */
86     while ( largest != 0 ) {
87        ++digits;
88        largest /= 10;
89     } /* end while */
90
91     return digits; /* return number of digits */
92
93  } /* end function numberOfDigits */
94
95  /* Distribute elements into buckets based on specified digit */
96  void distributeElements( int a[], int buckets[][ SIZE ], int digit )
97  {
98     int divisor = 10;  /* used to get specific digit */
99     int i;             /* loop counter */
```

Fig. S6.6   Solution for Exercise 6.31.   (Part 2 of 4.)

```
100      int bucketNumber;  /* current bucket number */
101      int elementNumber; /* current element number */
102
103      /* determine the divisor */
104      for ( i = 1; i < digit; i++ ) {
105         divisor *= 10;
106      } /* end for */
107
108      /* bucketNumber example for hundreds digit: */
109      /* ( 1234 % 1000 - 1234 % 100 ) / 100 --> 2    */
110      for ( i = 0; i < SIZE; i++ ) {
111         bucketNumber = ( a[ i ] % divisor - a[ i ] % ( divisor / 10 ) ) /
112            ( divisor / 10 );
113
114         /* retrieve value in buckets[ bucketNumber ][ 0 ] to determine */
115         /* which element of the row to store a[ i ] in.               */
116         elementNumber = ++buckets[ bucketNumber ][ 0 ];
117         buckets[ bucketNumber ][ elementNumber ] = a[ i ];
118      } /* end for */
119
120   } /* end function distributeElements */
121
122   /* Return elements to original array */
123   void collectElements( int a[], int buckets[][ SIZE ] )
124   {
125      int i;                 /* loop counter */
126      int j;                 /* loop counter */
127      int subscript = 0; /* current subscript */
128
129      /* retrieve elements from buckets */
130      for ( i = 0; i < 10; i++ ) {
131
132         for ( j = 1; j <= buckets[ i ][ 0 ]; j++ ) {
133            a[ subscript++ ] = buckets[ i ][ j ];
134         } /* end for */
135
136      } /* end for */
137
138   } /* end function collectElements */
139
140   /* Set all buckets to zero */
141   void zeroBucket( int buckets[][ SIZE ] )
142   {
143      int i; /* loop counter */
144      int j; /* loop counter */
145
146      for ( i = 0; i < 10; i++ ) {
147
148         for ( j = 0; j < SIZE; j++ ) {
149            buckets[ i ][ j ] = 0;
```

Fig. S6.6   Solution for Exercise 6.31.   (Part 3 of 4.)

```
150         } /* end for */
151
152     } /* end for */
153
154 } /* end function zeroBucket */
```

```
Array elements in original order:
 19 13  5 27  1 26 31 16  2  9 11 21

Array elements in sorted order:
  1  2  5  9 11 13 16 19 21 26 27 31
```

Fig. S6.6   Solution for Exercise 6.31. (Part 4 of 4.)

6.34   (*Linear Search*) Modify the program of Fig. 6.18 to use a recursive linearSearch function to perform the linear search of the array. The function should receive an integer array and the size of the array as arguments. If the search key is found, return the array subscript; otherwise, return –1.

ANS:

```
1   /* Exercise 6.34 Solution */
2   #include <stdio.h>
3   #define SIZE 100
4
5   /* function prototypes */
6   int linearSearch( int array[], int key, int low, int high );
7
8   int main()
9   {
10      int array[ SIZE ]; /* array to be searched */
11      int loop;          /* loop counter */
12      int searchKey;     /* element to search for */
13      int element;       /* result of linear search */
14
15      /* initialize array elements */
16      for ( loop = 0; loop < SIZE; loop++ ) {
17         array[ loop ] = 2 * loop;
18      } /* end for */
19
20      /* obtain search key from user */
21      printf( "Enter the integer search key: " );
22      scanf( "%d", &searchKey );
23
24      /* search array for search key */
25      element = linearSearch( array, searchKey, 0, SIZE - 1 );
26
27      /* display message if search key was found */
28      if ( element != -1 ) {
29         printf( "Found value in element %d\n", element );
```

Fig. S6.7   Solution for Exercise 6.34. (Part 1 of 2.)

```
30      } /* end if */
31      else {
32         printf( "Value not found\n" );
33      } /* end else */
34
35      return 0; /* indicate successful termination */
36
37   } /* end main */
38
39   /* function to search array for specified key */
40   int linearSearch( int array[], int key, int low, int high )
41   {
42
43      /* recursively search array */
44      if ( array[ low ] == key ) {
45         return low;
46      } /* end if */
47      else if ( low == high ) {
48         return -1;
49      } /* end else if */
50      else { /* recursive call */
51         return linearSearch( array, key, low + 1, high );
52      } /* end else */
53
54   } /* end function linearSearch */
```

```
Enter the integer search key: 8
Found value in element 4
```

Fig. S6.7   Solution for Exercise 6.34.   (Part 2 of 2.)

```
Enter the integer search key: 48
Found value in element 24
```

```
Enter the integer search key: 99
Value not found
```

6.37   (*Print an array*) Write a recursive function printArray that takes an array and the size of the array as arguments, and returns nothing. The function should stop processing and return when it receives an array of size zero.

ANS:

```
1   /* Exercise 6.37 Solution */
2   #include <stdio.h>
3   #include <stdlib.h>
4   #include <time.h>
5
6   #define SIZE 10
7
8   /* function prototype */
9   void printArray( int array[], int low, int high );
10
11  int main()
12  {
13     int array[ SIZE ]; /* array to be printed */
14     int loop;          /* loop counter */
15
16     srand( time( NULL ) );
17
18     /* initialize array elements to random numbers */
19     for ( loop = 0; loop < SIZE; loop++ ) {
20        array[ loop ] = 1 + rand() % 500;
21     } /* end for */
22
23     printf( "Array values printed in main:\n" );
24
25     /* print array elements */
26     for ( loop = 0; loop < SIZE; loop++ ) {
27        printf( "%d  ", array[ loop ] );
28     } /* end for */
29
30     printf( "\n\nArray values printed in printArray:\n" );
31     printArray( array, 0, SIZE - 1 );
32     printf( "\n" );
33
34     return 0; /* indicate successful termination */
35
36  } /* end main */
37
38  /* function to recursively print an array */
39  void printArray( int array[], int low, int high )
40  {
41     /* print first element of array passed */
42     printf( "%d  ", array[ low ] );
43
44     /* return if array only has 1 element */
45     if ( low == high ) {
46        return;
47     } /* end if */
48     else { /* call printArray with new subarray */
```

Fig. S6.8   Solution for Exercise 6.37.   (Part 1 of 2.)

```
49          printArray( array, low + 1, high );
50       } /* end else */
51
52    } /* end function printArray */
```

```
Array values printed in main:
22  180  7  321  486  366  69  304  273  213

Array values printed in printArray:
22  180  7  321  486  366  69  304  273  213
```

Fig. S6.8   Solution for Exercise 6.37.   (Part 2 of 2.)

6.39   (*Find the minimum value in an array*) Write a recursive function recursiveMinimum that takes an integer array and the array size as arguments and returns the smallest element of the array. The function should stop processing and return when it receives an array of one element.

ANS:

```
1   /* Exercise 6.39 Solution */
2   #include <stdio.h>
3   #include <stdlib.h>
4   #include <time.h>
5   #define SIZE 10
6   #define MAXRANGE 1000
7
8   /* function prototype */
9   int recursiveMinimum( int array[], int low, int high );
10
11  int main()
12  {
13     int array[ SIZE ]; /* array to be searched */
14     int loop;          /* loop counter */
15     int smallest;      /* smallest element */
16
17     srand( time( NULL ) );
18
19     /* initialize elements of array to random numbers */
20     for ( loop = 0; loop < SIZE; loop++ ) {
21        array[ loop ] = 1 + rand() % MAXRANGE;
22     } /* end for */
23
24     printf( "Array members are:\n" );
25
26     /* display array */
27     for ( loop = 0; loop < SIZE; loop++ ) {
28        printf( " %d ", array[ loop ] );
29     } /* end for */
30
```

Fig. S6.9   Solution for Exercise 6.39.   (Part 1 of 2.)

```
31      /* find and display smallest array element */
32      printf( "\n" );
33      smallest = recursiveMinimum( array, 0, SIZE - 1 );
34      printf( "\nSmallest element is: %d\n", smallest );
35
36      return 0; /* indicate successful termination */
37
38   } /* end main */
39
40   /* function to recursively find minimum array element */
41   int recursiveMinimum( int array[], int low, int high )
42   {
43      static int smallest = MAXRANGE; /* largest possible value */
44
45      /* if first element of array is smallest so far,
46         set smallest equal to that element */
47      if ( array[ low ] < smallest ) {
48         smallest = array[ low ];
49      } /* end if */
50
51      /* if only one element in array, return smallest */
52      if ( low == high ) {
53         return smallest;
54      } /* end if */
55      else { /* recursively call recursiveMinimum with new subarray */
56         return recursiveMinimum( array, low + 1, high );
57      } /* end else */
58
59   } /* end function recursiveMinimum */
```

```
Array members are:
 666   251   624   359   577   837   992   197   249   492

Smallest element is: 197
```

Fig. S6.9   Solution for Exercise 6.39.   (Part 2 of 2.)

7

Pointers

Solutions to Selected Exercises

7.9 Answer each of the following. Assume that unsigned integers are stored in 2 bytes and that the starting address of the array is at location 1002500 in memory.

    a) Define an array of type `unsigned int` called `values` with five elements, and initialize the elements to the even integers from 2 to 10. Assume the symbolic constant SIZE has been defined as 5.

ANS: **unsigned int** values[SIZE] = { 2, 4, 6, 8, 10 };

    b) Define a pointer vPtr that points to an object of type `unsigned int`.

ANS: **unsigned int** *vPtr;

    c) Print the elements of array `values` using array subscript notation. Use a `for` statement and assume integer control variable i has been defined.

ANS:
```
for ( i = 0; i < SIZE; i++ )
    printf( "%d ", values[ i ] );
```

    d) Give two separate statements that assign the starting address of array `values` to pointer variable vPtr.

ANS:
```
1) vPtr = values;
2) vPtr = &values[ 0 ];
```

    e) Print the elements of array `values` using pointer/offset notation.

ANS:
```
for  ( i = 0; i < SIZE; i++ )
    printf( "%d", *( vPtr + i ) );
```

    f) Print the elements of array `values` using pointer/offset notation with the array name as the pointer.

ANS:
```
for  ( i = 0; i < SIZE; i++ )
    printf( "%d", *( values + i ) );
```

g) Print the elements of array values by subscripting the pointer to the array.

ANS:
```
for  ( i = 0; i < SIZE; i++ )
    printf( "%d", vPtr[ i ] );
```

h) Refer to element 5 of array values using array subscript notation, pointer/offset notation with the array name as the pointer, pointer subscript notation, and pointer/offset notation.

ANS: values[4], *(values + 4), vPtr[4], *(vPtr + 4).

i) What address is referenced by vPtr + 3? What value is stored at that location?

ANS: 1002506; 8.

j) Assuming vPtr points to values[4], what address is referenced by vPtr -= 4. What value is stored at that location?

ANS: 1002500; 2.

7.22   What does this program do?

```
1    /* ex07_22.c */
2    /* what does this program do? */
3    #include <stdio.h>
4
5    int mystery2( const char *s ); /* prototype */
6
7    int main()
8    {
9       char string[ 80 ]; /* create char array */
10
11      printf( "Enter a string: " );
12      scanf( "%s", string );
13
14      printf( "%d\n", mystery2( string ) );
15
16      return 0; /* indicates successful termination */
17
18   } /* end main */
19
20   /* What does this function do? */
21   int mystery2( const char *s )
22   {
23      int x; /* counter */
24
25      /* loop through string */
26      for ( x = 0; *s != '\0'; s++ ) {
27         x++;
28      } /* end for */
29
30      return x;
31
32   } /* end function mystery2 */
```

Fig. S7.1   Exercise 7.22: What does this program do?

ANS: *Determines the length of a string.*

```
Enter a string: string1
7
```

Fig. S7.2   Solution for Exercise 7.22.

7.25   (*Maze Traversal*) The following grid is a double-subscripted array representation of a maze.

```
# # # # # # # # # # # #
# . . . # . . . . . . #
. . # . # . # # # # . #
# # # . # . . . . # . #
# . . . . # # # . # . .
# # # # . # . # . # . #
# . . # . # . # . # . #
# # . # . # . # . # . #
# . . . . . . . # . # #
# # # # # # . # # # . #
# . . . . . # . . . # #
# # # # # # # # # # # #
```

The # symbols represent the walls of the maze, and the periods (.) represent squares in the possible paths through the maze.

There is a simple algorithm for walking through a maze that guarantees finding the exit (assuming there is an exit). If there is not an exit, you will arrive at the starting location again. Place your right hand on the wall to your right and begin walking forward. Never remove your hand from the wall. If the maze turns to the right, you follow the wall to the right. As long as you do not remove your hand from the wall, eventually you will arrive at the exit of the maze. There may be a shorter path than the one you have taken, but you are guaranteed to get out of the maze.

Write recursive function mazeTraverse to walk through the maze. The function should receive as arguments a 12-by-12 character array representing the maze and the starting location of the maze. As mazeTraverse attempts to locate the exit from the maze, it should place the character X in each square in the path. The function should display the maze after each move so the user can watch as the maze is solved.

ANS:

```
1   /* Exercise 7.25 Solution */
2   /* This solution assumes that there is only one */
3   /* entrance and one exit for a given maze, and  */
4   /* these are the only two zeroes on the borders.*/
5   #include <stdio.h>
6   #include <stdlib.h>
7
8   #define DOWN  0   /* move down  */
9   #define RIGHT 1   /* move right */
10  #define UP    2   /* move up    */
11  #define LEFT  3   /* move left  */
12
13  #define X_START 2 /* starting X and Y coordinate for maze */
14  #define Y_START 0
15
16  /* function prototypes */
17  void mazeTraversal( char maze[ 12 ][ 12 ], int xCoord, int yCoord,
18                      int direction );
19  void printMaze( const char maze[][ 12 ] );
20  int validMove( const char maze[][ 12 ], int r, int c );
21  int coordsAreEdge( int x, int y );
22
23  int main()
24  {
25
26     /* maze grid */
27     char maze[ 12 ][ 12 ] =
28     { { '1', '1', '1', '1', '1', '1', '1', '1', '1', '1', '1', '1'},
29       { '1', '0', '0', '0', '1', '0', '0', '0', '0', '0', '0', '1'},
30       { '0', '0', '1', '0', '1', '0', '1', '1', '1', '1', '0', '1'},
31       { '1', '1', '1', '0', '1', '0', '0', '0', '0', '1', '0', '1'},
32       { '1', '0', '0', '0', '0', '1', '1', '1', '0', '1', '0', '0'},
33       { '1', '1', '1', '1', '0', '1', '0', '1', '0', '1', '0', '1'},
34       { '1', '0', '0', '1', '0', '1', '0', '1', '0', '1', '0', '1'},
35       { '1', '1', '0', '1', '0', '1', '0', '1', '0', '1', '0', '1'},
36       { '1', '0', '0', '0', '0', '0', '0', '0', '0', '1', '0', '1'},
37       { '1', '1', '1', '1', '1', '1', '0', '1', '1', '1', '0', '1'},
38       { '1', '0', '0', '0', '0', '0', '0', '1', '0', '0', '0', '1'},
39       { '1', '1', '1', '1', '1', '1', '1', '1', '1', '1', '1', '1' } };
40
41     mazeTraversal( maze, X_START, Y_START, RIGHT );
42
43     return 0; /* indicate successful termination */
44
45  } /* end main */
46
47  /* Assume that there is exactly 1 entrance and
48     exactly 1 exit to the maze. */
```

Fig. S7.3   Solution for Exercise 7.25.   (Part 1 of 5.)

```
49   void mazeTraversal( char maze[ 12 ][ 12 ], int xCoord, int yCoord,
50                       int direction )
51   {
52      static int flag = 0; /* starting position flag */
53
54      maze[ xCoord ][ yCoord ] = 'X'; /* mark current point */
55      printMaze( maze );
56
57      /* if maze completed */
58      if ( coordsAreEdge( xCoord, yCoord ) && xCoord != X_START &&
59         yCoord != Y_START ) {
60         printf( "\nMaze successfully exited!\n\n" );
61         return;
62      } /* end if */
63      else if ( xCoord == X_START && yCoord == Y_START && flag == 1 ) {
64         printf( "\nArrived back at the starting location.\n\n" );
65         return;
66      } /* end else if */
67      else { /* make next move */
68         int move;  /* next move */
69         int count; /* counter */
70
71         flag = 1;
72
73         /* loop 4 times and find first valid move */
74         for ( move = direction, count = 0; count < 4; ++count,
75            ++move, move %= 4 ) {
76
77            /* choose valid move */
78            switch( move ) {
79
80               case DOWN: /* move down */
81
82                  /* if move is valid, call mazeTraversal */
83                  if ( validMove( maze, xCoord + 1, yCoord ) ) {
84                     mazeTraversal( maze, xCoord + 1, yCoord, LEFT );
85                     return;
86                  } /* end if */
87
88                  break; /* exit switch */
89
90               case RIGHT: /* move right */
91
92                  /* if move is valid, call mazeTraversal */
93                  if ( validMove( maze, xCoord, yCoord + 1 ) ) {
94                     mazeTraversal( maze, xCoord, yCoord + 1, DOWN );
95                     return;
96                  } /* end if */
97
98                  break; /* exit switch */
```

Fig. S7.3   Solution for Exercise 7.25.   (Part 2 of 5.)

```
99
100              case UP: /* move up */
101
102                  /* if move is valid, call mazeTraversal */
103                  if ( validMove( maze, xCoord - 1, yCoord ) ) {
104                     mazeTraversal( maze, xCoord - 1, yCoord, RIGHT );
105                     return;
106                  } /* end if */
107
108                  break; /* exit switch */
109
110              case LEFT: /* move left */
111
112                  /* if move is valid, call mazeTraversal */
113                  if ( validMove( maze, xCoord, yCoord - 1 ) ) {
114                     mazeTraversal( maze, xCoord, yCoord - 1, UP );
115                     return;
116                  } /* end if */
117
118                  break; /* exit switch */
119           } /* end switch */
120
121        } /* end for */
122
123     } /* end else */
124
125 } /* end function mazeTraversal */
126
127 /* validate move */
128 int validMove( const char maze[][ 12 ], int r, int c )
129 {
130     return ( r >= 0 && r <= 11 && c >= 0 && c <= 11 &&
131        maze[ r ][ c ] != '1' );
132
133 } /* end function validMove */
134
135 /* function to check coordinates */
136 int coordsAreEdge( int x, int y )
137 {
138
139     /* if coordinate is not valid */
140     if ( ( x == 0 || x == 11 ) && ( y >= 0 && y <= 11 ) ) {
141        return 1;
142     } /* end if */
143     else if ( ( y == 0 || y == 11 ) && ( x >= 0 && x <= 11 ) ) {
144        return 1;
145     } /* end else if */
146     else { /* coordinate is valid */
147        return 0;
148     } /* end else */
```

Fig. S7.3   Solution for Exercise 7.25.   (Part 3 of 5.)

```
149
150  } /* end function coordsAreEdge */
151
152  /* print the current state of the maze */
153  void printMaze( const char maze[][ 12 ] )
154  {
155     int x; /* row counter */
156     int y; /* column counter */
157
158     /* iterate through the maze */
159     for ( x = 0; x < 12; x++ ) {
160
161        for ( y = 0; y < 12; y++ ) {
162           printf( "%c ", maze[ x ][ y ] );
163        } /* end for */
164
165        printf( "\n" );
166     } /* end for */
167
168     printf( "\nHit return to see next move" );
169     getchar();
170  } /* end function printMaze */
```

Fig. S7.3   Solution for Exercise 7.25.   (Part 4 of 5.)

```
Hit return to see next move
1 1 1 1 1 1 1 1 1 1 1 1
1 X X X 1 X X X X X X 1
X X 1 X 1 X 1 1 1 1 0 1
1 1 1 X 1 X X X X 1 0 1
1 X X X X 1 1 1 X 1 0 0
1 1 1 1 X 1 0 1 X 1 0 1
1 X X 1 X 1 0 1 X 1 0 1
1 1 X 1 X 1 0 1 X 1 0 1
1 X X X X X X X 1 0 1
1 1 1 1 1 X 1 1 1 0 1
1 X X X X X 1 0 0 0 1
1 1 1 1 1 1 1 1 1 1 1

Hit return to see next move
1 1 1 1 1 1 1 1 1 1 1 1
1 X X X 1 X X X X X X 1
X X 1 X 1 X 1 1 1 1 X 1
1 1 1 X 1 X X X X 1 0 1
1 X X X X 1 1 1 X 1 0 0
1 1 1 1 X 1 0 1 X 1 0 1
1 X X 1 X 1 0 1 X 1 0 1
1 1 X 1 X 1 0 1 X 1 0 1
1 X X X X X X X 1 0 1
1 1 1 1 1 X 1 1 1 0 1
1 X X X X X 1 0 0 0 1
1 1 1 1 1 1 1 1 1 1 1

...

Hit return to see next move
1 1 1 1 1 1 1 1 1 1 1 1
1 X X X 1 X X X X X X 1
X X 1 X 1 X 1 1 1 1 X 1
1 1 1 X 1 X X X X 1 X 1
1 X X X 1 1 1 X 1 X X
1 1 1 1 X 1 0 1 X 1 X 1
1 X X 1 X 1 0 1 X 1 X 1
1 1 X 1 X 1 0 1 X 1 X 1
1 X X X X X X X 1 X 1
1 1 1 1 1 X 1 1 1 X 1
1 X X X X X 1 X X X 1
1 1 1 1 1 1 1 1 1 1 1

Hit return to see next move

Maze successfully exited!
```

Fig. S7.3   Solution for Exercise 7.25.   (Part 5 of 5.)

7.26 (*Generating Mazes Randomly*) Write a function `mazeGenerator` that takes as an argument a double-subscripted 12-by-12 character array and randomly produces a maze. The function should also provide the starting and ending locations of the maze. Try your function `mazeTraverse` from Exercise 7.25 using several randomly generated mazes.

ANS:

```
1   /* Exercise 7.26 Solution */
2   #include <stdio.h>
3   #include <stdlib.h>
4   #include <time.h>
5
6   #define DOWN  0 /* move down */
7   #define RIGHT 1 /* move right */
8   #define UP    2 /* move up */
9   #define LEFT  3 /* move left */
10  #define POSSIBLE_ZEROS 100 /* maximum possible zeroes */
11
12  /* function prototypes */
13  void mazeTraversal( char maze[ 12 ][ 12 ], const int xCoord,
14                      const int yCoord, int row, int col, int direction );
15  void mazeGenerator( char maze[][ 12 ], int *xPtr, int *yPtr );
16  void printMaze( const char maze[][ 12 ] );
17  int validMove( const char maze[][ 12 ], int r, int c );
18  int coordsAreEdge( int x, int y );
19
20  int main()
21  {
22     char maze[ 12 ][ 12 ]; /* maze grid */
23     int loop;              /* row counter */
24     int loop2;             /* column counter */
25     int xStart;            /* starting x coordinate */
26     int yStart;            /* starting y coordinate */
27     int x;                 /* current x coordinate */
28     int y;                 /* current y coordinate */
29
30     /* initialize maze grid to 1's */
31     for ( loop = 0; loop < 12; loop++ ) {
32
33        for ( loop2 = 0; loop2 < 12; loop2++ ) {
34           maze[ loop ][ loop2 ] = '1';
35        } /* end for */
36
37     } /* end for */
38
39     /* generate the maze */
40     mazeGenerator( maze, &xStart, &yStart );
41
42     x = xStart; /* starting row */
43     y = yStart; /* starting col */
44
```

Fig. S7.4   Solution for Exercise 7.26.   (Part 1 of 6.)

```
45        mazeTraversal( maze, xStart, yStart, x, y, RIGHT );
46
47        return 0; /* indicate successful termination */
48
49     } /* end main */
50
51     /* Assume that there is exactly 1 entrance and
52        exactly 1 exit to the maze. */
53     void mazeTraversal( char maze[ 12 ][ 12 ], const int xCoord,
54                         const int yCoord, int row, int col, int direction )
55     {
56        static int flag = 0; /* starting position flag */
57
58        maze[ row ][ col ] = 'X'; /* insert X at current location */
59        printMaze( maze );
60
61        /* if maze completed */
62        if ( coordsAreEdge( row, col ) && row != xCoord && col != yCoord ) {
63           printf( "\nMaze successfully exited!\n\n" );
64           return;
65        } /* end if */
66        else if ( row == xCoord && col == yCoord && flag == 1 ) {
67           printf( "\nArrived back at the starting location.\n\n" );
68           return;
69        } /* end else if */
70        else { /* make next move */
71           int move;  /* next move */
72           int count; /* counter */
73
74           flag = 1;
75
76           /* loop 4 times and find first valid move */
77           for ( move = direction, count = 0; count < 4; ++count,
78              ++move, move %= 4 ) {
79
80              /* choose valid move */
81              switch( move ) {
82
83                 case DOWN: /* move down */
84
85                    /* if move is valid, call mazeTraversal */
86                    if ( validMove( maze, row + 1, col ) ) {
87                       mazeTraversal( maze, xCoord, yCoord, row + 1,
88                          col, LEFT );
89                       return;
90                    } /* end if */
91
92                    break; /* exit switch */
93
94                 case RIGHT: /* move right */
```

Fig. S7.4   Solution for Exercise 7.26.   (Part 2 of 6.)

```
 95
 96                    /* if move is valid, call mazeTraversal */
 97                    if ( validMove( maze, row, col + 1 ) ) {
 98                       mazeTraversal( maze, xCoord, yCoord, row,
 99                          col + 1, DOWN );
100                       return;
101                    } /* end if */
102
103                    break; /* exit switch */
104
105                 case UP: /* move up */
106
107                    /* if move is valid, call mazeTraversal */
108                    if ( validMove( maze, row - 1, col ) ) {
109                       mazeTraversal( maze, xCoord, yCoord, row - 1,
110                          col, RIGHT );
111                       return;
112                    } /* end if */
113
114                    break; /* exit switch */
115
116                 case LEFT: /* move left */
117
118                    /* if move is valid, call mazeTraversal */
119                    if ( validMove( maze, row, col - 1 ) ) {
120                       mazeTraversal( maze, xCoord, yCoord, row,
121                          col - 1, UP );
122                       return;
123                    } /* end if */
124
125                    break; /* exit switch */
126              } /* end switch */
127
128           } /* end for */
129
130     } /* end else */
131
132 } /* end function mazeTraversal */
133
134 /* validate move */
135 int validMove( const char maze[][ 12 ], int r, int c )
136 {
137    return ( r >= 0 && r <= 11 && c >= 0 && c <= 11 &&
138       maze[ r ][ c ] != '1' );
139
140 } /* end function validMove */
141
142 /* check boundaries of coordinates */
143 int coordsAreEdge( int x, int y )
144 {
```

Fig. S7.4   Solution for Exercise 7.26.   (Part 3 of 6.)

```
145
146     /* if coordinates not valid */
147     if ( ( x == 0 || x == 11 ) && ( y >= 0 && y <= 11 ) ) {
148        return 1;
149     } /* end if */
150     else if ( ( y == 0 || y == 11 ) && ( x >= 0 && x <= 11 ) ) {
151        return 1;
152     } /* end else if */
153     else { /* coordinates valid */
154        return 0;
155     } /* end else */
156
157  } /* end function coordsAreEdge */
158
159  /* print the maze */
160  void printMaze( const char maze[][ 12 ] )
161  {
162     int x; /* row counter */
163     int y; /* column counter */
164
165     /* loop through maze grid */
166     for ( x = 0; x < 12; x++ ) {
167
168        for ( y = 0; y < 12; y++ ) {
169           printf( "%c ", maze[ x ][ y ] );
170        } /* end for */
171
172        printf( "\n" );
173     } /* end for */
174
175     printf( "\nHit return to see next move" );
176     getchar();
177  } /* end function printMaze */
178
179  /* random maze generator */
180  void mazeGenerator( char maze[][ 12 ], int *xPtr, int *yPtr )
181  {
182     int a;      /* random number */
183     int x;      /* random number */
184     int y;      /* random number */
185     int entry; /* random entry */
186     int exit;  /* random exit */
187     int loop;  /* loop counter */
188
189     srand( time( NULL ) );
190
191     /* generate random entry and exit positions */
192     do {
193        entry = rand() % 4;
194        exit = rand() % 4;
```

Fig. S7.4   Solution for Exercise 7.26.   (Part 4 of 6.)

```
195      } while ( entry == exit ); /* end do...while */
196
197      /* Determine entry position while avoiding corners */
198      if ( entry == 0 ) {
199        *xPtr = 1 + rand() % 10;
200        *yPtr = 0;
201        maze[ *xPtr ][ 0 ] = '0';
202      } /* end if */
203      else if ( entry == 1 ) {
204        *xPtr = 0;
205        *yPtr = 1 + rand() % 10;
206        maze[ 0 ][ *yPtr ] = '0';
207      } /* end else if */
208      else if ( entry == 2 ) {
209        *xPtr = 1 + rand() % 10;
210        *yPtr = 11;
211        maze[ *xPtr ][ 11 ] = '0';
212      } /* end else if */
213      else {
214        *xPtr = 11;
215        *yPtr = 1 + rand() % 10;
216        maze[ 11 ][ *yPtr ] = '0';
217      } /* end else */
218
219      /* Determine exit location */
220      if ( exit == 0 ) {
221        a = 1 + rand() % 10;
222        maze[ a ][ 0 ] = '0';
223      } /* end if */
224      else if ( exit == 1 ) {
225        a = 1 + rand() % 10;
226        maze[ 0 ][ a ] = '0';
227      } /* end else if */
228      else if ( exit == 2 ) {
229        a = 1 + rand() % 10;
230        maze[ a ][ 11 ] = '0';
231      } /* end else if */
232      else {
233        a = 1 + rand() % 10;
234        maze[ 11 ][ a ] = '0';
235      } /* end else */
236
237      /* randomly add zeroes to maze grid */
238      for ( loop = 1; loop < POSSIBLE_ZEROS; loop++ ) {
239        x = 1 + rand() % 10;
240        y = 1 + rand() % 10;
241        maze[ x ][ y ] = '0';
242      } /* end for */
243
244   } /* end function mazeGenerator */
```

Fig. S7.4   Solution for Exercise 7.26.   (Part 5 of 6.)

```
Hit return to see next move
1 1 1 1 0 1 1 1 1 1 1 1
1 0 1 1 0 1 0 1 X X X 1
1 1 1 0 0 0 1 1 1 1 X 1
X X 1 0 0 1 X X X X X 1
1 X X X 1 X X 1 X X 1 1
1 X 1 X X X 1 0 1 X 1 1
1 1 X 1 X X X 1 X X 1 1
1 1 X X X X 1 1 X 1 0 1
1 X X 0 0 X 1 X X X 1 1
1 1 X 0 1 X 1 X X 1 0 1
1 1 X X X X X 1 1 0 0 1
1 1 1 1 1 1 1 1 1 1 1 1

Hit return to see next move
1 1 1 1 0 1 1 1 1 1 1 1
1 0 1 1 0 1 0 1 X X X 1
1 1 1 0 0 0 1 1 1 1 X 1
X X 1 0 0 1 X X X X X 1
1 X X X 1 X X 1 X X 1 1
1 X 1 X X X 1 0 1 X 1 1
1 1 X 1 X X X 1 X X 1 1
1 1 X X X X 1 1 X 1 0 1
1 X X 0 0 X 1 X X X 1 1
1 1 X 0 1 X 1 X X 1 0 1
1 1 X X X X X 1 1 0 0 1
1 1 1 1 1 1 1 1 1 1 1 1

. . .

Hit return to see next move
1 1 1 1 X 1 1 1 1 1 1 1
1 0 1 1 X 1 0 1 X X X 1
1 1 1 0 X X 1 1 1 1 X 1
X X 1 X X 1 X X X X X 1
1 X X X 1 X X 1 X X 1 1
1 X 1 X X X 1 0 1 X 1 1
1 1 X 1 X X X 1 X X 1 1
1 1 X X X X 1 1 X 1 0 1
1 X X 0 0 X 1 X X X 1 1
1 1 X 0 1 X 1 X X 1 0 1
1 1 X X X X X 1 1 0 0 1
1 1 1 1 1 1 1 1 1 1 1 1

Hit return to see next move

Maze successfully exited!
```

Fig. S7.4   Solution for Exercise 7.26.   (Part 6 of 6.)

7.27   (*Mazes of Any Size*) Generalize functions mazeTraverse and mazeGenerator of Exercise 7.25 and Exercise 7.26 to process mazes of any width and height.

ANS:

```
1   /* Exercise 7.27 Solution */
2   #include <stdio.h>
3   #include <stdlib.h>
4   #include <time.h>
5
6   #define ROW 10   /* height */
7   #define COL 10   /* width  */
8   #define DOWN  0 /* move down */
9   #define RIGHT 1 /* move right */
10  #define UP    2 /* move up */
11  #define LEFT  3 /* move left */
12
13  /* function prototypes */
14  void mazeTraversal( char maze[ ROW ][ COL ], const int xCoord,
15                    const int yCoord, int row, int col, int direction );
16  void mazeGenerator( char maze[][ COL ], int *xPtr, int *yPtr );
17  void printMaze( const char maze[][ COL ] );
18  int validMove( const char maze[][ COL ], int r, int c );
19  int coordsAreEdge( int x, int y );
20
21  int main()
22  {
23     char maze[ ROW ][ COL ]; /* maze grid */
24     int loop;               /* row counter */
25     int loop2;              /* column counter */
26     int xStart;             /* starting x coordinate */
27     int yStart;             /* starting y coordinate */
28     int x;                  /* current x coordinate */
29     int y;                  /* current y coordinate */
30
31     /* initialize maze grid to 1's */
32     for ( loop = 0; loop < ROW; loop++ ) {
33
34        for ( loop2 = 0; loop2 < COL; loop2++ ) {
35           maze[ loop ][ loop2 ] = '1';
36        } /* end for */
37
38     } /* end for */
39
40     /* generate the maze */
41     mazeGenerator( maze, &xStart, &yStart );
42
43     x = xStart; /* starting row */
44     y = yStart; /* starting col */
45
46     mazeTraversal( maze, xStart, yStart, x, y, RIGHT );
47
```

Fig. S7.5   Solution for Exercise 7.27.   (Part 1 of 6.)

```
48       return 0; /* indicate successful termination */
49
50   } /* end main */
51
52   /* Assume that there is exactly 1 entrance and
53       exactly 1 exit to the maze. */
54   void mazeTraversal( char maze[ ROW ][ COL ], const int xCoord,
55                       const int yCoord, int row, int col, int direction )
56   {
57       static int flag = 0; /* starting position flag */
58
59       maze[ row ][ col ] = 'X'; /* insert X at current location */
60       printMaze( maze );
61
62       /* if maze completed */
63       if ( coordsAreEdge( row, col ) && row != xCoord && col != yCoord ) {
64           printf( "\nMaze successfully exited!\n\n" );
65           return;
66       } /* end if */
67       else if ( row == xCoord && col == yCoord && flag == 1 ) {
68           printf( "\nArrived back at the starting location.\n\n" );
69           return;
70       } /* end else if */
71       else { /* make next move */
72           int move;  /* next move */
73           int count; /* counter */
74
75           flag = 1;
76
77           /* loop 4 times and find first valid move */
78           for ( move = direction, count = 0; count < 4; ++count,
79               ++move, move %= 4 ) {
80
81               /* choose valid move */
82               switch( move ) {
83
84                   case DOWN: /* move down */
85
86                       /* if move is valid, call mazeTraversal */
87                       if ( validMove( maze, row + 1, col ) ) {
88                           mazeTraversal( maze, xCoord, yCoord, row + 1,
89                               col, LEFT );
90                           return;
91                       } /* end if */
92
93                       break; /* exit switch */
94
95                   case RIGHT: /* move right */
96
97                       /* if move is valid, call mazeTraversal */
```

Fig. S7.5   Solution for Exercise 7.27.   (Part 2 of 6.)

```
 98              if ( validMove( maze, row, col + 1 ) ) {
 99                 mazeTraversal( maze, xCoord, yCoord, row,
100                    col + 1, DOWN );
101                 return;
102              } /* end if */
103
104              break; /* exit switch */
105
106           case UP: /* move up */
107
108              /* if move is valid, call mazeTraversal */
109              if ( validMove( maze, row - 1, col ) ) {
110                 mazeTraversal( maze, xCoord, yCoord, row - 1,
111                    col, RIGHT );
112                 return;
113              } /* end if */
114
115              break; /* exit switch */
116
117           case LEFT: /* move left */
118
119              /* if move is valid, call mazeTraversal */
120              if ( validMove( maze, row, col - 1 ) ) {
121                 mazeTraversal( maze, xCoord, yCoord, row,
122                    col - 1, UP );
123                 return;
124              } /* end if */
125
126              break; /* exit switch */
127        } /* end switch */
128
129     } /* end for */
130
131   } /* end else */
132
133 } /* end function mazeTraversal */
134
135 /* validate move */
136 int validMove( const char maze[][ COL ], int r, int c )
137 {
138    return ( r >= 0 && r <= ROW - 1 && c >= 0 && c <= COL - 1 &&
139       maze[ r ][ c ] != '1' );  /* a valid move */
140
141 } /* end function validMove */
142
143 /* check boundaries of coordinates */
144 int coordsAreEdge( int x, int y )
145 {
146
147    /* if coordinates not valid */
```

Fig. S7.5   Solution for Exercise 7.27.   (Part 3 of 6.)

```
148     if ( ( x == 0 || x == ROW - 1 ) && ( y >= 0 && y <= COL - 1 ) ) {
149        return 1;
150     } /* end if */
151     else if ( ( y == 0 || y == COL - 1 ) && ( x >= 0 &&
152        x <= ROW - 1 ) ) {
153        return 1;
154     } /* end else if */
155     else { /* coordinates valid */
156        return 0;
157     } /* end else */
158
159  } /* end function coordsAreEdge */
160
161  /* print the maze */
162  void printMaze( const char maze[][ COL ] )
163  {
164     int x; /* row counter */
165     int y; /* column counter */
166
167     /* loop through maze grid */
168     for ( x = 0; x < ROW; x++ ) {
169
170        for ( y = 0; y < COL; y++ ) {
171           printf( "%c ", maze[ x ][ y ] );
172        } /* end for */
173
174        printf( "\n" );
175     } /* end for */
176
177     printf( "\nHit return to see next move" );
178     getchar();
179  } /* end function printMaze */
180
181  /* random maze generator */
182  void mazeGenerator( char maze[][ COL ], int *xPtr, int *yPtr )
183  {
184     int a;     /* random number */
185     int x;     /* random number */
186     int y;     /* random number */
187     int entry; /* random entry */
188     int exit;  /* random exit */
189     int loop;  /* loop counter */
190
191     srand( time( NULL ) );
192
193     /* generate random entry and exit positions */
194     do {
195        entry = rand() % 4;
196        exit = rand() % 4;
197     } while ( entry == exit ); /* end do...while */
```

Fig. S7.5   Solution for Exercise 7.27.   (Part 4 of 6.)

```
198
199        /* Determine entry position while avoiding corners */
200        if ( entry == 0 ) {
201           *xPtr = 1 + rand() % ( ROW - 2 );
202           *yPtr = 0;
203           maze[ *xPtr ][ *yPtr ] = '0';
204        } /* end if */
205        else if ( entry == 1 ) {
206           *xPtr = 0;
207           *yPtr = 1 + rand() % ( COL - 2 );
208           maze[ *xPtr ][ *yPtr ] = '0';
209        } /* end else if */
210        else if ( entry == 2 ) {
211           *xPtr = 1 + rand() % ( ROW - 2 );
212           *yPtr = COL - 1;
213           maze[ *xPtr ][ *yPtr ] = '0';
214        } /* end else if */
215        else {
216           *xPtr = ROW - 1;
217           *yPtr = 1 + rand() % ( COL - 2 );
218           maze[ *xPtr ][ *yPtr ] = '0';
219        } /* end else */
220
221        /* Determine exit location */
222        if ( exit == 0 ) {
223           a = 1 + rand() % ( ROW - 2 );
224           maze[ a ][ 0 ] = '0';
225        } /* end if */
226        else if ( exit == 1 ) {
227           a = 1 + rand() % ( COL - 2 );
228           maze[ 0 ][ a ] = '0';
229        } /* end else if */
230        else if ( exit == 2 ) {
231           a = 1 + rand() % ( ROW - 2 );
232           maze[ a ][ COL - 1 ] = '0';
233        } /* end else if */
234        else {
235           a = 1 + rand() % ( COL - 2 );
236           maze[ ROW - 1 ][ a ] = '0';
237        } /* end else */
238
239        /* randomly add zeroes to maze grid */
240        for ( loop = 1; loop < ( ROW - 2 ) * ( COL - 2 ); loop++ ) {
241           x = 1 + rand() % ( ROW - 2 );
242           y = 1 + rand() % ( COL - 2 );
243           maze[ x ][ y ] = '0';
244        } /* end for */
245
246     } /* end function mazeGenerator */
```

Fig. S7.5   Solution for Exercise 7.27.   (Part 5 of 6.)

```
1 1 X 1 1 1 1 1 1 1
1 0 0 1 1 0 1 0 0 1
0 0 0 1 1 1 1 1 0 1
1 0 0 0 0 0 1 0 1 1
1 1 1 0 0 0 1 0 0 1
1 1 1 0 1 0 1 1 0 1
1 0 0 0 1 0 0 1 0 1
1 0 0 0 1 1 0 0 0 1
1 0 0 0 0 1 1 0 0 1
1 1 1 1 1 1 1 1 1 1

Hit return to see next move
1 1 X 1 1 1 1 1 1 1
1 0 X 1 1 0 1 0 0 1
0 0 0 1 1 1 1 1 0 1
1 0 0 0 0 0 1 0 1 1
1 1 1 0 0 0 1 0 0 1
1 1 1 0 1 0 1 1 0 1
1 0 0 0 1 0 0 1 0 1
1 0 0 0 1 1 0 0 0 1
1 0 0 0 0 1 1 0 0 1
1 1 1 1 1 1 1 1 1 1

. . .

Hit return to see next move
1 1 X 1 1 1 1 1 1 1
1 X X 1 1 0 1 0 0 1
X X 0 1 1 1 1 1 0 1
1 0 0 0 0 0 1 0 1 1
1 1 1 0 0 0 1 0 0 1
1 1 1 0 1 0 1 1 0 1
1 0 0 0 1 0 0 1 0 1
1 0 0 0 1 1 0 0 0 1
1 0 0 0 0 1 1 0 0 1
1 1 1 1 1 1 1 1 1 1

Hit return to see next move

Maze successfully exited!
```

Fig. S7.5   Solution for Exercise 7.27.   (Part 6 of 6.)

7.30   What does this program do?

```
1   /* ex07_30.c */
2   /* What does this program do? */
3   #include <stdio.h>
```

Fig. S7.6   Exercise 7.30: What does this program do? (Part 1 of 2.)

```
4
5   int mystery3( const char *s1, const char *s2 ); /* prototype */
6
7   int main()
8   {
9      char string1[ 80 ]; /* create char array */
10     char string2[ 80 ]; /* create char array */
11
12     printf( "Enter two strings: " );
13     scanf( "%s%s", string1 , string2 );
14
15     printf( "The result is %d\n", mystery3( string1, string2 ) );
16
17     return 0; /* indicates successful termination */
18
19  } /* end main */
20
21  int mystery3( const char *s1, const char *s2 )
22  {
23     for ( ; *s1 != '\0' && *s2 != '\0'; s1++, s2++ ) {
24
25        if ( *s1 != *s2 ) {
26           return 0;
27        } /* end if */
28
29     } /* end for */
30
31     return 1;
32
33  } /* end function mystery3 */
```

Fig. S7.6   Exercise 7.30: What does this program do? (Part 2 of 2.)

ANS: *The program compares two strings, element by element, for equality.*

```
Enter two strings:  string1 string2
The result is 0
```

Fig. S7.7   Solution for Exercise 7.30.

```
Enter two strings:  string2 string2
The result is 1
```

C Characters and Strings

Solutions to Selected Exercises

8.6   Write a program that inputs a line of text with function gets into char array s[100]. Output the line in uppercase letters and in lowercase letters.

ANS:

```
1   /* Exercise 8.6 Solution */
2   #include <stdio.h>
3   #include <ctype.h>
4
5   int main()
6   {
7      char s[ 100 ]; /* define character array of size 100 */
8      int i; /* loop counter */
9
10     /* use gets to get text from user */
11     printf( "Enter a line of text:\n" );
12     gets( s );
13     printf( "\nThe line in uppercase is:\n" );
14
15     /* convert each character to uppercase and output */
16     for ( i = 0; s[ i ] != '\0'; i++ ) {
17        printf( "%c", toupper( s[ i ] ) );
18     } /* end for */
19
20     printf( "\n\nThe line in lowercase is:\n" );
21
22     /* convert each character to lowercase and output */
23     for ( i = 0; s[ i ] != '\0'; i++ ) {
24        printf( "%c", tolower( s[ i ] ) );
25     } /* end for */
26
27     return 0; /* indicate successful termination */
28
```

Fig. S8.1   Solution for Exercise 8.6.   (Part 1 of 2.)

```
29   } /* end main */
```

```
Enter a line of text:
A line with UPPER- and lowercase LeTters

The line in uppercase is:
A LINE WITH UPPER- AND LOWERCASE LETTERS

The line in lowercase is:
a line with upper- and lowercase letters
```

Fig. S8.1   Solution for Exercise 8.6.   (Part 2 of 2.)

8.7   Write a program that inputs four strings that represent integers, converts the strings to integers, sums the values and prints the total of the four values.

ANS:

```
1   /* Exercise 8.7 Solution */
2   #include <stdio.h>
3   #include <stdlib.h>
4
5   int main()
6   {
7      char stringValue[ 6 ]; /* integer string input by user */
8      int sum = 0;              /* result of four integers */
9      int i;                    /* loop counter */
10
11     /* loop 4 times */
12     for ( i = 1; i <= 4; i++ ) {
13        printf( "Enter an integer string: " );
14        scanf( "%s", stringValue );
15
16        /* atoi converts stringValue to integer */
17        sum += atoi( stringValue );
18     } /* end for */
19
20     printf( "\nThe total of the values is %d\n", sum );
21
22     return 0; /* indicate successful termination */
23
24  } /* end main */
```

```
Enter an integer string: 43
Enter an integer string: 77
Enter an integer string: 120
Enter an integer string: 9999

The total of the values is 10239
```

Fig. S8.2   Solution for Exercise 8.7.

8.9   Write a program that uses function `strcmp` to compare two strings input by the user. The program should state whether the first string is less than, equal to or greater than the second string.

ANS:

```
1   /* Exercise 8.9 Solution */
2   #include <stdio.h>
3   #include <string.h>
4
5   int main()
6   {
7      char string1[ 20 ]; /* first string input by user */
8      char string2[ 20 ]; /* second string input by user */
9      int result;         /* result of comparing two strings */
10
11     printf( "Enter two strings: " );
12     scanf( "%s%s", string1, string2 ); /* read two strings */
13
14     result = strcmp( string1, string2 );
15
16     /* display appropriate message for result */
17     if ( result > 0 ) {
18        printf( "\"%s\" is greater than \"%s\"\n", string1, string2 );
19     } /* end if */
20     else if ( result == 0 ) {
21        printf( "\"%s\" is equal to \"%s\"\n", string1, string2 );
22     } /* end else if */
23     else {
24        printf( "\"%s\" is less than \"%s\"\n", string1, string2 );
25     } /* end else */
26
27     return 0; /* indicate successful termination */
28
29  } /* end main */
```

```
Enter two strings: Greg Dave
"Greg" is greater than "Dave"
```

Fig. S8.3   Solution for Exercise 8.9.

```
Enter two strings: Bill Bill
"Bill" is equal to "Bill"
```

```
Enter two strings: Pete Tim
"Pete" is less than "Tim"
```

8.11   Write a program that uses random number generation to create sentences. The program should use four arrays of pointers to char called article, noun, verb and preposition. The program should create a sentence by selecting a word at random from each array in the following order: article, noun, verb, preposition, article and noun. As each word is picked, it should be concatenated to the previous words in an array large enough to hold the entire sentence. The words should be separated by spaces. When the final sentence is output, it should start with a capital letter and end with a period. The program should generate 20 such sentences.

The arrays should be filled as follows: The article array should contain the articles "the", "a", "one", "some" and "any"; the noun array should contain the nouns "boy", "girl", "dog", "town" and "car"; the verb array should contain the verbs "drove", "jumped", "ran", "walked" and "skipped"; the preposition array should contain the prepositions "to", "from", "over", "under" and "on".

After the preceding program is written and working, modify the program to produce a short story consisting of several of these sentences. (How about the possibility of a random term paper writer?)

ANS:

```
1    /* Exercise 8.11 Solution */
2    #include <stdio.h>
3    #include <stdlib.h>
4    #include <time.h>
5    #include <string.h>
6    #include <ctype.h>
7
8    int main()
9    {
10       /* initialize 4 arrays of char pointers */
11       char *article[] = { "the", "a", "one", "some", "any" };
12       char *noun[] = { "boy", "girl", "dog", "town", "car" };
13       char *verb[] = { "drove", "jumped", "ran", "walked", "skipped" };
14       char *preposition[] = { "to", "from", "over", "under", "on" };
15       char sentence[ 100 ] = ""; /* completed sentence */
16       int i; /* loop counter */
17
18       /* create 20 sentences */
19       for ( i = 1; i <= 20; i++ ) {
20
21          /* randomly choose pieces of sentence */
22          strcat( sentence, article[ rand() % 5 ] );
23          strcat( sentence, " " );
24
25          strcat( sentence, noun[ rand() % 5 ] );
26          strcat( sentence, " " );
27
28          strcat( sentence, verb[ rand() % 5 ] );
29          strcat( sentence, " " );
30
31          strcat( sentence, preposition[ rand() % 5 ] );
32          strcat( sentence, " " );
```

Fig. S8.4   Solution for Exercise 8.11.   (Part 1 of 2.)

```
33
34          strcat( sentence, article[ rand() % 5 ] );
35          strcat( sentence, " " );
36
37          strcat( sentence, noun[ rand() % 5 ] );
38
39          /* capitalize first letter and print sentence */
40          putchar( toupper( sentence[ 0 ] ) );
41          printf( "%s.\n", &sentence[ 1 ] );
42          sentence[ 0 ] = '\0';
43      } /* end for */
44
45      return 0; /* indicate successful termination */
46
47  } /* end main */
```

```
A dog skipped to any car.
Some town ran on the boy.
A dog jumped from the dog.
One girl jumped on one town.
One dog jumped from some boy.
One girl jumped under any dog.
One car drove on some girl.
One town walked on a girl.
Some town ran on one dog.
One car walked from any town.
A boy drove over some girl.
The dog skipped under a boy.
The car drove to a girl.
Some town skipped under any car.
A boy jumped from a town.
Any car jumped under one town.
Some dog skipped from some boy.
Any town skipped to one girl.
Some girl jumped to any dog.
The car ran under one dog.
```

Fig. S8.4   Solution for Exercise 8.11.   (Part 2 of 2.)

8.15   Write a program that inputs a line of text, tokenizes the line with function strtok and outputs the tokens in reverse order.

ANS:

```
1   /* Exercise 8.15 solution */
2   #include <stdio.h>
3   #include <string.h>
4
5   void reverseTokens( char *sentence ); /* function prototype */
```

Fig. S8.5   Solution for Exercise 8.15.   (Part 1 of 2.)

```
6
7   int main()
8   {
9      char text[ 80 ]; /* line of text from user */
10
11     printf( "Enter a line of text:\n" );
12     gets( text );
13
14     reverseTokens( text ); /* call to function reverseTokens */
15
16     return 0; /* indicate successful termination */
17
18  } /* end main */
19
20  /* function to reverse the individual tokens */
21  void reverseTokens( char *sentence )
22  {
23     char *pointers[ 50 ]; /* array to store entire sentence */
24     char *temp;           /* pointer to each token */
25     int count = 0;        /* token counter */
26     int i;                /* loop counter */
27
28     /* function strtok takes first word of sentence */
29     temp = strtok( sentence, " " );
30
31     /* while temp does not equal NULL */
32     while ( temp ) {
33
34        /* add the word into the array and get next token */
35        pointers[ count++ ] = temp;
36        temp = strtok( NULL, " " );
37     } /* end while */
38
39     printf( "The tokens in reverse order are:\n" );
40
41     /* loop through the array backwards */
42     for ( i = count - 1; i >= 0; i-- ) {
43        printf( "%s ", pointers[ i ] );
44     } /* end for */
45
46  } /* end function reverseTokens */
```

```
Enter a line of text:
testing 1 2 3
The tokens in reverse order are:
3 2 1 testing
```

Fig. S8.5   Solution for Exercise 8.15.   (Part 2 of 2.)

8.16   Write a program that inputs a line of text and a search string from the keyboard. Using function strstr, locate the first occurrence of the search string in the line of text, and assign the location to variable searchPtr of type char *. If the search string is found, print the remainder of the line of text beginning with the search string. Then, use strstr again to locate the next occurrence of the search string in the line of text. If a second occurrence is found, print the remainder of the line of text beginning with the second occurrence. [*Hint:* The second call to strstr should contain searchPtr + 1 as its first argument.]

ANS:

```
1   /* Exercise 8.16 Solution */
2   #include <stdio.h>
3   #include <string.h>
4   int main()
5   {
6      char text[ 80 ];    /* line of text */
7      char search[ 15 ];  /* search string */
8      char *searchPtr;    /* poiner to search string */
9
10     /* get line of text from user */
11     printf( "Enter a line of text:\n" );
12     gets( text );
13
14     /* get search string from user */
15     printf( "Enter a search string: " );
16     scanf( "%s", search );
17
18     /* search for search string in text */
19     searchPtr = strstr( text, search );
20
21     /* if searchPtr is not NULL */
22     if ( searchPtr ) {
23        printf( "\n%s\n%s\"%s\":\n%s\n",
24               "The remainder of the line beginning with",
25               "the first occurrence of ", search, searchPtr );
26
27        /* search for a second occurrence */
28        searchPtr = strstr( searchPtr + 1, search );
29
30        /* if searchPtr is not NULL */
31        if ( searchPtr )  {
32           printf( "\n%s\n%s\"%s\":\n%s\n",
33                  "The remainder of the line beginning with",
34                  "the second occurrence of ", search, searchPtr );
35        } /* end if */
36        else {
37           printf( "The search string appeared only once.\n" );
38        } /* end else */
39
40     } /* end if */
41     else {
42        printf( "\"%s\" not found.\n", search );
43     } /* end else */
```

Fig. S8.6   Solution for Exercise 8.16. (Part 1 of 2.)

```
44
45      return 0; /* indicate successful termination */
46
47  } /* end main */
```

```
Enter a line of text:
To be or not to be; that is the question.
Enter a search string: be

The remainder of the line beginning with
the first occurrence of "be":
be or not to be; that is the question.

The remainder of the line beginning with
the second occurrence of "be":
be; that is the question.
```

Fig. S8.6   Solution for Exercise 8.16.   (Part 2 of 2.)

8.18   Write a program that inputs several lines of text and a search character, and uses function strchr to determine the total occurrences of the character in the lines of text.

ANS:

```
1   /* Exercise 8.18 Solution */
2   #include <stdio.h>
3   #include <string.h>
4   #include <ctype.h>
5
6   int main()
7   {
8      char text[ 3 ][ 80 ]; /* array to hold text entered by user */
9      char search;          /* search character */
10     char *searchPtr;      /* pointer to search character */
11     int count = 0;        /* total search characters found */
12     int i;                /* loop counter */
13     int j;                /* loop counter */
14
15     printf( "Enter three lines of text:\n" );
16
17     /* read 3 lines of text */
18     for ( i = 0; i <= 2; i++ ) {
19        gets( &text[ i ][ 0 ] );
20     } /* end for */
21
22     /* convert all letters to lowercase */
23     for ( i = 0; i <= 2; i++ ) {
24
25        /* loop through each character */
26        for ( j = 0; text[ i ][ j ] != '\0'; j++ ) {
```

Fig. S8.7   Solution for Exercise 8.18.   (Part 1 of 2.)

```
27                text[ i ][ j ] = tolower( text[ i ][ j ] );
28            } /* end for */
29
30        } /* end for */
31
32        /* get search character */
33        printf( "\nEnter a search character: " );
34        scanf( "%c", &search );
35
36        /* loop through 3 lines of text */
37        for ( i = 0; i <= 2; i++ ) {
38
39            /* set pointer to first character in line */
40            searchPtr = &text[ i ][ 0 ];
41
42            /* loop while strchr does not return NULL */
43            while ( searchPtr = strchr( searchPtr, search ) ) {
44                ++count;
45                searchPtr++;
46            } /* end while */
47
48        } /* end for */
49
50        printf( "\nThe total occurrences of '%c' in the text is %d\n",
51                search, count );
52
53        return 0; /* indicate successful termination */
54
55    } /* end main */
```

```
Enter three lines of text:
This program inputs three lines of text
and counts the number of occurrences of
the specified search character in the text

Enter a search character: e

The total occurrences of 'e' in the text is 15
```

Fig. S8.7   Solution for Exercise 8.18.   (Part 2 of 2.)

8.20   Write a program that inputs several lines of text and uses `strtok` to count the total number of words. Assume that the words are separated either by spaces or newline characters.

ANS:

```
1    /* Exercise 8.20 Solution */
2    #include <stdio.h>
3    #include <string.h>
4
```

Fig. S8.8   Solution for Exercise 8.20.   (Part 1 of 2.)

```
5   int main()
6   {
7      char text[ 4 ][ 80 ]; /* text entered by user */
8      char *tokenPtr;        /* pointer to current token */
9      int i;                 /* loop counter */
10     int counter = 0;       /* token counter */
11
12     printf( "Enter 4 lines of text: \n" );
13
14     /* read 4 lines of text */
15     for ( i = 0; i <= 3; i++ ) {
16        gets( &text[ i ][ 0 ] );
17     } /* end for */
18
19     /* loop through 4 lines of text */
20     for ( i = 0; i <= 3; i++ ) {
21
22        /* get first token */
23        tokenPtr = strtok( &text[ i ][ 0 ], " \n" );
24
25        /* while tokenPtr does not equal NULL */
26        while ( tokenPtr ) {
27           ++counter;
28           tokenPtr = strtok( NULL, " \n" ); /* get next token */
29        } /* end while */
30
31     } /* end for */
32
33     printf( "\nThe total number of words is %d\n", counter );
34
35     return 0; /* indicate successful termination */
36
37  } /* end main */
```

```
Enter 4 lines of text:
This line of text has seven words
This line has five words
There are two words on the next line
I am

The total number of words is 22
```

Fig. S8.8   Solution for Exercise 8.20.   (Part 2 of 2.)

8.21   Use the string comparison functions discussed in Section 8.6 and the techniques for sorting arrays developed in Chapter 6 to write a program that alphabetizes a list of strings. Use the names of 10 or 15 towns in your area as data for your program.

ANS:

```
 1   /* Exercise 8.21 solution */
 2   #include <stdio.h>
 3   #include <string.h>
 4
 5   void bubbleSort( char a[][ 50 ] ); /* function prototype */
 6
 7   int main()
 8   {
 9      char array[ 10 ][ 50 ]; /* 10 lines of text from user */
10      int i; /* counter */
11
12      /* read in 10 lines of text */
13      for ( i = 0; i <= 9; i++ ) {
14         printf( "Enter a string: " );
15         scanf( "%s", &array[ i ][ 0 ] );
16      } /* end for */
17
18      bubbleSort( array ); /* sort the array of strings */
19      printf( "\nThe strings in sorted order are:\n" );
20
21      /* display text in sorted order */
22      for ( i = 0; i <= 9; i++ ) {
23         printf( "%s\n", &array[ i ][ 0 ] );
24      } /* end for */
25
26      return 0; /* indicate successful termination */
27
28   } /* end main */
29
30   /* sort the array */
31   void bubbleSort( char a[][ 50 ] )
32   {
33      int i;          /* loop counter */
34      int j;          /* loop counter */
35      char temp[ 50 ]; /* temporary array */
36
37      /* make 9 passes */
38      for ( i = 0; i <= 8; i++ ) {
39
40         for ( j = 0; j <= 8; j++ ) {
41
42            /* swap strings if necessary */
43            if ( strcmp( &a[ j ][ 0 ], &a[ j + 1 ][ 0 ] ) > 0 ) {
44               strcpy( temp, &a[ j ][ 0 ] );
45               strcpy( &a[ j ][ 0 ], &a[ j + 1 ][ 0 ] );
46               strcpy( &a[ j + 1 ][ 0 ], temp );
47            } /* end if */
48
49         } /* end for */
```

Fig. S8.9   Solution for Exercise 8.21.   (Part 1 of 2.)

```
50
51     } /* end for */
52
53  } /* end function bubbleSort */
```

```
Enter a string: Westborough
Enter a string: Wellesley
Enter a string: Natick
Enter a string: Waltham
Enter a string: Framingham
Enter a string: Marlborough
Enter a string: Boston
Enter a string: Ashland
Enter a string: Hopkington
Enter a string: Shrewsbury

The strings in sorted order are:
Ashland
Boston
Framingham
Hopkington
Marlborough
Natick
Shrewsbury
Waltham
Wellesley
Westborough
```

Fig. S8.9   Solution for Exercise 8.21.   (Part 2 of 2.)

8.24   Write a program that reads a series of strings and prints only those strings that end with the letters "ed."

ANS:

```
1    /* Exercise 8.24 solution */
2    #include <stdio.h>
3    #include <string.h>
4
5    int main()
6    {
7       int i;                  /* loop counter */
8       int length;             /* length of current string */
9       char array[ 5 ][ 20 ]; /* 5 strings from user */
10
11      /* read in 5 strings from user */
12      for ( i = 0; i <= 4; i++ ) {
13         printf( "Enter a string: " );
14         scanf( "%s", &array[ i ][ 0 ] );
```

Fig. S8.10   Solution for Exercise 8.24.   (Part 1 of 2.)

```
15      } /* end for */
16
17      printf( "\nThe strings ending with \"ED\" are:\n" );
18
19      /* loop through 5 strings */
20      for ( i = 0; i <= 4; i++ ) {
21
22          /* find length of current string */
23          length = strlen( &array[ i ][ 0 ] );
24
25          /* print string if it ends with "ED" */
26          if ( strcmp( &array[ i ][ length - 2 ], "ED" ) == 0 ) {
27              printf( "%s\n", &array[ i ][ 0 ] );
28          } /* end if */
29
30      } /* end for */
31
32      return 0; /* indicate successful termination */
33
34  } /* end main */
```

```
Enter a string: WALKED
Enter a string: SKIPPED
Enter a string: JUMPED
Enter a string: FLEW
Enter a string: DROVE

The strings ending with "ED" are:
WALKED
SKIPPED
JUMPED
```

Fig. S8.10   Solution for Exercise 8.24.   (Part 2 of 2.)

8.34   *(Text Analysis)* The availability of computers with string manipulation capabilities has resulted in some rather interesting approaches to analyzing the writings of great authors. Much attention has been focused on whether William Shakespeare ever lived. Some scholars believe that there is substantial evidence indicating that Christopher Marlowe actually penned the masterpieces attributed to Shakespeare. Researchers have used computers to find similarities in the writings of these two authors. This exercise examines three methods for analyzing texts with a computer.

    a) Write a program that reads several lines of text and prints a table indicating the number of occurrences of each letter of the alphabet in the text. For example, the phrase

        `To be, or not to be: that is the question:`

        contains one "a," two "b's," no "c's," etc.

ANS:

```
1    /* Exercise 8.34 Part A Solution */
2    #include <stdio.h>
3    #include <ctype.h>
4
5    int main()
6    {
7       char letters[ 26 ] = { 0 }; /* letters of the alphabet */
8       char text[ 3 ][ 80 ];      /* three lines of text */
9       int i;                     /* loop counter */
10      int j;                     /* loop counter */
11
12      printf( "Enter three lines of text:\n" );
13
14      /* read 3 lines of text */
15      for ( i = 0; i <= 2; i++ ) {
16         gets( &text[ i ][ 0 ] );
17      } /* end for */
18
19      /* loop through 3 strings */
20      for ( i = 0; i <= 2; i++ ) {
21
22         /* loop through each character */
23         for ( j = 0; text[ i ][ j ] != '\0'; j++ ) {
24
25            /* if letter, update corresponding array element */
26            if ( isalpha( text[ i ][ j ] ) ) {
27               ++letters[ tolower( text[ i ][ j ] ) - 'a' ];
28            } /* end if */
29
30         } /* end for */
31
32      } /* end for */
33
34      printf( "\nTotal letter counts:\n" );
35
36      /* print letter totals */
37      for ( i = 0; i <= 25; i++ ) {
38         printf( "%c:%3d\n", 'a' + i, letters[ i ] );
39      } /* end for */
40
41      return 0; /* indicate successful termination */
42
43   } /* end main */
```

Fig. S8.11   Solution for Exercise 8.34, Part A.   (Part 1 of 2.)

```
Enter three lines of text:
This program counts the occurrences of each
letter of the alphabet in the input text. Then,
it prints a summary of the occurrences.

Total letter counts:
a:  6
b:  1
c:  8
d:  0
e: 14
f:  3
g:  1
h:  8
i:  5
j:  0
k:  0
l:  2
m:  3
n:  7
o:  7
p:  4
q:  0
r:  9
s:  6
t: 15
u:  5
v:  0
w:  0
x:  1
y:  1
z:  0
```

Fig. S8.11   Solution for Exercise 8.34, Part A.   (Part 2 of 2.)

b) Write a program that reads several lines of text and prints a table indicating the number of one-letter words, two-letter words, three-letter words, etc., appearing in the text. For example, the phrase

```
Whether 'tis nobler in the mind to suffer
```

contains

Word length	Occurrences
1	0
2	2
3	1
4	2 (including 'tis)

Word length	Occurrences
5	0
6	2
7	1

ANS:

```
1   /* Exercise 8.34 Part B solution */
2   #include <stdio.h>
3   #include <string.h>
4
5   int main()
6   {
7      char text[ 3 ][ 80 ];        /* 3 strings from user */
8      char *temp;                  /* token pointer */
9      int lengths[ 20 ] = { 0 };   /* array of length counts */
10     int i;                       /* loop counter */
11
12     printf( "Enter three lines of text:\n" );
13
14     /* read 3 lines of text */
15     for ( i = 0; i <= 2; i++ ) {
16        gets( &text[ i ][ 0 ] );
17     } /* end for */
18
19     /* loop through each string */
20     for ( i = 0; i <= 2; i++ ) {
21
22        /* get first token */
23        temp = strtok( &text[ i ][ 0 ], ". \n" );
24
25        /* while temp does not equal NULL */
26        while ( temp ) {
27
28           /* increment corresponding array element */
29           ++lengths[ strlen( temp ) ];
30           temp = strtok( NULL, ". \n" );
31        } /* end while */
32
33     } /* end for */
34
35     putchar( '\n' );
36
37     /* display results in array */
38     for ( i = 1; i <= 19; i++ ) {
39
40        /* if length is not zero */
41        if ( lengths[ i ] ) {
```

Fig. S8.12 Solution for Exercise 8.34, Part B. (Part 1 of 2.)

```
42              printf( "%d word%s of length %d\n",
43                  lengths[ i ], lengths[ i ] == 1 ? "" : "s", i );
44          } /* end if */
45
46      } /* end for */
47
48      return 0; /* indicate successful termination */
49
50  } /* end main */
```

```
Enter three lines of text:
This program determines the length of each word
in the input text.  The input text here has words
of several different lengths.

3 words of length 2
4 words of length 3
6 words of length 4
3 words of length 5
1 word of length 6
3 words of length 7
1 word of length 9
1 word of length 10
```

Fig. S8.12   Solution for Exercise 8.34, Part B.   (Part 2 of 2.)

c) Write a program that reads several lines of text and prints a table indicating the number of occurrences of each different word in the text. The first version of your program should include the words in the table in the same order in which they appear in the text. A more interesting (and useful) printout should then be attempted in which the words are sorted alphabetically. For example, the lines

```
To be, or not to be: that is the question:
Whether 'tis nobler in the mind to suffer
```

contain the words "to" three times, the word "be" two times, the word "or" once, etc.

ANS:

```
1   /* Exercise 8.34 Part C solution */
2   #include <stdio.h>
3   #include <string.h>
4
5   int main()
6   {
7      char text[ 3 ][ 80 ];            /* 3 string from user */
8      char *temp;                       /* token pointer */
9      char words[ 100 ][ 20 ] = { "" }; /* array of words */
10     int i;                            /* loop counter */
```

Fig. S8.13   Solution for Exercise 8.34, Part C.   (Part 1 of 3.)

```
11      int j;                                    /* loop counter */
12      int count[ 100 ] = { 0 };                 /* array of word counts */
13
14      printf( "Enter three lines of text:\n" );
15
16      /* read three lines of text */
17      for ( i = 0; i <= 2; i++ ) {
18         gets( &text[ i ][ 0 ] );
19      } /* end for */
20
21      /* loop through 3 strings */
22      for ( i = 0; i <= 2; i++ ) {
23
24         /* get first token */
25         temp = strtok( &text[ i ][ 0 ], ". \n" );
26
27         /* while temp does not equal NULL */
28         while ( temp ) {
29
30            /* loop through words for match */
31            for ( j = 0; words[ j ][ 0 ] && strcmp( temp,
32               &words[ j ][ 0 ] ) != 0; j++ ) {
33               ; /* empty body */
34            } /* end for */
35
36            ++count[ j ]; /* increment count */
37
38            /* if temp could not be found in words array */
39            if ( !words[ j ][ 0 ] ) {
40               strcpy( &words[ j ][ 0 ], temp );
41            } /* end if */
42
43            temp = strtok( NULL, ". \n" );
44         } /* end while */
45
46      } /* end for */
47
48      putchar( '\n' );
49
50      /* loop through words array */
51      for ( j = 0; words[ j ][ 0 ] != '\0' && j <= 99; j++ ) {
52         printf( "\"%s\" appeared %d time%s\n",
53            &words[ j ][ 0 ], count[ j ], count[ j ] == 1 ? "" : "s" );
54      } /* end for */
55
56      return 0; /* indicate successful termination */
57
58   } /* end main */
```

Fig. S8.13   Solution for Exercise 8.34, Part C.   (Part 2 of 3.)

```
Enter three lines of text:
This program counts the number
of occurrences of each word in
the input text.

"This" appeared 1 time
"program" appeared 1 time
"counts" appeared 1 time
"the" appeared 2 times
"number" appeared 1 time
"of" appeared 2 times
"occurrences" appeared 1 time
"each" appeared 1 time
"word" appeared 1 time
"in" appeared 1 time
"input" appeared 1 time
"text" appeared 1 time
```

Fig. S8.13   Solution for Exercise 8.34, Part C.   (Part 3 of 3.)

8.36   *(Printing Dates in Various Formats)* Dates are commonly printed in several different formats in business correspondence. Two of the more common formats are

    07/21/2003 and July 21, 2003

Write a program that reads a date in the first format and prints that date in the second format.

        ANS:

```
1    /* Exercise 8.36 solution */
2    #include <stdio.h>
3
4    int main()
5    {
6
7       /* array of month names */
8       char *months[ 13 ] = { "", "January", "February", "March",
9                              "April", "May", "June", "July",
10                             "August", "September", "October",
11                             "November", "December"};
12      int m; /* integer month */
13      int d; /* integer day */
14      int y; /* integer year */
15
16      /* read a date from user */
17      printf( "Enter a date in the form mm/dd/yyyy: " );
18      scanf( "%d/%d/%d", &m, &d, &y );
19
20      /* output date in new format */
21      printf( "The date is: %s %d, %d\n", months[ m ], d, y );
```

Fig. S8.14   Solution for Exercise 8.36.   (Part 1 of 2.)

```
22
23      return 0; /* indicate successful termination */
24
25  } /* end main */
```

```
Enter a date in the form mm/dd/yyyy: 06/18/2003
The date is: June 18, 2003
```

Fig. S8.14   Solution for Exercise 8.36.   (Part 2 of 2.)

8.38   *(Writing the Word Equivalent of a Check Amount)* Continuing the discussion of the previous example, we reiterate the importance of designing check-writing systems to prevent alteration of check amounts. One common security method requires that the check amount be both written in numbers and "spelled out" in words. Even if someone is able to alter the numerical amount of the check, it is extremely difficult to change the amount in words.

Many computerized check-writing systems do not print the amount of the check in words. Perhaps the main reason for this omission is the fact that most high-level languages used in commercial applications do not contain adequate string manipulation features. Another reason is that the logic for writing word equivalents of check amounts is somewhat involved.

Write a program that inputs a numeric check amount and writes the word equivalent of the amount. For example, the amount 112.43 should be written as

ONE HUNDRED TWELVE and 43/100

ANS:

```
1   /* Exercise 8.38 solution */
2   /* NOTE THAT THIS PROGRAM ONLY HANDLES VALUES UP TO $99.99 */
3   /* The program is easily modified to process larger values */
4   #include <stdio.h>
5
6   int main()
7   {
8
9       /* word equivalents of single digits */
10      char *digits[ 10 ] = { "", "ONE", "TWO", "THREE", "FOUR",
11                             "FIVE", "SIX", "SEVEN", "EIGHT", "NINE"};
12
13      /* word equivalents of 10-19 */
14      char *teens[ 10 ] = { "TEN", "ELEVEN", "TWELVE", "THIRTEEN",
15                            "FOURTEEN", "FIFTEEN", "SIXTEEN",
16                            "SEVENTEEN", "EIGHTEEN", "NINETEEN"};
17
18      /* word equivalents of tens digits */
19      char *tens[ 10 ] = { "", "TEN", "TWENTY", "THIRTY", "FORTY",
20                           "FIFTY", "SIXTY", "SEVENTY", "EIGHTY",
21                           "NINETY"};
```

Fig. S8.15   Solution for Exercise 8.38.   (Part 1 of 2.)

```
22
23        int dollars;  /* check dollar amount */
24        int cents;    /* check cents amount */
25        int digit1;   /* ones digit */
26        int digit2;   /* tens digit */
27
28        /* get check amount */
29        printf( "Enter the check amount ( 0.00 to 99.99 ): " );
30        scanf( "%d.%d", &dollars, &cents );
31        printf( "\nThe check amount in words is:\n" );
32
33        /* print equivalent words */
34        if ( dollars < 10 ) {
35           printf( "%s ", digits[ dollars ] );
36        } /* end if */
37        else if ( dollars < 20 ) {
38           printf( "%s ", teens[ dollars - 10 ] );
39        } /* end else if */
40        else {
41           digit1 = dollars / 10; /* ones digit */
42           digit2 = dollars % 10; /* tens digit */
43
44           /* if ones digit is zero */
45           if ( digit2 == 0 ) {
46              printf( "%s ", tens[ digit1 ] );
47           } /* end if */
48           else {
49              printf( "%s-%s ", tens[ digit1 ], digits[ digit2 ] );
50           } /* end else */
51
52        } /* end else */
53
54        printf( "and %d/100\n", cents );
55
56        return 0; /* indicate successful termination */
57
58     } /* end main */
```

```
Enter the check amount ( 0.00 to 99.99 ): 72.63

The check amount in words is:
SEVENTY-TWO and 63/100
```

Fig. S8.15   Solution for Exercise 8.38.   (Part 2 of 2.)

```
Enter the check amount ( 0.00 to 99.99 ): 13.22

The check amount in words is:
THIRTEEN and 22/100
```

```
Enter the check amount ( 0.00 to 99.99 ): 5.75

The check amount in words is:
FIVE and 75/100
```

C Formatted Input/Output

Solutions to Selected Exercises

9.5 Show what is printed by each of the following statements. If a statement is incorrect, indicate why.

a) `printf( "%-10d\n", 10000 );`
ANS: `10000`

b) `printf( "%c\n", "This is a string" );`
ANS: A string cannot be printed with the %c specifier.

c) `printf( "%*.*lf\n", 8, 3, 1024.987654 );`
ANS: `1024.988`

d) `printf( "%#o\n%#X\n%#e\n", 17, 17, 1008.83689 );`
ANS:
```
021
0X11
1.008837e+03
```

e) `printf( "% ld\n%+ld\n", 1000000, 1000000 );`
ANS:
```
 1000000
+1000000
```

f) `printf( "%10.2E\n", 444.93738 );`
ANS: `4.45E+02`   *preceded by two spaces*

g) `printf( "%10.2g\n", 444.93738 );`
ANS: `4.4e+02`   *preceded by three spaces*

h) `printf( "%d\n", 10.987 );`
ANS: *A floating point value cannot be printed with the* %d *conversion specifier.*

9.10 Write a program to test the results of printing the integer value `12345` and the floating-point value `1.2345` in various size fields. What happens when the values are printed in fields containing fewer digits than the values?

ANS:

```
1   /* Exercise 9.10 Solution */
2   #include <stdio.h>
3
4   int main()
5   {
6
7      /* print the integer 12345 */
8      printf( "%10d\n", 12345 );
9      printf( "%5d\n", 12345 );
10     printf( "%2d\n\n", 12345 );
11
12     /* print the floating-point value 1.2345 */
13     printf( "%10f\n", 1.2345 );
14     printf( "%6f\n", 1.2345 );
15     printf( "%2f\n", 1.2345 );
16
17     return 0; /* indicate successful termination */
18
19   } /* end main */
```

```
     12345
12345
12345

   1.234500
1.234500
1.234500
```

Fig. S9.1   Solution for Exercise 9.10.

9.11   Write a program that prints the value 100.453627 rounded to the nearest digit, tenth, hundredth, thousandth and ten thousandth.

ANS:

```
1   /* Exercise 9.11 Solution */
2   #include <stdio.h>
3
4   int main()
5   {
6      printf( "%.0f\n", 100.453627 );
7      printf( "%.1f\n", 100.453627 );
8      printf( "%.2f\n", 100.453627 );
9      printf( "%.3f\n", 100.453627 );
10     printf( "%.4f\n", 100.453627 );
11
12     return 0; /* indicate successful termination */
```

Fig. S9.2   Solution for Exercise 9.11. (Part 1 of 2.)

```
13
14   } /* end main */
```

```
100
100.5
100.45
100.454
100.4536
```

Fig. S9.2   Solution for Exercise 9.11. (Part 2 of 2.)

9.13   Write a program that converts integer Fahrenheit temperatures from 0 to 212 degrees to floating-point Celsius temperatures with 3 digits of precision. Use the formula

```
celsius = 5.0 / 9.0 * ( fahrenheit - 32 );
```

to perform the calculation. The output should be printed in two right-justified columns of 10 characters each, and the Celsius temperatures should be preceded by a sign for both positive and negative values.

ANS:

```
1    /* Exercise 9.13 Solution */
2    #include <stdio.h>
3
4    int main()
5    {
6       int fahrenheit; /* holds fahrenheit temperature */
7       double celcius; /* holds celcius temperature */
8
9       printf( "%10s%12s\n", "Fahrenheit", "Celcius" );
10
11      /* convert fahrenheit to celsius and display temperatures
12         showing the sign for celsius temperatures */
13      for ( fahrenheit = 0; fahrenheit <= 212; fahrenheit++ ) {
14         celcius = 5.0 / 9.0 * ( fahrenheit - 32 );
15         printf( "%10d%+12.3f\n", fahrenheit, celcius );
16      } /* end for */
17
18      return 0; /* indicate successful termination */
19
20   } /* end main */
```

Fig. S9.3   Solution for Exercise 9.13.   (Part 1 of 2.)

```
Fahrenheit     Celcius
         0     -17.778
         1     -17.222
         2     -16.667
         3     -16.111
         4     -15.556
         5     -15.000
         6     -14.444
         7     -13.889
         .
         .
         .
       204     +95.556
       205     +96.111
       206     +96.667
       207     +97.222
       208     +97.778
       209     +98.333
       210     +98.889
       211     +99.444
       212     +100.000
```

Fig. S9.3   Solution for Exercise 9.13.   (Part 2 of 2.)

9.16   Write a program that inputs the value 437 using each of the scanf integer conversion specifiers.
Print each input value using all the integer conversion specifiers.

      ANS:

```
1   /* Exercise 9.16 Solution */
2   #include <stdio.h>
3
4   int main()
5   {
6      int array[ 5 ]; /* holds the value 437 five times */
7      int loop;       /* loop counter */
8
9      /* array of table headers */
10     char *s[] = { "Read with %d:", "Read with %i:", "Read with %o:",
11                   "Read with %u:", "Read with %x:"};
12
13     /* prompt the user and read 5 values */
14     printf( "Enter the value 437 five times: " );
15     scanf( "%d%i%o%u%x", &array[ 0 ], &array[ 1 ], &array[ 2 ],
16        &array[ 3 ], &array[ 4 ] );
17
18     /* loop through all 5 values */
19     for ( loop = 0; loop <= 4; loop++ ) {
20
```

Fig. S9.4   Solution for Exercise 9.16.   (Part 1 of 2.)

```
21          /* print each of the 5 values */
22          printf( "%s\n%d %i %o %u %x\n\n", s[ loop ], array[ loop ],
23             array[ loop ], array[ loop ], array[ loop ], array[ loop ] );
24       } /* end for */
25
26       return 0; /* indicate successful termination */
27
28    } /* end main */
```

```
Enter the value 437 five times: 437 437 437 437 437
Read with %d:
437 437 665 437 1b5

Read with %i:
437 437 665 437 1b5

Read with %o:
287 287 437 287 11f

Read with %u:
437 437 665 437 1b5

Read with %x:
1079 1079 2067 1079 437
```

Fig. S9.4   Solution for Exercise 9.16.   (Part 2 of 2.)

9.18   In some programming languages, strings are entered surrounded by either single *or* double quo-
tation marks. Write a program that reads the three strings suzy, "suzy" and 'suzy'. Are the single and
double quotes ignored by C or read as part of the string?

    ANS:

```
1    /* Exercise 9.18 Solution */
2    #include <stdio.h>
3
4    int main()
5    {
6       char a[ 10 ]; /* first string */
7       char b[ 10 ]; /* second string */
8       char c[ 10 ]; /* third string */
9
10      /* prompt user and read three strings */
11      printf( "Enter the strings suzy, \"suzy\", and 'suzy':\n" );
12      scanf( "%s%s%s", a, b, c );
13
14      printf( "%s %s %s\n", a, b, c ); /* display strings */
15
16      return 0; /* indicate successful termination */
```

Fig. S9.5   Solution for Exercise 9.18.   (Part 1 of 2.)

```
17
18    } /* end main */
```

```
Enter the strings suzy, "suzy", and 'suzy':
suzy
"suzy"
'suzy'
suzy "suzy" 'suzy'
```

Fig. S9.5   Solution for Exercise 9.18.   (Part 2 of 2.)

Structures, Unions, Bit Manipulations and Enumerations

Solutions to Selected Exercises

10.8   Create union `integer` with members `char c`, `short s`, `int i` and `long b`. Write a program that inputs value of type `char`, `short`, `int` and `long` and stores the values in union variables of type `union integer`. Each union variable should be printed as a `char`, a `short`, an `int` and a `long`. Do the values always print correctly?

ANS:

```
1   /* Exercise 10.8 Solution */
2   /* NOTE: The program output is machine dependent */
3   #include <stdio.h>
4
5   /* integer union definition */
6   union integer {
7      char c;  /* character input by user */
8      short s; /* short integer input by user */
9      int i;   /* integer input by user */
10     long l;  /* long integer input by user */
11  }; /* end union integer */
12
13  int main()
14  {
15     union integer a; /* define union a */
16
17     /* read a character from user into the union */
18     printf( "Enter a character: " );
19     scanf( "%c", &a.c );
20
21     /* print each value of union */
22     printf( "\'%c'\ printed as a character is %c\n", a.c, a.c );
23     printf( "\'%c'\ printed as a short integer is %hd\n", a.c, a.s );
24     printf( "\'%c'\ printed as an integer is %d\n", a.c, a.i );
```

Fig. S10.1   Solution for Exercise 10.8.   (Part 1 of 3.)

```
25        printf( "\'%c'\ printed as a long integer is %ld\n", a.c, a.l );
26
27        /* read a short integer from user into the union */
28        printf( "\nEnter a short integer: " );
29        scanf( "%hd", &a.s );
30
31        /* print each value of union */
32        printf( "%hd printed as a character is %c\n", a.s, a.c );
33        printf( "%hd printed as a short integer is %hd\n", a.s, a.s );
34        printf( "%hd printed as an integer is %d\n", a.s, a.i );
35        printf( "%hd printed as a long integer is %ld\n", a.s, a.l );
36
37        /* read an integer from user into the union */
38        printf( "\nEnter an integer: " );
39        scanf( "%d", &a.i );
40
41        /* print each value of union */
42        printf( "%d printed as a character is %c\n", a.i, a.c );
43        printf( "%d printed as a short integer is %hd\n", a.i, a.s );
44        printf( "%d printed as an integer is %d\n", a.i, a.i );
45        printf( "%d printed as a long integer is %ld\n", a.i, a.l );
46
47        /* read a long integer from user into the union */
48        printf( "\nEnter a long integer: " );
49        scanf( "%ld", &a.l );
50
51        /* print each value of union */
52        printf( "%ld printed as a character is %c\n", a.l, a.c );
53        printf( "%ld printed as a short integer is %hd\n", a.l, a.s );
54        printf( "%ld printed as an integer is %d\n", a.l, a.i );
55        printf( "%ld printed as a long integer is %ld\n", a.l, a.l );
56
57        return 0; /* indicate successful termination */
58
59    } /* end main */
```

Fig. S10.1   Solution for Exercise 10.8.   (Part 2 of 3.)

```
Enter a character: A
'A' printed as a character is A
'A' printed as a short integer is -13247
'A' printed as an integer is -858993599
'A' printed as a long integer is -858993599

Enter a short integer: 97
97 printed as a character is a
97 printed as a short integer is 97
97 printed as an integer is -859045791
97 printed as a long integer is -859045791

Enter an integer: 32700
32700 printed as a character is +
32700 printed as a short integer is 32700
32700 printed as an integer is 32700
32700 printed as a long integer is 32700

Enter a long integer: 10000000
10000000 printed as a character is Ç
10000000 printed as a short integer is -27008
10000000 printed as an integer is 10000000
10000000 printed as a long integer is 10000000
```

Fig. S10.1   Solution for Exercise 10.8.   (Part 3 of 3.)

10.10   Write a program that right shifts an integer variable 4 bits. The program should print the integer in bits before and after the shift operation. Does your system place 0s or 1s in the vacated bits?

   ANS:

```
 1    /* Exercise 10.10 Solution */
 2    #include <stdio.h>
 3
 4    void displayBits( unsigned value ); /* prototype */
 5
 6    int main()
 7    {
 8       unsigned val; /* value from user */
 9
10       /* prompt user and read value */
11       printf( "Enter an integer: " );
12       scanf( "%u", &val );
13
14       /* display value before shifting */
15       printf( "%u before right shifting 4 bits is:\n", val );
16       displayBits( val );
17
18       /* display value after shifting */
```

Fig. S10.2   Solution for Exercise 10.10.   (Part 1 of 2.)

```
19      printf( "%u after right shifting 4 bits is:\n", val );
20      displayBits( val >> 4 );
21
22      return 0; /* indicate successful termination */
23
24   } /* end main */
25
26   /* function displayBits prints each bit of value */
27   void displayBits( unsigned value )
28   {
29      unsigned c; /* bit counter */
30      unsigned displayMask = 1 << 15; /* bit mask */
31
32      printf( "%7u = ", value );
33
34      /* loop through bits */
35      for ( c = 1; c <= 16; c++ ) {
36         value & displayMask ? putchar( '1' ) : putchar( '0' );
37         value <<= 1; /* shift value 1 bit to the left */
38
39         if ( c % 8 == 0 ) { /* print a space */
40            putchar( ' ' );
41         } /* end if */
42
43      } /* end for */
44
45      putchar( '\n' );
46   } /* end function displayBits */
```

```
Enter an integer: 1234
1234 before right shifting 4 bits is:
   1234 = 00000100 11010010
1234 after right shifting 4 bits is:
     77 = 00000000 01001101
```

Fig. S10.2 Solution for Exercise 10.10. (Part 2 of 2.)

10.13 The left-shift operator can be used to pack two character values into an unsigned integer variable. Write a program that inputs two characters from the keyboard and passes them to function pack-
Characters. To pack two characters into an unsigned integer variable, assign the first character to the
unsigned variable, shift the unsigned variable left by 8 bit positions and combine the unsigned variable with the second character using the bitwise inclusive OR operator. The program should output the
characters in their bit format before and after they are packed into the unsigned integer to prove that the
characters are in fact packed correctly in the unsigned variable.

     ANS:

```
1   /* Exercise 10.13 Solution */
2   #include <stdio.h>
```

Fig. S10.3 Solution for Exercise 10.13. (Part 1 of 3.)

```
 3
 4   /* prototypes */
 5   unsigned packCharacters( char x, char y );
 6   void displayBits( unsigned value );
 7
 8   int main()
 9   {
10      char a;           /* first character from user */
11      char b;           /* second character from user */
12      unsigned result; /* result of packing both characters */
13
14      /* prompt user and read two characters */
15      printf( "Enter two characters: " );
16      scanf( "%c %c", &a, &b );
17
18      /* display first character as bits */
19      printf( "\'%c\' in bits as an unsigned integers is:\n", a );
20      displayBits( a );
21
22      /* display second character as bits */
23      printf( "\n\'%c\' in bits as an unsigned integers is:\n", b );
24      displayBits( b );
25
26      /* pack characters and display result */
27      result = packCharacters( a, b );
28      printf( "\n\'%c\' and \'%c\' packed in an unsigned integer:\n",
29         a, b );
30      displayBits( result );
31
32      return 0; /* indicate successful termination */
33
34   } /* end main */
35
36   /* function packCharacters packs two characters into an unsigned int */
37   unsigned packCharacters( char x, char y )
38   {
39      unsigned pack = x; /* initialize pack to x */
40
41      pack <<= 8; /* shift pack 8 bits to the left */
42      pack |= y; /* pack y using inclusive OR operator */
43      return pack;
44
45   } /* end function packCharacters */
46
47   /* display the bits of value */
48   void displayBits( unsigned value )
49   {
50      unsigned c; /* bit counter */
51      unsigned displayMask = 1 << 15; /* bit mask */
52
```

Fig. S10.3   Solution for Exercise 10.13.   (Part 2 of 3.)

```
53      printf( "%7u = ", value );
54
55      /* loop through bits */
56      for ( c = 1; c <= 16; c++ ) {
57         value & displayMask ? putchar( '1' ) : putchar( '0' );
58         value <<= 1; /* shift value 1 bit to the left */
59
60         if ( c % 8 == 0 ) { /* print a space */
61            putchar( ' ' );
62         } /* end if */
63
64      } /* end for */
65
66      putchar( '\n' );
67   } /* end function displayBits */
```

```
Enter two characters: A B
'A' in bits as an unsigned integers is:
    65 = 00000000 01000001

'B' in bits as an unsigned integers is:
    66 = 00000000 01000010

'A' and 'B' packed in an unsigned integer:
  16706 = 01000001 01000010
```

Fig. S10.3   Solution for Exercise 10.13.   (Part 3 of 3.)

10.19   The following program uses function `multiple` to determine if the integer entered from the keyboard is a multiple of some integer X. Examine the function multiple, then determine the value of X.

```
1    /* ex10_19.c */
2    /* This program determines if a value is a multiple of X. */
3    #include <stdio.h>
4
5    int multiple( int num ); /* prototype */
6
7    int main()
8    {
9       int y; /* y will hold an integer entered by the user  */
10
11      printf( "Enter an integer between 1 and 32000: " );
12      scanf( "%d", &y );
13
14      /* if y is a multiple of X */
15      if ( multiple( y ) ) {
16         printf( "%d is a multiple of X\n", y );
17      } /* end if */
```

Fig. S10.4   Exercise 10.19: What does this program do?   (Part 1 of 2.)

```
18      else {
19         printf( "%d is not a multiple of X\n", y );
20      } /* end else */
21
22      return 0; /* indicates successful termination */
23   } /* end main */
24
25   /* determine if num is a multiple of X */
26   int multiple( int num )
27   {
28      int i;          /* counter */
29      int mask = 1; /* initialize mask */
30      int mult = 1; /* initialize mult */
31
32      for ( i = 1; i <= 10; i++, mask <<= 1 ) {
33
34         if ( ( num & mask ) != 0 ) {
35            mult = 0;
36            break;
37         } /* end if */
38
39      } /* end for */
40
41      return mult;
42   } /* end function multiple */
```

Fig. S10.4   Exercise 10.19: What does this program do?   (Part 2 of 2.)

ANS:

```
Enter an integer between 1 and 32000: 1024
1024 is a multiple of X
```

Fig. S10.5   Solution for Exercise 10.19.

10.20   What does the following program do?

```
1    /* ex10_20.c */
2    #include <stdio.h>
3
4    int mystery( unsigned bits ); /* prototype */
5
6    int main()
7    {
8       unsigned x; /* x will hold an integer entered by the user */
9
```

Fig. S10.6   Exercise 10.20: What does this program do?   (Part 1 of 2.)

```
10        printf( "Enter an integer: " );
11        scanf( "%u", &x );
12
13        printf( "The result is %d\n", mystery( x ) );
14
15        return 0; /* indicates successful termination */
16     } /* end main */
17
18     /* What does this function do? */
19     int mystery( unsigned bits )
20     {
21        unsigned i;                    /* counter */
22        unsigned mask = 1 << 31; /* initialize mask */
23        unsigned total = 0;         /* initialize total */
24
25        for ( i = 1; i <= 32; i++, bits <<= 1 ) {
26
27           if ( ( bits & mask ) == mask ) {
28              total++;
29           } /* end if */
30
31        } /* end for */
32
33        return !( total % 2 ) ? 1 : 0;
34     } /* end function mystery */
```

Fig. S10.6   Exercise 10.20: What does this program do?   (Part 2 of 2.)

ANS:

```
Enter an integer: 5678
The result is 0
```

Fig. S10.7   Solution for Exercise 10.20.

```
Enter an integer: 65
The result is 1
```

C File Processing

Solutions to Selected Exercises

11.7 Exercise 11.3 asked the reader to write a series of single statements. Actually, these statements form the core of an important type of file-processing program, namely, a file-matching program. In commercial data processing, it is common to have several files in each system. In an accounts receivable system, for example, there is generally a master file containing detailed information about each customer such as the customer's name, address, telephone number, outstanding balance, credit limit, discount terms, contract arrangements and possibly a condensed history of recent purchases and cash payments.

As transactions occur (i.e., sales are made and cash payments arrive in the mail), they are entered into a file. At the end of each business period (i.e., a month for some companies, a week for others and a day in some cases) the file of transactions (called "`trans.dat`" in Exercise 11.3) is applied to the master file (called "`oldmast.dat`" in Exercise 11.3), thus updating each account's record of purchases and payments. After each of these updatings run, the master file is rewritten as a new file ("`newmast.dat`"), which is then used at the end of the next business period to begin the updating process again.

File-matching programs must deal with certain problems that do not exist in single-file programs. For example, a match does not always occur. A customer on the master file might not have made any purchases or cash payments in the current business period, and therefore no record for this customer will appear on the transaction file. Similarly, a customer who did make some purchases or cash payments might have just moved to this community, and the company may not have had a chance to create a master record for this customer.

Use the statements written in Exercise 11.3 as a basis for writing a complete file-matching accounts receivable program. Use the account number on each file as the record key for matching purposes. Assume that each file is a sequential file with records stored in increasing account number order.

When a match occurs (i.e., records with the same account number appear on both the master file and the transaction file), add the dollar amount on the transaction file to the current balance on the master file and write the "`newmast.dat`" record. (Assume that purchases are indicated by positive amounts on the transaction file, and that payments are indicated by negative amounts.) When there is a master record for a particular account but no corresponding transaction record, merely write the master record to "`newmast.dat`". When there is a transaction record but no corresponding master record, print the message "`Unmatched transaction record for account number` ..." (fill in the account number from the transaction record).

ANS:

```
1    /* Exercise 11.7 Solution */
2    /* NOTE: This program was run using the */
3    /* data in Exercise 11.8  */
4    #include <stdio.h>
5    #include <stdlib.h>
6
7    int main()
8    {
9       int masterAccount;          /* account from old master file */
10      int transactionAccount;     /* account from transactions file */
11      double masterBalance;       /* balance from old master file */
12      double transactionBalance;  /* balance from transactions file */
13      char masterName[ 30 ];      /* name from master file */
14      FILE *ofPtr;                /* old master file pointer */
15      FILE *tfPtr;                /* transactions file pointer */
16      FILE *nfPtr;                /* new master file pointer */
17
18      /* terminate application if old master file cannot be opened */
19      if ( ( ofPtr = fopen( "oldmast.dat", "r" ) ) == NULL ) {
20         printf( "Unable to open oldmast.dat\n" );
21         exit( 1 );
22      } /* end if */
23
24      /* terminate application if transactions file cannot be opened */
25      if ( ( tfPtr = fopen( "trans.dat", "r" ) ) == NULL ) {
26         printf( "Unable to open trans.dat\n" );
27         exit( 1 );
28      } /* end if */
29
30      /* terminate application if new master file cannot be opened */
31      if ( ( nfPtr = fopen( "newmast.dat", "w" ) ) == NULL ) {
32         printf( "Unable to open newmast.dat\n" );
33         exit( 1 );
34      } /* end if */
35
36      /* display account currently being processed */
37      printf( "Processing....\n" );
38      fscanf( tfPtr, "%d%lf", &transactionAccount, &transactionBalance );
39
40      /* while not the end of transactions file */
41      while ( !feof( tfPtr ) ) {
42
43         /* read next record from old master file */
44         fscanf( ofPtr, "%d%[^0-9-]%lf", &masterAccount, masterName,
45            &masterBalance );
46
47         /* display accounts from master file until number of
48            new account is reached */
49         while ( masterAccount < transactionAccount && !feof( ofPtr ) ) {
```

Fig. S11.1   Solution for Exercise 11.7.   (Part 1 of 3.)

```
50          fprintf( nfPtr, "%d %s %.2f\n", masterAccount, masterName,
51              masterBalance );
52          printf( "%d %s %.2f\n", masterAccount, masterName,
53              masterBalance );
54
55          /* read next record from old master file */
56          fscanf( ofPtr, "%d%[^0-9-]%lf", &masterAccount,
57              masterName, &masterBalance );
58       } /* end while */
59
60       /* if matching account found, update balance and output
61          account info */
62       if ( masterAccount == transactionAccount ) {
63          masterBalance += transactionBalance;
64          fprintf( nfPtr, "%d %s %.2f\n", masterAccount, masterName,
65              masterBalance );
66          printf( "%d %s %.2f\n", masterAccount, masterName,
67              masterBalance );
68       } /* end if */
69
70       /* tell user if account from transactions file does
71          not match account from master file */
72       else if ( masterAccount > transactionAccount ) {
73          printf( "Unmatched transaction record for account %d\n",
74              transactionAccount );
75          fprintf( nfPtr, "%d %s %.2f\n", masterAccount, masterName,
76              masterBalance );
77          printf( "%d %s %.2f\n", masterAccount, masterName,
78              masterBalance );
79       } /* end else if */
80       else {
81          printf( "Unmatched transaction record for account %d\n",
82              transactionAccount );
83       } /* end else */
84
85       /* get next account and balance from transactions file */
86       fscanf( tfPtr, "%d%lf", &transactionAccount, &transactionBalance );
87    } /* end while */
88
89    /* loop through file and display account number, name and balance */
90    while ( !feof( ofPtr ) ) {
91       fscanf( ofPtr, "%d%[^0-9-]%lf", &masterAccount, masterName,
92           &masterBalance );
93       fprintf( nfPtr, "%d %s %.2f", masterAccount, masterName,
94           masterBalance );
95       printf( "%d %s %.2f", masterAccount, masterName, masterBalance );
96    } /* end while */
97
98    fclose( ofPtr ); /* close all file pointers */
99    fclose( tfPtr );
```

Fig. S11.1   Solution for Exercise 11.7.   (Part 2 of 3.)

```
100     fclose( nfPtr );
101
102     return 0; /* indicate successful termination */
103
104  } /* end main */
```

```
Processing....
100    Alan Jones    375.31
300    Mary Smith    89.30
Unmatched transaction record for account 400
500    Sam Sharp     0.00
700    Suzy Green    -14.22
Unmatched transaction record for account 900
```

Fig. S11.1   Solution for Exercise 11.7.   (Part 3 of 3.)

11.16   Write a program that uses the sizeof operator to determine the sizes in bytes of the various data types on your computer system. Write the results to the file "datasize.dat" so you may print the results later. The format for the results in the file should be as follows:

```
Data type              Size
char                      1
unsigned char             1
short int                 2
unsigned short int        2
int                       4
unsigned int              4
long int                  4
unsigned long int         4
float                     4
double                    8
long double              16
```

[*Note:* The type sizes on your computer might be different from those listed above.]
     ANS:

```
1  /* Exercise 11.16 Solution */
2  #include <stdio.h>
3
4  int main()
5
6  {
7     FILE *outPtr; /* output file pointer */
8
```

Fig. S11.2   Solution for Exercise 11.16.   (Part 1 of 2.)

```
 9      /* open datasize.dat for writing */
10      outPtr = fopen( "datasize.dat", "w" );
11
12      /* write size of various data types */
13      fprintf( outPtr, "%s%16s\n", "Data type", "Size" );
14      fprintf( outPtr, "%s%21d\n", "char", sizeof( char ) );
15      fprintf( outPtr, "%s%12d\n", "unsigned char",
16         sizeof( unsigned char ) );
17      fprintf( outPtr, "%s%16d\n", "short int", sizeof( short int ) );
18      fprintf( outPtr, "%s%7d\n", "unsigned short int",
19         sizeof( unsigned short int ) );
20      fprintf( outPtr, "%s%22d\n", "int", sizeof( int ) );
21      fprintf( outPtr, "%s%13d\n", "unsigned int",
22         sizeof( unsigned int ) );
23      fprintf( outPtr, "%s%17d\n", "long int", sizeof( long int ) );
24      fprintf( outPtr, "%s%8d\n", "unsigned long int",
25         sizeof( unsigned long int ) );
26      fprintf( outPtr, "%s%20d\n", "float", sizeof( float ) );
27      fprintf( outPtr, "%s%19d\n", "double", sizeof( double ) );
28      fprintf( outPtr, "%s%14d\n", "long double", sizeof( long double ) );
29
30      fclose( outPtr ); /* close file pointer */
31
32      return 0; /* indicate successful termination */
33
34   } /* end main */
```

Fig. S11.2   Solution for Exercise 11.16.   (Part 2 of 2.)

Contents of datasize.dat

```
Data type          Size
char                1
unsigned char       1
short int           2
unsigned short int  2
int                 4
unsigned int        4
long int            4
unsigned long int   4
float               4
double              8
long double         8
```

Data Structures

Solutions to Selected Exercises

12.6   Write a program that concatenates two linked lists of characters. The program should include function `concatenate` that takes pointers to both lists as arguments and concatenates the second list to the first list.

      ANS:

```
1   /* Exercise 12.6 Solution */
2   #include <stdio.h>
3   #include <stdlib.h>
4
5   /* ListNode structure definition */
6   struct ListNode {
7      char data;                 /* node data */
8      struct ListNode *nextPtr; /* pointer to next node */
9   }; /* end struct ListNode */
10
11  typedef struct ListNode ListNode;
12  typedef ListNode *ListNodePtr;
13
14  /* function prototypes */
15  void concatenate( ListNodePtr a, ListNodePtr b );
16  void insert( ListNodePtr *sPtr, char value );
17  void printList( ListNodePtr currentPtr );
18
19  int main()
20  {
21     ListNodePtr list1Ptr = NULL; /* pointer to first list */
22     ListNodePtr list2Ptr = NULL; /* pointer to second list */
23     char i; /* loop counter */
24
25     /* assign letters from A to C into first list */
26     for ( i = 'A'; i <= 'C'; i++ ) {
27        insert( &list1Ptr, i );
```

Fig. S12.1   Solution for Exercise 12.6.   (Part 1 of 4.)

```
28         } /* end for */
29
30         printf( "List 1 is: " );
31         printList( list1Ptr );
32
33         /* assign letters from D to F into second list */
34         for ( i = 'D'; i <= 'F'; i++ ) {
35            insert( &list2Ptr, i );
36         } /* end for */
37
38         printf( "List 2 is: " );
39         printList( list2Ptr );
40
41         concatenate( list1Ptr, list2Ptr );
42         printf( "The concatenated list is: " );
43         printList( list1Ptr );
44
45         return 0; /* indicate successful termination */
46
47      } /* end main */
48
49      /* Concatenate two lists */
50      void concatenate( ListNodePtr a, ListNodePtr b )
51      {
52         ListNodePtr currentPtr; /* temporary pointer */
53
54         currentPtr = a; /* set currentPtr to first linked list */
55
56         /* while currentPtr does not equal NULL */
57         while( currentPtr->nextPtr != NULL ) {
58            currentPtr = currentPtr->nextPtr;
59         } /* end while */
60
61         currentPtr->nextPtr = b; /* concatenate both lists */
62      } /* end function concatenate */
63
64      /* Insert a new value into the list in sorted order */
65      void insert( ListNodePtr *sPtr, char value )
66      {
67         ListNodePtr newPtr;      /* new node */
68         ListNodePtr previousPtr; /* previous node */
69         ListNodePtr currentPtr;  /* current node */
70
71         /* dynamically allocate memory */
72         newPtr = malloc( sizeof( ListNode ) );
73
74         /* if newPtr does not equal NULL */
75         if ( newPtr ) {
76            newPtr->data = value;
77            newPtr->nextPtr = NULL;
```

Fig. S12.1   Solution for Exercise 12.6.   (Part 2 of 4.)

```
78
79        previousPtr = NULL;
80        currentPtr = *sPtr; /* set currentPtr to start of list */
81
82        /* loop to find correct location in list */
83        while ( currentPtr != NULL && value > currentPtr->data ) {
84           previousPtr = currentPtr;
85           currentPtr = currentPtr->nextPtr;
86        } /* end while */
87
88        /* insert at beginning of list */
89        if ( previousPtr == NULL ) {
90           newPtr->nextPtr = *sPtr;
91           *sPtr = newPtr;
92        } /* end if */
93        else { /* insert node between previousPtr and currentPtr */
94           previousPtr->nextPtr = newPtr;
95           newPtr->nextPtr = currentPtr;
96        } /* end else */
97
98     } /* end if */
99     else {
100        printf( "%c not inserted. No memory available.\n", value );
101     } /* end else */
102
103 } /* end function insert */
104
105 /* Print the list */
106 void printList( ListNodePtr currentPtr )
107 {
108
109     /* if list is empty */
110     if ( !currentPtr ) {
111        printf( "List is empty.\n\n" );
112     } /* end if */
113     else {
114
115        /* loop while currentPtr does not equal NULL */
116        while ( currentPtr ) {
117           printf( "%c ", currentPtr->data );
118           currentPtr = currentPtr->nextPtr;
119        } /* end while */
120
121        printf( "*\n\n" );
122     } /* end else */
123
124 } /* end function printList */
```

Fig. S12.1   Solution for Exercise 12.6.   (Part 3 of 4.)

```
List 1 is: A B C *

List 2 is: D E F *

The concatenated list is: A B C D E F *
```

Fig. S12.1   Solution for Exercise 12.6.   (Part 4 of 4.)

12.8   Write a program that inserts 25 random integers from 0 to 100 in order in a linked list. The program should calculate the sum of the elements and the floating-point average of the elements.

ANS: .

```
1   /* Exercise 12.8 Solution */
2   #include <stdio.h>
3   #include <stdlib.h>
4   #include <time.h>
5
6   /* ListNode structure definition */
7   typedef struct ListNode {
8      int data;                  /* node data */
9      struct ListNode *nextPtr; /* pointer to next node */
10  } ListNode; /* end struct ListNode */
11
12  typedef ListNode *ListNodePtr;
13
14  /* function prototypes */
15  int sumList( ListNodePtr a );
16  double averageList( ListNodePtr a );
17  void insert( ListNodePtr *sPtr, int value );
18  void printList( ListNodePtr currentPtr );
19
20  int main()
21  {
22     ListNodePtr listPtr = NULL; /* list pointer */
23     int i; /* loop counter */
24
25     srand( time( NULL ) ); /* randomize */
26
27     /* build list with random numbers from 0 to 100 */
28     for ( i = 1; i <= 25; i++ ) {
29        insert( &listPtr, rand() % 101 );
30     } /* end for */
31
32     printf( "The list is:\n" );
33     printList( listPtr );
34
35     /* calculate and display the sum and average of list values */
36     printf( "The sum is %d\n", sumList( listPtr ) );
```

Fig. S12.2   Solution for Exercise 12.8.   (Part 1 of 4.)

```
37       printf( "The average is %f\n", averageList( listPtr ) );
38
39     return 0; /* indicate successful termination */
40
41   } /* end main */
42
43   /* Sum the integers in a list */
44   int sumList( ListNodePtr a )
45   {
46      ListNodePtr currentPtr; /* temporary pointer to list a */
47      int total = 0;             /* sum of node values */
48
49      currentPtr = a; /* set currentPtr to list a */
50
51      /* loop through list */
52      while ( currentPtr != NULL ) {
53
54         /* add node value to total */
55         total += currentPtr->data;
56         currentPtr = currentPtr->nextPtr;
57      } /* end while */
58
59      return total;
60
61   } /* end function sumList */
62
63   /* Average the integers in a list */
64   double averageList( ListNodePtr a )
65   {
66      ListNodePtr currentPtr; /* temporary pointer to list a */
67      double total = 0.0;       /* sum of node values */
68      int count = 0;             /* number of nodes in list */
69
70      currentPtr = a; /* set currentPtr to list a */
71
72      /* loop through list */
73      while ( currentPtr != NULL ) {
74         ++count; /* increment count */
75         total += currentPtr->data; /* update total */
76         currentPtr = currentPtr->nextPtr;
77      } /* end while */
78
79      return total / count; /* return average */
80
81   } /* end function averageList */
82
83   /* Insert a new value into the list in sorted order */
84   void insert( ListNodePtr *sPtr, int value )
85   {
86      ListNodePtr newPtr;         /* new node */
```

Fig. S12.2   Solution for Exercise 12.8.   (Part 2 of 4.)

```
87         ListNodePtr previousPtr; /* previous node */
88         ListNodePtr currentPtr;  /* current node */
89
90         /* dynamically allocate memory */
91         newPtr = malloc( sizeof( ListNode ) );
92
93         /* if newPtr does not equal NULL */
94         if ( newPtr ) {
95            newPtr->data = value;
96            newPtr->nextPtr = NULL;
97
98            previousPtr = NULL;
99            currentPtr = *sPtr; /* set currentPtr to start of list */
100
101           /* loop to find correct location in list */
102           while ( currentPtr != NULL && value > currentPtr->data ) {
103              previousPtr = currentPtr;
104              currentPtr = currentPtr->nextPtr;
105           } /* end while */
106
107           /* insert at beginning of list */
108           if ( previousPtr == NULL ) {
109              newPtr->nextPtr = *sPtr;
110              *sPtr = newPtr;
111           } /* end if */
112           else { /* insert node between previousPtr and currentPtr */
113              previousPtr->nextPtr = newPtr;
114              newPtr->nextPtr = currentPtr;
115           } /* end else */
116
117        } /* end if */
118        else {
119           printf( "%c not inserted. No memory available.\n", value );
120        } /* end else */
121
122     } /* end function insert */
123
124     /* Print the list */
125     void printList( ListNodePtr currentPtr )
126     {
127
128        /* if list is empty */
129        if ( !currentPtr ) {
130           printf( "List is empty.\n\n" );
131        } /* end if */
132        else {
133
134           /* loop while currentPtr does not equal NULL */
135           while ( currentPtr ) {
136              printf( "%d ", currentPtr->data );
```

Fig. S12.2   Solution for Exercise 12.8.   (Part 3 of 4.)

```
137            currentPtr = currentPtr->nextPtr;
138         } /* end while */
139
140         printf( "*\n\n" );
141      } /* end else */
142
143   } /* end function printList */
```

```
The list is:
6 12 14 20 27 31 31 34 37 38 56 59 63 66 72 73 73 76 77 79 88 94 95 96 97 *

The sum is 1414
The average is 56.560000
```

Fig. S12.2   Solution for Exercise 12.8.   (Part 4 of 4.)

12.10   Write a program that inputs a line of text and uses a stack to print the line reversed.
         ANS:

```
1   /* Exercise 12.10 Solution */
2   #include <stdio.h>
3   #include <stdlib.h>
4
5   /* stackNode structure definition */
6   struct stackNode {
7      char data;                   /* node data */
8      struct stackNode *nextPtr; /* pointer to next node */
9   }; /* end struct stackNode */
10
11  typedef struct stackNode StackNode;
12  typedef StackNode *StackNodePtr;
13
14  /* function prototypes */
15  void push( StackNodePtr *topPtr, char info );
16  char pop( StackNodePtr *topPtr );
17  int isEmpty( StackNodePtr topPtr );
18
19  int main()
20  {
21     StackNodePtr stackPtr = NULL; /* points to the stack top */
22     char c; /* current character from text */
23
24     printf( "Enter a line of text:\n" );
25
26     /* read each letter with getchar and push on stack */
27     while ( ( c = getchar() ) != '\n' ) {
28        push( &stackPtr, c );
29     } /* end while */
30
```

Fig. S12.3   Solution for Exercise 12.10.   (Part 1 of 3.)

```
31       printf( "\nThe line is reverse is:\n" );
32
33       /* while the stack is not empty, pop next character */
34       while ( !isEmpty( stackPtr ) ) {
35          printf( "%c", pop( &stackPtr ) );
36       } /* end while */
37
38       return 0; /* indicate successful termination */
39
40    } /* end main */
41
42    /* Insert a node at the stack top */
43    void push( StackNodePtr *topPtr, char info )
44    {
45       StackNodePtr newPtr; /* temporary node pointer */
46
47       /* dynamically allocate memory */
48       newPtr = malloc( sizeof( StackNode ) );
49
50       /* if memory was allocated, insert node at top of stack */
51       if ( newPtr ) {
52          newPtr->data = info;
53          newPtr->nextPtr = *topPtr;
54          *topPtr = newPtr;
55       } /* end if */
56       else {
57          printf( "%d not inserted. No memory available.\n", info );
58       } /* end else */
59
60    } /* end function push */
61
62    /* Remove a node from the stack top */
63    char pop( StackNodePtr *topPtr )
64    {
65       StackNodePtr tempPtr; /* temporary node pointer */
66       int popValue;          /* value of popped node */
67
68       tempPtr = *topPtr;
69       popValue = ( *topPtr )->data;
70       *topPtr = ( *topPtr )->nextPtr; /* reset topPtr */
71       free( tempPtr ); /* free memory */
72
73       return popValue; /* return value of popped node */
74
75    } /* end function pop */
76
77    /* Is the stack empty? */
78    int isEmpty( StackNodePtr topPtr )
79    {
80       return !topPtr; /* return NULL if stack is empty */
```

Fig. S12.3   Solution for Exercise 12.10.   (Part 2 of 3.)

```
81
82    } /* end function isEmpty */
```

```
Enter a line of text:
this is a line of text

The line is reverse is:
txet fo enil a si siht
```

Fig. S12.3   Solution for Exercise 12.10.   (Part 3 of 3.)

12.11   Write a program that uses a stack to determine if a string is a palindrome (i.e., the string is spelled identically backward and forward). The program should ignore spaces and punctuation.

　　　ANS:

```
1     /* Exercise 12.11 Solution   */
2     #include <stdio.h>
3     #include <stdlib.h>
4     #include <ctype.h>
5
6     #define YES 1
7     #define NO 0
8
9     /* stackNode structure definition */
10    struct stackNode {
11       char data;                  /* node data */
12       struct stackNode *nextPtr; /* pointer to next node */
13    }; /* end struct stackNode */
14
15    typedef struct stackNode STACKNODE;
16    typedef STACKNODE *STACKNODEPTR;
17
18    /* function prototypes */
19    void push( STACKNODEPTR *topPtr, char info );
20    char pop( STACKNODEPTR *topPtr );
21    int isEmpty( STACKNODEPTR topPtr );
22
23    int main()
24    {
25       STACKNODEPTR stackPtr = NULL; /* points to the stack top */
26       char c;                       /* current character from text */
27       char line[ 50 ];              /* text from user */
28       char condensedLine[ 50 ];     /* text with only letters */
29       int i = 0;                    /* length of condensed line */
30       int j = 0;                    /* length of line */
31       int palindrome = YES;         /* result of palindrome test */
32
33       printf( "Enter a line of text:\n" );
```

Fig. S12.4   Solution for Exercise 12.11.   (Part 1 of 3.)

```
34
35          /* read each letter with getchar and add to line */
36          while ( ( c = getchar() ) != '\n' ) {
37             line[ j++ ] = c;
38
39             /* remove all spaces and punctuation */
40             if ( isalpha( c ) ) {
41                condensedLine[ i++ ] = tolower( c );
42                push( &stackPtr, tolower( c ) );
43             } /* end if */
44
45          } /* end while */
46
47          line[ j ] = '\0';
48
49          /* loop through condensedLine */
50          for ( j = 0; j < i; j++ ) {
51
52             /* if condensedLine does not equal stack */
53             if ( condensedLine[ j ] != pop( &stackPtr ) ) {
54                palindrome = NO;
55                break; /* exit loop */
56             } /* end if */
57
58          } /* end for */
59
60          /* if text is a palindrome */
61          if ( palindrome ) {
62             printf( "\"%s\" is a palindrome\n", line );
63          } /* end if */
64          else {
65             printf( "\"%s\" is not a palindrome\n", line );
66          } /* end else */
67
68          return 0; /* indicate successful termination */
69
70       } /* end main */
71
72    /* Insert a node at the stack top */
73    void push( STACKNODEPTR *topPtr, char info )
74    {
75       STACKNODEPTR newPtr; /* temporary node pointer */
76
77       /* dynamically allocate memory */
78       newPtr = malloc( sizeof( STACKNODE ) );
79
80       /* if memory was allocated, insert node at top of stack */
81       if ( newPtr ) {
82          newPtr->data = info;
83          newPtr->nextPtr = *topPtr;
```

Fig. S12.4   Solution for Exercise 12.11.   (Part 2 of 3.)

```
84        *topPtr = newPtr;
85     } /* end if */
86     else {
87        printf( "%d not inserted. No memory available.\n", info );
88     } /* end else */
89
90  } /* end function push */
91
92  /* Remove a node from the stack top */
93  char pop( STACKNODEPTR *topPtr )
94  {
95     STACKNODEPTR tempPtr; /* temporary node pointer */
96     int popValue;          /* value of popped node */
97
98     tempPtr = *topPtr;
99     popValue = ( *topPtr )->data;
100    *topPtr = ( *topPtr )->nextPtr; /* reset topPtr */
101    free( tempPtr ); /* free memory */
102
103    return popValue; /* return value of popped node */
104
105 } /* end function pop */
106
107 /* Is the stack empty? */
108 int isEmpty( STACKNODEPTR topPtr )
109 {
110    return !topPtr; /* return NULL if stack is empty */
111
112 } /* end function isEmpty */
```

```
Enter a line of text:
able was i ere i saw elba
"able was i ere i saw elba" is a palindrome
```

Fig. S12.4   Solution for Exercise 12.11.   (Part 3 of 3.)

```
Enter a line of text:
this is not a palindrome
"this is not a palindrome" is not a palindrome
```

12.17 Write a program based on the program of Fig. 12.19 that inputs a line of text, tokenizes the sentence into separate words, inserts the words in a binary search tree, and prints the inorder, preorder, and postorder traversals of the tree.

[*Hint:* Read the line of text into an array. Use `strtok` to tokenize the text. When a token is found, create a new node for the tree, assign the pointer returned by `strtok` to member `string` of the new node, and insert the node in the tree.]

ANS:

```
1   /* Exercise 12.17 Solution */
2   #include <stdio.h>
3   #include <stdlib.h>
4   #include <string.h>
5
6   /* TreeNode structure definition */
7   struct TreeNode {
8      struct TreeNode *leftPtr;  /* pointer to left subtree */
9      char *token;                /* node data */
10     struct TreeNode *rightPtr; /* pointer to right subtree */
11  }; /* end struct TreeNode */
12
13  typedef struct TreeNode TreeNode;
14  typedef TreeNode *TreeNodePtr;
15
16  /* function prototypes */
17  void insertNode( TreeNodePtr *treePtr, char *tokenPtr );
18  void inOrder( TreeNodePtr treePtr );
19  void preOrder( TreeNodePtr treePtr );
20  void postOrder( TreeNodePtr treePtr );
21
22  int main()
23  {
24     TreeNodePtr rootPtr = NULL; /* points to the tree root */
25     char sentence[ 80 ];       /* text from user */
26     char *tokenPtr;            /* pointer to current token */
27
28     /* prompt user and read a sentence */
29     printf( "Enter a sentence:\n" );
30     gets( sentence );
31
32     /* tokenize the sentence */
33     tokenPtr = strtok( sentence, " " );
34
35     /* insert the tokens in the tree */
36     while ( tokenPtr ) {
37        insertNode( &rootPtr, tokenPtr );
38        tokenPtr = strtok( NULL, " " );
39     } /* end while */
40
41     /* traverse the tree preorder */
42     printf( "\nThe preorder traversal is:\n" );
43     preOrder( rootPtr );
44
45     /* traverse the tree inorder */
46     printf( "\n\nThe inorder traversal is:\n" );
47     inOrder( rootPtr );
48
49     /* traverse the tree postorder */
```

Fig. S12.5 Solution for Exercise 12.17. (Part 1 of 3.)

```
50      printf( "\n\nThe postorder traversal is:\n" );
51      postOrder( rootPtr );
52
53      return 0; /* indicate successful termination */
54
55   } /* end main */
56
57   /* insert a node into the tree */
58   void insertNode( TreeNodePtr *treePtr, char *tokenPtr )
59   {
60
61      /* if treePtr is NULL */
62      if ( !*treePtr ) {
63
64         /* dynamically allocate memory */
65         *treePtr = malloc( sizeof( TreeNode ) );
66
67         /* if memory was allocated, insert node */
68         if ( *treePtr ) {
69            ( *treePtr )->token = tokenPtr;
70            ( *treePtr )->leftPtr = NULL;
71            ( *treePtr )->rightPtr = NULL;
72         } /* end if */
73         else {
74            printf( "\"%s\" not inserted. No memory available.\n",
75               tokenPtr );
76         } /* end else */
77
78         return;
79      } /* end if */
80      else { /* recursively call insertNode */
81
82         /* insert node in left subtree */
83         if ( strcmp( tokenPtr, ( *treePtr )->token ) <= 0 ) {
84            insertNode( &( ( *treePtr )->leftPtr ), tokenPtr );
85         } /* end if */
86         else { /* insert node in right subtree */
87            insertNode( &( ( *treePtr )->rightPtr ), tokenPtr );
88         } /* end else */
89
90      } /* end else */
91
92   } /* end function insertNode */
93
94   /* traverse the tree inorder */
95   void inOrder( TreeNodePtr treePtr )
96   {
97
98      /* traverse left subtree, print node, traverse right subtree */
99      if ( treePtr ) {
```

Fig. S12.5   Solution for Exercise 12.17.   (Part 2 of 3.)

```
100        inOrder( treePtr->leftPtr );
101        printf( "%s ", treePtr->token );
102        inOrder( treePtr->rightPtr );
103     } /* end if */
104
105  } /* end function inOrder */
106
107  /* traverse the tree preorder */
108  void preOrder( TreeNodePtr treePtr )
109  {
110
111     /* print node, traverse left subtree, traverse right subtree */
112     if ( treePtr ) {
113        printf( "%s ", treePtr->token );
114        preOrder( treePtr->leftPtr );
115        preOrder( treePtr->rightPtr );
116     } /* end if */
117
118  } /* end function preOrder */
119
120  /* traverse the tree postorder */
121  void postOrder( TreeNodePtr treePtr )
122  {
123
124     /* traverse left subtree, traverse right subtree, print node */
125     if ( treePtr ) {
126        postOrder( treePtr->leftPtr );
127        postOrder( treePtr->rightPtr );
128        printf( "%s ", treePtr->token );
129     } /* end if */
130
131  } /* end function postOrder */
```

```
Enter a sentence:
this program inserts strings of different lengths in a tree

The preorder traversal is:
this program inserts different a in of lengths strings tree

The inorder traversal is:
a different in inserts lengths of program strings this tree

The postorder traversal is:
a in different lengths of inserts strings program tree this
```

Fig. S12.5   Solution for Exercise 12.17.   (Part 3 of 3.)

12.20 (*Recursively Print a List Backwards*) Write a function printListBackwards that recursively outputs the items in a list in reverse order. Use your function in a test program that creates a sorted list of integers and prints the list in reverse order.

ANS:

```
1    /* Exercise 12.20 Solution */
2    #include <stdio.h>
3    #include <stdlib.h>
4
5    /* ListNode structure definition */
6    struct ListNode {
7       int data;                    /* node data */
8       struct ListNode *nextPtr; /* pointer to next node */
9    }; /* end struct ListNode */
10
11   typedef struct ListNode ListNode;
12   typedef ListNode *ListNodePtr;
13
14   /* function prototype */
15   void printList( ListNodePtr currentPtr );
16   void printListBackwards( ListNodePtr currentPtr );
17   void insertItem( ListNodePtr *sPtr, int value );
18
19   int main()
20   {
21      ListNodePtr startPtr = NULL; /* list pointer */
22      int item; /* loop counter */
23
24      /* insert integers into list */
25      for ( item = 1; item < 11; item++ ) {
26         insertItem( &startPtr, item );
27      } /* end for */
28
29      printList( startPtr );
30      printf( "\n" );
31      printListBackwards( startPtr );
32
33      return 0; /* indicate successful termination */
34
35   } /* end main */
36
37   /* Insert a new value into the list in sorted order */
38   void insertItem( ListNodePtr *sPtr, int value )
39   {
40      ListNodePtr newPtr;        /* new node */
41      ListNodePtr previousPtr; /* previous node */
42      ListNodePtr currentPtr;  /* current node */
43
44      /* dynamically allocate memory */
45      newPtr = malloc( sizeof( ListNode ) );
46
47      /* if newPtr does not equal NULL */
48      if ( newPtr ) {
49         newPtr->data = value;
```

Fig. S12.6   Solution for Exercise 12.20. (Part 1 of 3.)

```
50          newPtr->nextPtr = NULL;
51
52          previousPtr = NULL;
53          currentPtr = *sPtr; /* set currentPtr to start of list */
54
55          /* loop to find correct location in list */
56          while ( currentPtr != NULL && value > currentPtr->data ) {
57             previousPtr = currentPtr;
58             currentPtr = currentPtr->nextPtr;
59          } /* end while */
60
61          /* insert at beginning of list */
62          if ( previousPtr == NULL ) {
63             newPtr->nextPtr = *sPtr;
64             *sPtr = newPtr;
65          } /* end if */
66          else { /* insert node between previousPtr and currentPtr */
67             previousPtr->nextPtr = newPtr;
68             newPtr->nextPtr = currentPtr;
69          } /* end else */
70
71       } /* end if */
72       else {
73          printf( "%c not inserted. No memory available.\n", value );
74       } /* end else */
75
76    } /* end function insertItem */
77
78    /* Print the list */
79    void printList( ListNodePtr currentPtr )
80    {
81
82       /* if list is empty */
83       if ( !currentPtr ) {
84          printf( "List is empty.\n\n" );
85       } /* end if */
86       else {
87
88          /* loop while currentPtr does not equal NULL */
89          while ( currentPtr ) {
90             printf( "%d ", currentPtr->data );
91             currentPtr = currentPtr->nextPtr;
92          } /* end while */
93
94          printf( "*\n\n" );
95       } /* end else */
96
97    } /* end function printList */
98
99    /* Print the list recursively backwards */
```

Fig. S12.6   Solution for Exercise 12.20. (Part 2 of 3.)

```
100  void printListBackwards( ListNodePtr currentPtr )
101  {
102
103     /* if at end of list */
104     if ( currentPtr == NULL ) {
105        printf( "The list reversed is:\n" );
106     } /* end if */
107     else { /* recursive call */
108        printListBackwards( currentPtr->nextPtr );
109        printf( "%d ", currentPtr->data );
110     } /* end else */
111
112  } /* end function printListBackwards */
```

```
the list is:
1 2 3 4 5 6 7 8 9 10

The list reversed is:
10 9 8 7 6 5 4 3 2 1
```

Fig. S12.6   Solution for Exercise 12.20. (Part 3 of 3.)

12.24 (*Level Order Binary Tree Traversal*) The program of Fig. 12.19 illustrated three recursive methods of traversing a binary tree—inorder traversal, preorder traversal, and postorder traversal. This exercise presents the *level order traversal* of a binary tree in which the node values are printed level-by-level starting at the root node level. The nodes on each level are printed from left to right. The level order traversal is not a recursive algorithm. It uses the queue data structure to control the output of the nodes. The algorithm is as follows:

    1) Insert the root node in the queue
    2) While there are nodes left in the queue,
        Get the next node in the queue
        Print the node's value
        If the pointer to the left child of the node is not null
        Insert the left child node in the queue
        If the pointer to the right child of the node is not null
        Insert the right child node in the queue.

Write function `levelOrder` to perform a level order traversal of a binary tree. The function should take as an argument a pointer to the root node of the binary tree. Modify the program of Fig. 12.19 to use this function. Compare the output from this function to the outputs of the other traversal algorithms to see that it worked correctly. [*Note:* You will also need to modify and incorporate the queue processing functions of Fig. 12.13 in this program.]

    ANS:

```
1   /* Exercise 12.24 solution */
2   #include <stdio.h>
3   #include <stdlib.h>
```

Fig. S12.7   Solution for Exercise 12.24. (Part 1 of 5.)

```
 4   #include <time.h>
 5
 6   /* TreeNode structure definition */
 7   struct TreeNode {
 8      struct TreeNode *leftPtr;  /* pointer to left subtree */
 9      int data;                  /* node data */
10      struct TreeNode *rightPtr; /* pointer to right subtree */
11   }; /* end struct TreeNode */
12
13   typedef struct TreeNode TreeNode;
14   typedef TreeNode *TreeNodePtr;
15
16   /* tree function prototypes */
17   void insertNode( TreeNodePtr *treePtr, int value );
18   void levelOrderTraversal( TreeNodePtr treePtr );
19
20   /* QueueNode structure definition */
21   struct QueueNode {
22      TreeNodePtr data;          /* node data */
23      struct QueueNode *nextPtr; /* pointer to next node */
24   }; /* end struct QueueNode */
25
26   typedef struct QueueNode QueueNode;
27   typedef QueueNode *QueueNodePtr;
28
29   /* queue function prototypes */
30   int isEmpty( QueueNodePtr headPtr );
31   TreeNodePtr dequeue( QueueNodePtr *headPtr, QueueNodePtr * tailPtr );
32   void enqueue( QueueNodePtr *headPtr, QueueNodePtr *tailPtr,
33               TreeNodePtr node );
34
35   int main()
36   {
37      int i;                       /* loop counter */
38      int item;                    /* random value to insert in tree */
39      TreeNodePtr rootPtr = NULL; /* points to the tree root */
40
41      srand( time( NULL ) ); /* randomize */
42      printf( "The values being inserted in the tree are:\n" );
43
44      /* insert random values between 1 and 15 in the tree */
45      for ( i = 1; i <= 15; i++ ) {
46         item = 1 + rand() % 20;
47         printf( " %d", item );
48         insertNode( &rootPtr, item );
49      } /* end for */
50
51      /* traverse the tree level order */
52      printf( "\n\nThe level order traversal is:\n" );
53      levelOrderTraversal( rootPtr );
```

Fig. S12.7   Solution for Exercise 12.24.   (Part 2 of 5.)

```
54        printf( "\n" );
55
56        return 0; /* indicate successful termination */
57
58   } /* end main */
59
60   /* Level order traversal of a binary tree */
61   void levelOrderTraversal( TreeNodePtr ptr )
62   {
63        QueueNodePtr head = NULL; /* points to queue head */
64        QueueNodePtr tail = NULL; /* points to queue tail */
65        TreeNodePtr node;         /* current tree node */
66
67        /* if tree is not empty */
68        if ( ptr != NULL ) {
69           enqueue( &head, &tail, ptr ); /* enqueue root nood */
70
71           /* while queue is not empty */
72           while ( !isEmpty( head ) ) {
73
74              /* dequeue next node and print data */
75              node = dequeue( &head, &tail );
76              printf( "%d ", node->data );
77
78              /* insert left child node in the queue */
79              if ( node->leftPtr != NULL ) {
80                 enqueue( &head, &tail, node->leftPtr );
81              } /* end if */
82
83              /* insert right child node in the queue */
84              if ( node->rightPtr != NULL ) {
85                 enqueue( &head, &tail, node->rightPtr );
86              } /* end if */
87
88           } /* end while */
89
90        } /* end if */
91
92   } /* end function levelOrderTraversal */
93
94   /* insert a node into the tree */
95   void insertNode( TreeNodePtr *treePtr, int value )
96   {
97
98        /* if treePtr is NULL */
99        if ( *treePtr == NULL ) {
100
101           /* dynamically allocate memory */
102           *treePtr = malloc( sizeof( TreeNode ) );
103
```

Fig. S12.7   Solution for Exercise 12.24.   (Part 3 of 5.)

```
104          /* if memory was allocated, insert node */
105          if ( *treePtr != NULL ) {
106             ( *treePtr )->data = value;
107             ( *treePtr )->leftPtr = NULL;
108             ( *treePtr )->rightPtr = NULL;
109          } /* end if */
110          else {
111             printf( "%d not inserted. No memory available.\n", value );
112          } /* end else */
113
114       } /* end if */
115       else { /* recursively call insertNode */
116
117          /* insert node in left subtree */
118          if ( value < ( *treePtr )->data ) {
119             insertNode( &( ( *treePtr )->leftPtr ), value );
120          } /* end if */
121          else {
122
123             /* insert node in right subtree */
124             if ( value > ( *treePtr )->data ) {
125                insertNode( &( ( *treePtr )->rightPtr ), value );
126             } /* end if */
127             else { /* duplicate value */
128                printf( "dup" );
129             } /* end else */
130
131          } /* end else */
132
133       } /* end else */
134
135    } /* end function insertNode */
136
137    /* enqueue node */
138    void enqueue( QueueNodePtr *headPtr, QueueNodePtr *tailPtr, TreeNodePtr node )
139    {
140       QueueNodePtr newPtr; /* temporary node pointer */
141
142       /* dynamically allocate memory */
143       newPtr = malloc( sizeof( QueueNode ) );
144
145       /* if newPtr does not equal NULL */
146       if ( newPtr != NULL ) {
147          newPtr->data = node;
148          newPtr->nextPtr = NULL;
149
150          /* if queue is empty, insert at head */
151          if ( isEmpty( *headPtr ) ) {
152             *headPtr = newPtr;
153          } /* end if */
```

Fig. S12.7   Solution for Exercise 12.24.   (Part 4 of 5.)

```
154          else { /* insert at tail */
155             ( *tailPtr )->nextPtr = newPtr;
156          } /* end else */
157
158          *tailPtr = newPtr;
159       } /* end if */
160       else {
161          printf( "Node not inserted\n" );
162       } /* end else */
163
164    } /* end function enqueue */
165
166    /* dequeue node from queue */
167    TreeNodePtr dequeue( QueueNodePtr *headPtr, QueueNodePtr *tailPtr )
168    {
169       TreeNodePtr node;      /* dequeued node */
170       QueueNodePtr tempPtr; /* temporary node pointer */
171
172       /* dequeue node and reset queue headPtr */
173       node = ( *headPtr )->data;
174       tempPtr = *headPtr;
175       *headPtr = ( *headPtr )->nextPtr;
176
177       /* if queue is empty */
178       if ( *headPtr == NULL ) {
179          *tailPtr = NULL;
180       } /* end if */
181
182       free( tempPtr ); /* free memory */
183
184       return node; /* return dequeued node */
185
186    } /* end function dequeue */
187
188    /* is queue empty? */
189    int isEmpty( QueueNodePtr headPtr )
190    {
191       return headPtr == NULL; /* return NULL is queue is empty */
192
193    } /* end function isEmpty */
```

```
The values being inserted in the tree are:
 5 10 7 5dup 11 9 15 1 7dup 20 6 20dup 4 16 4dup

The level order traversal is:
5 1 10 4 7 11 6 9 15 20 16
```

Fig. S12.7   Solution for Exercise 12.24.   (Part 5 of 5.)

The Preprocessor

Solutions to Selected Exercises

13.4   Write a program that defines a macro with one argument to compute the volume of a sphere. The program should compute the volume for spheres of radius 1 to 10 and print the results in tabular format. The formula for the volume of a sphere is

$$(\ 4.0 \ / \ 3 \ ) \ * \ \pi \ * \ r^3$$

where π is 3.14159.

     ANS:

```
1   /* Exercise 13.4 Solution: sphere volume macro */
2   #include <stdio.h>
3
4   #define PI 3.14159 /* constant representing Pi */
5
6   /* define preprocessor directive sphere volume */
7   #define SPHEREVOLUME( r ) ( 4.0 / 3.0 * PI * ( r ) * ( r ) * ( r ) )
8
9   int main()
10  {
11     int i; /* loop counter */
12
13     /* print header */
14     printf( "%10s%10s\n", "Radius", "Volume" );
15
16     /* use sphere volume macro */
17     for ( i = 1; i <= 10; i++ ) {
18        printf( "%10d%10.3f\n", i, SPHEREVOLUME( i ) );
19     } /* end for */
20
21     return 0; /* indicate successful termination */
22
23  } /* end main */
```

Fig. S13.1   Solution for Exercise 13.4.   (Part 1 of 2.)

```
    Radius    Volume
         1     4.189
         2    33.510
         3   113.097
         4   268.082
         5   523.598
         6   904.778
         7  1436.754
         8  2144.659
         9  3053.625
        10  4188.787
```

Fig. S13.1   Solution for Exercise 13.4.   (Part 2 of 2.)

13.6   Write a program that defines and uses macro MINIMUM2 to determine the smallest of two numeric values. Input the values from the keyboard.

ANS:

```
1   /* Exercise 13.6 Solution */
2   #include <stdio.h>
3
4   /* macro to determine smallest of two values */
5   #define MINIMUM2( x, y ) ( ( x ) < ( y ) ? ( x ) : ( y ) )
6
7   int main()
8   {
9      int a;     /* first integer */
10     int b;     /* second integer */
11     double c;  /* first double */
12     double d;  /* second double */
13
14     /* prompt user and read two integers */
15     printf( "Enter two integers: " );
16     scanf( "%d%d", &a, &b );
17
18     /* use macro MINIMUM to determine and display
19        smallest user entered integer */
20     printf( "The minimum of %d and %d is %d\n\n", a, b,
21        MINIMUM2( a,b ) );
22
23     /* prompt user and read two doubles */
24     printf( "Enter two doubles: " );
25     scanf( "%lf%lf", &c, &d );
26
27     /* use macro MINIMUM to determine and display
28        smallest user entered double */
29     printf( "The minimum of %.2f and %.2f is %.2f\n\n",
30             c, d, MINIMUM2( c,d ) );
31
```

Fig. S13.2   Solution for Exercise 13.6.   (Part 1 of 2.)

```
32      return 0; /* indicate successful termination */
33
34  } /* end main */
```

```
Enter two integers: 4 9
The minimum of 4 and 9 is 4

Enter two doubles: 45.7 13.2
The minimum of 45.70 and 13.20 is 13.20
```

Fig. S13.2   Solution for Exercise 13.6.   (Part 2 of 2.)

13.8   Write a program that defines and uses macro PRINT to print a string value.

ANS:

```
1   /* Exercise 13.8 Solution */
2   #include <stdio.h>
3
4   /* macro that prints its argument */
5   #define PRINT( string ) printf( "%s", ( string ) )
6
7   int main()
8   {
9      char text[ 20 ]; /* array to hold user input string */
10
11     /* prompt user and read string */
12     PRINT( "Enter a string: " );
13     scanf( "%s", text );
14
15     /* use macro to output string entered by user */
16     PRINT( "The string entered was: " );
17     PRINT( text );
18     PRINT( "\n" );
19
20     return 0; /* indicate successful termination */
21
22  } /* end main */
```

```
Enter a string: Hello
The string entered was: Hello
```

Fig. S13.3   Solution for Exercise 13.8.

13.10   Write a program that defines and uses macro SUMARRAY to sum the values in a numeric array. The macro should receive the array and the number of elements in the array as arguments.

ANS:

```
1    /* Exercise 13.10 Solution */
2    #include <stdio.h>
3
4    /* macro that adds values of a numeric array */
5    #define SUMARRAY( a, n ) for ( i = 0; i < ( n ); i++ ) \
6                             sum += a[ i ]
7
8    int main()
9    {
10      int i;        /* loop counter */
11      int sum = 0; /* sum of array elements */
12
13      /* initialize array whose values will be added */
14      int b[ 10 ] = { 1, 2, 3, 4, 5, 6, 7, 8, 9, 10};
15
16      /* use macro SUMARRAY to add elements of array */
17      SUMARRAY( b, 10 );
18      printf( "The sum of the elements of array b is %d\n", sum );
19
20      return 0; /* indicate successful termination */
21
22   } /* end main */
```

```
The sum of the elements of array b is 55
```

Fig. S13.4   Solution for Exercise 13.10.

Other C Topics

Solutions to Selected Exercises

14.3 Write a program that prints the command-line arguments of the program.
ANS:

```
1   /* Exercise 14.3 Solution */
2   #include <stdio.h>
3
4   int main( int argc, char *argv[] )
5   {
6      int i; /* loop counter */
7
8      printf( "The command line arguments are:\n" );
9
10     /* display arguments given to program at command line */
11     for ( i = 0; i < argc; i++ ) {
12        printf( "%s ", argv[ i ] );
13     } /* end for */
14
15     return 0; /* indicate successful termination */
16
17   } /* end main */
```

```
The command line arguments are:
C:\P14_3.exe arg1 arg2 arg3
```

Fig. S14.1 Solution for Exercise 14.3.

14.9 Write a program that uses goto statements to simulate a nested looping structure that prints a square of asterisks as follows:

```
*****
*   *
*   *
*   *
*****
```

The program should use only the following three `printf` statements:

```
printf( "*" );
printf( " " );
printf( "\n" );
```

ANS:

```
1   /* Exercise 14.9 Solution */
2   #include <stdio.h>
3
4   int main()
5   {
6      int size;      /* length of square sides */
7      int row = 0;   /* number of rows */
8      int col;       /* number of columns */
9
10     /* obtain length of side of square from user */
11     printf( "Enter the side length of the square: " );
12     scanf( "%d", &size );
13
14     start: /* label */
15        ++row;
16        printf( "\n" );
17
18        /* if all rows have been made end program */
19        if ( row > size ) {
20           goto end;
21        } /* end if */
22
23        col = 1; /* set column variable to first character of line */
24
25        innerLoop: /* label */
26
27           /* if all columns have been displayed return to top of loop */
28           if ( col > size ) {
29              goto start;
30           } /* end if */
31
32           /* display stars and spaces in appropriate positions */
33           if ( row == 1 || row == size || col == 1 || col == size ) {
```

Fig. S14.2   Solution for Exercise 14.9. (Part 1 of 2.)

```
34              printf( "*" );
35          } /* end if */
36          else {
37              printf( " " );
38          } /* end else */
39
40          ++col; /* increment column */
41          goto innerLoop; /* continue displaying columns */
42
43      end: /* label */
44
45      return 0; /* indicate successful termination */
46
47  } /* end main */
```

Fig. S14.2   Solution for Exercise 14.9.   (Part 2 of 2.)

C++ as a "Better C"

Solutions to Selected Exercises

15.5 Write a C++ program that uses an `inline` function `circleArea` to prompt the user for the radius of a circle and to calculate and print the area of that circle.

ANS:

```
1    // Exercise 15.5 Solution
2    #include <iostream>
3
4    using std::cout;
5    using std::endl;
6    using std::cin;
7
8    double pi = 3.14159;    // global variable
9
10   inline double circleArea( double r ) { return pi * r * r; }
11
12   int main()
13   {
14      double radius;
15
16      cout << "Enter the radius of the circle: ";
17      cin >> radius;
18      cout << "The area of the circle is " << circleArea( radius ) << endl;
19
20      return 0;
21   }
```

```
Enter the radius of the circle: 10
The area of the circle is 314.159
```

Fig. S15.1   Solution for Exercise 15.5.

15.8   Write a program that uses a function template called `min` to determine the smaller of two arguments. Test the program using integer, character and floating-point number pairs.

ANS:

```
1   // Exercise 15.8 Solution
2   #include <iostream>
3
4   using std::cout;
5   using std::endl;
6
7   template < class T >
8   void minimum( T value1, T value2 )    // find the smallest value
9   {
10      if ( value1 > value2 )
11         cout << value2 << " is smaller than " << value1;
12      else
13         cout << value1 << " is smaller than " << value2;
14
15      cout << endl;
16  }
17
18  int main()
19  {
20      minimum( 7, 54 );        // integers
21      minimum( 4.35, 8.46 ); // doubles
22      minimum( 'g', 'T' );   // characters
23
24      return 0;
25  }
```

```
7 is smaller than 54
4.35 is smaller than 8.46
T is smaller than g
```

Fig. S15.2   Solution for Exercise 15.8.

15.10 Determine whether the following program segments contain errors. For each error, explain how it can be corrected. [*Note*: For a particular program segment, it is possible that no errors are present in the segment.]

a) `template < class A >`
   `int sum( int num1, int num2, int num3 )`
      `{ return num1 + num2 + num3; }`

ANS: *The function return type and parameter types should be* A.

b) `void printResults( int x, int y )`
   `{`
      `cout << "The sum is " << x + y << '\n';`
      `return x + y;`
   `}`

ANS: *The function specifies a* void *return type and attempts to return a value. Two possible solutions: (1) change* void *to* int *or (2) remove the line* return x + y;.

c) **template** < A >
     A product(A num1, A num2, A num3)
     {
       return num1 * num2 * num3;
     }

ANS: *The keyword class is needed in the template declaration* template <class A>.

d) **double** cube(**int**);
     int cube(**int**);

ANS: *The signatures are not different. Overloaded functions must have different signatures meaning that the name and parameter list must be different. If only return types differ, the compiler generates an error message.*

C++ Classes and Data Abstraction

Solutions to Selected Exercises

16.4 Provide a constructor that is capable of using the current time from the `time` function—declared in the C Standard Library header `ctime`—to initialize an object of the `Time` class.

ANS:

```
1   // p16_4.H
2   #ifndef p16_4_H
3   #define p16_4_H
4
5   class Time {
6   public:
7       Time();
8       void setHour( int );
9       void setMinute( int );
10      void setSecond( int );
11      int getHour( void ) const;
12      int getMinute( void ) const;
13      int getSecond( void ) const;
14      void printStandard( void ) const;
15  private:
16      int hour;
17      int minute;
18      int second;
19  };
20
21  #endif
```

Fig. S16.1   Solution for Exercise 16.4: p16_4.H.

```
1   // p16_4.cpp
2   // member function definitions for p16_4.cpp
3   #include <iostream.h>
```

Fig. S16.2   Solution for Exercise 16.4: p16_4.cpp.   (Part 1 of 3.)

```
4
5   using std::cout;
6
7   #include <ctime>
8   #include "p16_4.h"
9
10  Time::Time()
11  {
12     long int totalTime;              // time in seconds since 1970
13     int currentYear = 1994 - 1970;   // current year
14     double totalYear;                // current time in years
15     double totalDay;                 // days since beginning of year
16     double day;                      // current time in days
17     long double divisor;             // conversion divisor
18     int timeShift = 7;               // time returned by time() is
19                                      // given as the number of seconds
20                                      // elapsed since 1/1/70 GMT.
21                                      // Depending on the time zone
22                                      // you are in, you must shift
23                                      // the time by a certain
24                                      // number of hours. For this
25                                      // problem, 7 hours is the
26                                      // current shift for EST.
27
28     totalTime = time( NULL );
29     divisor = ( 60.0 * 60.0 * 24.0 * 365.0 );
30     totalYear = totalTime / divisor - currentYear;
31     totalDay = 365 * totalYear;       // leap years ignored
32     day = totalDay - ( int ) totalDay;
33
34     setHour( day * 24 + timeShift );
35     setMinute( ( day * 24 - ( int )( day * 24 ) ) * 60 );
36     setSecond( ( minute * 60 - ( int )( minute * 60 ) ) * 60 );
37  }
38
39  void Time::setHour( int h ) {  hour = ( h >= 0 && h < 24 ) ? h : 0; }
40
41  void Time::setMinute( int m ) {  minute = ( m >= 0 && m < 60 ) ? m : 0; }
42
43  void Time::setSecond( int s ) {  second = ( s >= 0 && s < 60 ) ? s : 0; }
44
45  int Time::getHour() const {  return hour; }
46
47  int Time::getMinute() const {  return minute; }
48
49  int Time::getSecond() const {  return second; }
50
51  void Time::printStandard() const
52  {
53     cout << ( ( hour % 12 == 0 ) ? 12 : hour % 12 ) << ":"
54        << ( minute < 10 ? "0" : "" ) << minute << ":"
```

Fig. S16.2 Solution for Exercise 16.4: p16_4.cpp. (Part 2 of 3.)

```
55    << ( second < 10 ? "0" : "" ) << second
56    << ( hour < 12 ? " AM" : " PM" );
57  }
```

Fig. S16.2   Solution for Exercise 16.4: p16_4.cpp.   (Part 3 of 3.)

```
1   // driver for p16_4.cpp
2   #include "p16_4.h"
3
4   int main( void )
5   {
6       Time t;
7
8       t.printStandard();
9
10      return 0;
11  }
```

```
12:15:00 PM
```

Fig. S16.3   Solution for Exercise 16.4: Driver for p16_4.cpp.

16.6   Create a class called `Rational` for performing arithmetic with fractions. Write a driver program to test your class.

Use integer variables to represent the `private` data of the class—the numerator and the denominator. Provide a constructor function that enables an object of this class to be initialized when it is declared. The constructor should contain default values in case no initializers are provided and should store the fraction in reduced form (i.e., the fraction

$$\frac{2}{4}$$

would be stored in the object as 1 in the numerator and 2 in the denominator). Provide `public` member functions for each of the following:

    a) Addition of two `Rational` numbers. The result should be stored in reduced form.
    b) Subtraction of two `Rational` numbers. The result should be stored in reduced form.
    c) Multiplication of two `Rational` numbers. The result should be stored in reduced form.
    d) Division of two `Rational` numbers. The result should be stored in reduced form.
    e) Printing `Rational` numbers in the form a/b where a is the numerator and b is the denominator.
    f) Printing `Rational` numbers in floating-point format.

    ANS:

```
1   // P16_6.H
2   #ifndef P16_6_H
3   #define P16_6_H
```

Fig. S16.4   Solution for Exercise 16.6: P16_6.H.

```
 4
 5   class RationalNumber {
 6   public:
 7      RationalNumber( int = 0, int = 1 );   // default constructor
 8      RationalNumber addition( const RationalNumber& );
 9      RationalNumber subtraction( const RationalNumber& );
10      RationalNumber multiplication( const RationalNumber& );
11      RationalNumber division( RationalNumber& );
12      void printRational( void ) const;
13      void printRationalF( void ) const;
14   private:
15      int numerator;
16      int denominator;
17      void reduction( void );
18   };
19
20   #endif
```

Fig. S16.4   Solution for Exercise 16.6: P16_6.H.

```
 1   // P16_6M.cpp
 2   // member function definitions for p16_6.cpp
 3   #include <iostream>
 4
 5   using std::cout;
 6
 7   #include "p16_6.h"
 8
 9   RationalNumber::RationalNumber( int n, int d )
10   {
11      numerator = n;
12      denominator = d;
13   }
14
15   RationalNumber RationalNumber::addition( const RationalNumber &a )
16   {
17      RationalNumber t;
18
19      t.numerator = a.numerator * denominator + a.denominator * numerator;
20
21      t.denominator = a.denominator * denominator;
22      t.reduction();
23
24      return t;
25   }
26
27   RationalNumber RationalNumber::subtraction( const RationalNumber &s )
28   {
29      RationalNumber t;
```

Fig. S16.5   Solution for Exercise 16.6: P16_6M.cpp.   (Part 1 of 3.)

```
30
31      t.numerator = s.denominator * numerator - denominator * s.numerator;
32      t.denominator = s.denominator * denominator;
33      t.reduction();
34
35      return t;
36  }
37
38  RationalNumber RationalNumber::multiplication( const RationalNumber &m )
39  {
40      RationalNumber t;
41
42      t.numerator = m.numerator * numerator;
43      t.denominator = m.denominator * denominator;
44      t.reduction();
45
46      return t;
47  }
48
49  RationalNumber RationalNumber::division( RationalNumber &v )
50  {
51      RationalNumber t;
52
53      t.numerator = v.denominator * numerator;
54      t.denominator = denominator * v.numerator;
55      t.reduction();
56
57      return t;
58  }
59
60  void RationalNumber::printRational( void ) const
61  {
62      if ( denominator == 0 )
63         cout << "\nDIVIDE BY ZERO ERROR!!!\n";
64      else if ( numerator == 0 )
65         cout << 0;
66      else
67         cout << numerator << "/" << denominator;
68  }
69
70  void RationalNumber::printRationalF( void ) const
71  {   cout << ( double ) numerator / denominator; }
72
73  void RationalNumber::reduction( void )
74  {
75      int largest;
76
77      largest = numerator > denominator ? numerator : denominator;
78
79      int gcd = 0;  // greatest common divisor
```

Fig. S16.5   Solution for Exercise 16.6: P16_6M.cpp.   (Part 2 of 3.)

```
80        for ( int loop = 2; loop <= largest; loop++ )
81           if ( numerator % loop == 0 && denominator % loop == 0 )
82              gcd = loop;
83
84        if ( gcd != 0 ) {
85           numerator /= gcd;
86           denominator /= gcd;
87        }
88  }
```

Fig. S16.5   Solution for Exercise 16.6: P16_6M.cpp.   (Part 3 of 3.)

```
1   // driver for P16_6.cpp
2   #include <iostream>
3
4   using std::cout;
5
6   #include "p16_6.h"
7
8   int main( void )
9   {
10     RationalNumber c( 1,3 ), d( 7,8 ), x;
11
12     c.printRational();
13     cout << " + ";
14     d.printRational();
15     x = c.addition( d );
16     cout << " = ";
17     x.printRational();
18     cout << "\n";
19     x.printRational();
20     cout << " = ";
21     x.printRationalF();
22     cout << "\n\n";
23
24     c.printRational();
25     cout << " - ";
26     d.printRational();
27     x = c.subtraction( d );
28     cout << " = ";
29     x.printRational();
30     cout << "\n";
31     x.printRational();
32     cout << " = ";
33     x.printRationalF();
34     cout << "\n\n";
35
36     c.printRational();
37     cout << " x ";
38     d.printRational();
```

Fig. S16.6   Solution for Exercise 16.6: Driver for P16_6.cpp.   (Part 1 of 2.)

```
39        x = c.multiplication( d );
40        cout << " = ";
41        x.printRational();
42        cout << "\n";
43        x.printRational();
44        cout << " = ";
45        x.printRationalF();
46        cout << "\n\n";
47
48        c.printRational();
49        cout << " / ";
50        d.printRational();
51        x = c.division( d );
52        cout << " = ";
53        x.printRational();
54        cout << "\n";
55        x.printRational();
56        cout << " = ";
57        x.printRationalF();
58        cout << "\n";
59
60        return 0;
61    }
```

```
1/3 + 7/8 = 29/24
29/24 = 1.20833

1/3 - 7/8 = -13/24
-13/24 = -0.541667

1/3 x 7/8 = 7/24
7/24 = 0.291667

1/3 / 7/8 = 8/21
8/21 = 0.380952
```

Fig. S16.6   Solution for Exercise 16.6: Driver for P16_6.cpp.   (Part 2 of 2.)

16.7   Create a class Rectangle. The class has attributes length and width, each of which defaults to 1. It has member functions that calculate the perimeter and the area of the rectangle. It has *set* and *get* functions for both length and width. The *set* functions should verify that length and width are each floating-point numbers larger than 0.0 and less than 20.0.

    ANS:

```
1    // P16_7.H
2    #ifndef P16_7_H
3    #define P16_7_H
4
```

Fig. S16.7   Solution for Exercise 16.7: P16_7.H.

```
 5   class Rectangle {
 6   public:
 7      Rectangle( double = 1.0, double = 1.0 );
 8      double perimeter( void );
 9      double area( void );
10      void setWidth( double w );
11      void setLength( double l );
12      double getWidth( void );
13      double getLength( void );
14   private:
15      double length;
16      double width;
17   };
18
19   #endif
```

Fig. S16.7   Solution for Exercise 16.7: P16_7.H.

```
 1   // P16_7M.cpp
 2   // member function definitions for p16_7.cpp
 3
 4   #include "p16_7.h"
 5
 6   Rectangle::Rectangle( double w, double l )
 7   {
 8      setWidth(w);
 9      setLength(l);
10   }
11
12   double Rectangle::perimeter( void )
13   {
14   return 2 * ( width + length );
15   }
16
17   double Rectangle::area( void )
18   {
19   return width * length;
20   }
21
22   void Rectangle::setWidth( double w )
23   {
24   width = w > 0 && w < 20.0 ? w : 1.0;
25   }
26
27   void Rectangle::setLength( double l )
28   {
29   length = l > 0 && l < 20.0 ? l : 1.0;
30   }
31
```

Fig. S16.8   Solution for Exercise 16.7: P16_7M.cpp.   (Part 1 of 2.)

```
32   double Rectangle::getWidth( void ) { return width; }
33
34   double Rectangle::getLength( void ) { return length; }
```

Fig. S16.8   Solution for Exercise 16.7: P16_7M.cpp.   (Part 2 of 2.)

```
1    // driver for p16_7.cpp
2    #include <iostream>
3
4    using std::cout;
5    using std::endl;
6    using std::ios;
7
8    #include <iomanip>
9
10   using std::setprecision;
11   using std::setiosflags;
12
13   #include "p16_7.h"
14
15   int main()
16   {
17      Rectangle a, b( 4.0, 5.0 ), c( 67.0, 888.0 );
18
19      cout << setiosflags( ios::fixed | ios::showpoint );
20      cout << setprecision( 1 );
21
22      // output Rectangle a
23      cout << "a: length = " << a.getLength()
24       << "; width = " << a.getWidth()
25          << "; perimeter = " << a.perimeter() << "; area = "
26          << a.area() << '\n';
27
28      // output Rectangle b
29      cout << "b: length = " << b.getLength()
30       << "; width = " << b.getWidth()
31          << "; perimeter = " << b.perimeter() << "; area = "
32          << b.area() << '\n';
33
34      // output Rectangle c; bad values attempted
35      cout << "c: length = " << c.getLength()
36       << "; width = " << c.getWidth()
37          << "; perimeter = " << c.perimeter() << "; area = "
38          << c.area() << endl;
39
40      return 0;
41   }
```

Fig. S16.9   Solution for Exercise 16.7: Driver for P16_7.cpp.   (Part 1 of 2.)

```
a: length = 1.0; width = 1.0; perimeter = 4.0; area = 1.0
b: length = 5.0; width = 4.0; perimeter = 18.0; area = 20.0
c: length = 1.0; width = 1.0; perimeter = 4.0; area = 1.0
```

Fig. S16.9   Solution for Exercise 16.7: Driver for P16_7.cpp.   (Part 2 of 2.)

16.11   Create a class `TicTacToe` that will enable you to write a complete program to play the game of tic-tac-toe. The class contains as `private` data a 3-by-3 double array of integers. The constructor should initialize the empty board to all zeros. Allow two human players. Wherever the first player moves, place a 1 in the specified square; place a 2 wherever the second player moves. Each move must be to an empty square. After each move, determine if the game has been won or if the game is a draw. If you feel ambitious, modify your program so that the computer makes the moves for one of the players automatically. Also, allow the player to specify whether he or she wants to go first or second. If you feel exceptionally ambitious, develop a program that will play three-dimensional tic-tac-toe on a 4-by-4-by-4 board (Caution: This is an extremely challenging project that could take many weeks of effort!).

   ANS:

```
1   // p16_11.H
2   #ifndef P16_11_H
3   #define P16_11_H
4
5   class TicTacToe {
6   private:
7      enum Status { WIN, DRAW, CONTINUE };
8      int board[ 3 ][ 3 ];
9   public:
10      TicTacToe();
11      void makeMove( void );
12      void printBoard( void );
13      bool validMove( int, int );
14      bool xoMove( int );
15      Status gameStatus( void );
16   };
17
18   #endif
```

Fig. S16.10   Solution for Exercise 16.11: P16_11.H.

```
1   // P16_11M.cpp
2   // member function definitions for p16_9.cpp
3   #include <iostream>
4
5   using std::cout;
6   using std::cin;
7
8   #include <iomanip>
9
```

Fig. S16.11   Solution for Exercise 16.11: P16_11M.cpp.   (Part 1 of 4.)

```
10   using std::setw;
11
12   #include "p16_11.h"
13
14   TicTacToe::TicTacToe()
15   {
16      for ( int j = 0; j < 3; ++j )    // initialize board
17         for ( int k = 0; k < 3; ++k )
18            board[ j ][ k ] = ' ';
19   }
20
21   bool TicTacToe::validMove( int r, int c )
22   {
23      return r >= 0 && r < 3 && c >= 0 && c < 3 && board[ r ][ c ] == ' ';
24   }
25
26   // must specify that type Status is part of the TicTacToe class.
27   // See Chapter 21 for a discussion of namespaces.
28   TicTacToe::Status TicTacToe::gameStatus( void )
29   {
30      int a;
31
32      // check for a win on diagonals
33      if ( board[ 0 ][ 0 ] != ' ' && board[ 0 ][ 0 ] == board[ 1 ][ 1 ] &&
34         board[ 0 ][ 0 ] == board[ 2 ][ 2 ] )
35         return WIN;
36      else if ( board[ 2 ][ 0 ] != ' ' && board[ 2 ][ 0 ] ==
37      board[ 1 ][ 1 ] && board[ 2 ][ 0 ] == board[ 0 ][ 2 ] )
38         return WIN;
39
40      // check for win in rows
41      for ( a = 0; a < 3; ++a )
42         if ( board[ a ][ 0 ] != ' ' && board[ a ][ 0 ] ==
43      board[ a ][ 1 ] && board[ a ][ 0 ] == board[ a ][ 2 ] )
44            return WIN;
45
46      // check for win in columns
47      for ( a = 0; a < 3; ++a )
48         if ( board[ 0 ][ a ] != ' ' && board[ 0 ][ a ] ==
49      board[ 1 ][ a ] && board[ 0 ][ a ] == board[ 2 ][ a ] )
50            return WIN;
51
52      // check for a completed game
53      for ( int r = 0; r < 3; ++r )
54         for ( int c = 0; c < 3; ++c )
55            if ( board[ r ][ c ] == ' ' )
56               return CONTINUE; // game is not finished
57
58      return DRAW; // game is a draw
59   }
```

Fig. S16.11 Solution for Exercise 16.11: P16_11M.cpp.   (Part 2 of 4.)

```
60
61   void TicTacToe::printBoard( void )
62   {
63      cout << "   0    1    2\n\n";
64
65      for ( int r = 0; r < 3; ++r ) {
66         cout << r;
67
68         for ( int c = 0; c < 3; ++c ) {
69            cout << setw( 3 ) << static_cast< char > ( board[ r ][ c ] );
70
71            if ( c != 2 )
72               cout << " |";
73         }
74
75         if ( r != 2 )
76            cout << "\n ____|____|____ "
77                 << "\n     |    |     \n";
78      }
79
80      cout << "\n\n";
81   }
82
83   void TicTacToe::makeMove( void )
84   {
85      printBoard();
86
87      while ( true ) {
88         if ( xoMove( 'X' ) )
89            break;
90         else if ( xoMove( 'O' ) )
91            break;
92      }
93   }
94
95   bool TicTacToe::xoMove( int symbol )
96   {
97      int x, y;
98
99      do {
100        cout << "Player " << static_cast< char >( symbol )
101     << " enter move: ";
102        cin >> x >> y;
103        cout << '\n';
104     } while ( !validMove( x, y ) );
105
106     board[ x ][ y ] = symbol;
107     printBoard();
108     Status xoStatus = gameStatus();
109
```

Fig. S16.11 Solution for Exercise 16.11: P16_11M.cpp.   (Part 3 of 4.)

```
110    if ( xoStatus == WIN ) {
111       cout << "Player " << static_cast< char >( symbol ) << " wins!\n";
112       return true;
113    }
114    else if ( xoStatus == DRAW ) {
115       cout << "Game is a draw.\n";
116       return true;
117    }
118    else // CONTINUE
119       return false;
120 }
```

Fig. S16.11 Solution for Exercise 16.11: P16_11M.cpp.   (Part 4 of 4.)

```
1    // driver for p16_11.cpp
2    #include "p16_11.h"
3
4    int main()
5    {
6       TicTacToe g;
7       g.makeMove();
8
9       return 0;
10   }
```

Fig. S16.12 Solution for Exercise 16.11: Driver for P16_11.cpp.   (Part 1 of 2.)

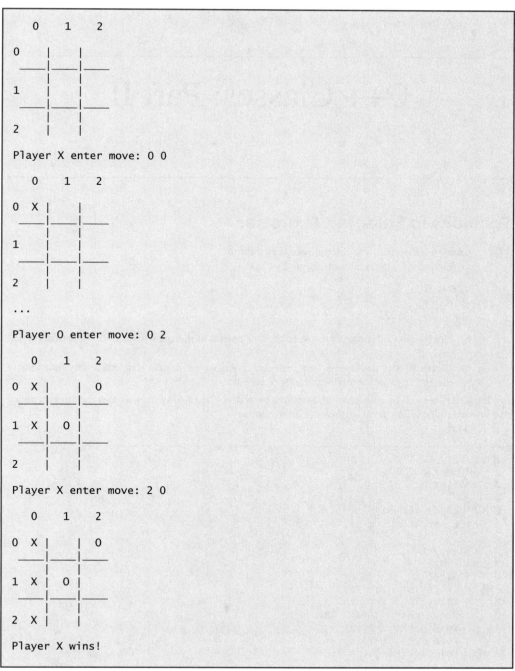

Fig. S16.12 Solution for Exercise 16.11: Driver for P16_11.cpp.   (Part 2 of 2.)

C++ Classes: Part II

Solutions to Selected Exercises

17.7 Create a `Date` class with the following capabilities:
a) Output the date in multiple formats such as

```
DDD YYYY
MM/DD/YY
June 14, 1992
```

b) Use overloaded constructors to create `Date` objects initialized with dates of the formats in part (a).
c) Create a `Date` constructor that reads the system date using the standard library functions of the `<ctime>` header and sets the `Date` members.

In Chapter 18, we will be able to create operators for testing the equality of two dates and for comparing dates to determine if one date is prior to, or after, another.

ANS:

```
1   // P17_07.H
2   #ifndef p17_07_H
3   #define p17_07_H
4
5   #include <ctime>
6   #include <cstring>
7
8   class Date {
9   public:
10      Date();
11      Date( int, int );
12      Date( int, int, int );
13      Date( char *, int, int );
14      void setMonth( int );
15      void setDay( int );
16      void setYear( int );
```

Fig. S17.1   Solution for Exercise 17.7: P17_07.H.   (Part 1 of 2.)

```
17      void printDateSlash( void ) const;
18      void printDateMonth( void ) const;
19      void printDateDay( void ) const;
20      const char *monthName( void ) const;
21      bool leapYear( void ) const;
22      int daysOfMonth( void ) const;
23      void convert1( int );
24      int convert2( void ) const;
25      void convert3( const char * const );
26      const char *monthList( int ) const;
27      int days( int ) const;
28   private:
29      int day;
30      int month;
31      int year;
32   };
33
34   #endif
```

Fig. S17.1   Solution for Exercise 17.7: P17_07.H.   (Part 2 of 2.)

```
1    // P17_07M.cpp
2    // member function definitions for p17_07.cpp
3    #include <iostream>
4
5    using std::cout;
6
7    #include <ctime>
8
9    #include "p17_07.h"
10
11   // Date constructor
12   Date::Date()
13   {
14      long int totalTime;
15      double totalYear;
16      long double divisor;
17
18      totalTime = time( NULL );        // time in seconds since 1970
19      divisor = ( 60.0 * 60.0 * 24.0 * 365.25 );   //seconds in a year
20      totalYear = totalTime / divisor + 1970;
21      year = ( int ) totalYear;
22      totalYear -= year;
23      day = ( int ) ( 365 * totalYear );
24      month = 1;
25
26      while ( day - days( month + 1 ) > 0 )
27         day -= days( month++ );
28   }
```

Fig. S17.2   Solution for Exercise 17.7: P17_07M.cpp.   (Part 1 of 4.)

```
29
30    // Date constructor that uses day of year and year
31    Date::Date( int ddd, int yyyy )
32    {
33       setYear( yyyy );
34       convert1( ddd );  // convert to month and day
35    }
36
37    // Date constructor that uses month, day and year
38    Date::Date( int mm, int dd, int yy )
39    {
40       setYear( yy + 1900 );
41       setMonth( mm );
42       setDay( dd );
43    }
44
45    // Date constructor that uses month name, day and year
46    Date::Date( char *mPtr, int dd, int yyyy )
47    {
48       setYear( yyyy );
49       convert3( mPtr );
50       setDay( dd );
51    }
52
53    // Set the day
54    void Date::setDay( int d )
55       { day = d >= 1 && d <= daysOfMonth() ? d : 1; }
56
57    // Set the month
58    void Date::setMonth( int m ) { month = m >= 1 && m <= 12 ? m : 1; }
59
60    // Set the year
61    void Date::setYear( int y ) { year = y >= 1900 && y <= 1999 ? y : 1900; }
62
63    // Print Date in the form: mm/dd/yyyy
64    void Date::printDateSlash( void ) const
65       { cout << month << '/' << day << '/' << year << '\n'; }
66
67    // Print Date in the form: monthname dd, yyyy
68    void Date::printDateMonth( void ) const
69       { cout << monthName() << ' ' << day << ", " << year << '\n'; }
70
71    // Print Date in the form: ddd yyyy
72    void Date::printDateDay( void ) const
73       { cout << convert2() << ' ' << year << '\n'; }
74
75    // Return the month name
76    const char *Date::monthName( void ) const
77       { return monthList( month - 1 ); }
78
```

Fig. S17.2   Solution for Exercise 17.7: P17_07M.cpp.   (Part 2 of 4.)

```
79   // Return the number of days in the month
80   int Date::daysOfMonth( void ) const
81     { return leapYear() && month == 2 ? 29 : days( month ); }
82
83   // Test for a leap year
84   bool Date::leapYear( void ) const
85   {
86      if ( year % 400 == 0 || ( year % 4 == 0 && year % 100 != 0 ) )
87         return true;
88      else
89         return false;
90   }
91
92   // Convert ddd to mm and dd
93   void Date::convert1( int ddd )   // convert to mm / dd / yyyy
94   {
95      int dayTotal = 0;
96
97      if ( ddd < 1 || ddd > 366 )   // check for invalid day
98         ddd = 1;
99
100     setMonth( 1 );
101
102     int m = 1;
103
104     for ( ; m < 13 && ( dayTotal + daysOfMonth() ) < ddd; ++m ) {
105        dayTotal += daysOfMonth();
106        setMonth( m + 1 );
107     }
108
109     setDay( ddd - dayTotal );
110     setMonth( m );
111  }
112
113  // Convert mm and dd to ddd
114  int Date::convert2( void ) const    // convert to a ddd yyyy format
115  {
116     int ddd = 0;
117
118     for ( int m = 1; m < month; ++m )
119        ddd += days( m );
120
121     ddd += day;
122     return ddd;
123  }
124
125  // Convert from month name to month number
126  void Date::convert3( const char * const mPtr )    // convert to mm/dd/yyyy
127  {
128     bool flag = false;
```

Fig. S17.2   Solution for Exercise 17.7: P17_07M.cpp.   (Part 3 of 4.)

```
129
130        for ( int subscript = 0; subscript < 12; ++subscript )
131          if ( !strcmp( mPtr, monthList( subscript ) ) ) {
132             setMonth( subscript + 1 );
133             flag = true; // set flag
134             break;      // stop checking for month
135          }
136
137        if ( !flag )
138          setMonth( 1 ); // invalid month default is january
139     }
140
141     // Return the name of the month
142     const char *Date::monthList( int mm ) const
143     {
144        char *months[] = { "January", "February", "March", "April", "May",
145                           "June", "July", "August", "September", "October",
146                           "November", "December" };
147
148        return months[ mm ];
149     }
150
151     // Return the days in the month
152     int Date::days( int m ) const
153     {
154        const int monthDays[] = { 31, 28, 31, 30, 31, 30, 31,
155           31, 30, 31, 30, 31 };
156
157        return monthDays[ m - 1 ];
158     }
```

Fig. S17.2   Solution for Exercise 17.7: P17_07M.cpp.   (Part 4 of 4.)

```
1    // driver for p17_07.cpp
2    #include <iostream>
3
4    using std::cout;
5    using std::endl;
6
7    #include "p17_07.h"
8
9    int main()
10   {
11      Date d1( 7, 4, 98 ), d2( 86, 1999 ),
12         d3, d4( "September", 1, 1998 );
13
14      d1.printDateSlash();   // format m / dd / yy
15      d2.printDateSlash();
16      d3.printDateSlash();
```

Fig. S17.3   Solution for Exercise 17.7: Driver for P17_07.cpp.   (Part 1 of 2.)

```
17        d4.printDateSlash();
18        cout << '\n';
19
20        d1.printDateDay();      // format ddd yyyy
21        d2.printDateDay();
22        d3.printDateDay();
23        d4.printDateDay();
24        cout << '\n';
25
26        d1.printDateMonth();    // format "month" d, yyyy
27        d2.printDateMonth();
28        d3.printDateMonth();
29        d4.printDateMonth();
30        cout << endl;
31
32        return 0;
33    }
```

```
7/4/1998
3/27/1999
7/26/2000
9/1/1998

185 1998
86 1999
207 2000
244 1998

July 4, 1998
March 27, 1999
July 26, 2000
September 1, 1998
```

Fig. S17.3   Solution for Exercise 17.7: Driver for P17_07.cpp.   (Part 2 of 2.)

17.8   Create a SavingsAccount class. Use a static data member to contain the annualInterestRate for each of the savers. Each member of the class contains a private data member savingsBalance indicating the amount the saver currently has on deposit. Provide a calculateMonthlyInterest member function that calculates the monthly interest by multiplying the balance by annualInterestRate divided by 12; this interest should be added to savingsBalance. Provide a static member function modifyInterestRate that sets the static annualInterestRate to a new value. Write a driver program to test class SavingsAccount. Instantiate two different savingsAccount objects, saver1 and saver2, with balances of $2000.00 and $3000.00, respectively. Set annualInterestRate to 3%, then calculate the monthly interest and print the new balances for each of the savers. Then set the annualInterestRate to 4% and calculate the next month's interest and print the new balances for each of the savers.

ANS:

```
1    // P17_08.H
2    #ifndef P17_08_H
3    #define P17_08_H
4
5    class SavingsAccount {
6    public:
7       SavingsAccount( double b ) { savingsBalance = b >= 0 ? b : 0; }
8       void calculateMonthlyInterest( void );
9       static void modifyInterestRate( double );
10      void printBalance( void ) const;
11   private:
12      double savingsBalance;
13      static double annualInterestRate;
14   };
15
16   #endif
```

Fig. S17.4   Solution for Exercise 17.8: P17_08.H.

```
1    // P17.08M.cpp
2    // Member function defintions for p17_08.cpp
3    #include "p17_08.h"
4    #include <iostream>
5
6    using std::cout;
7    using std::ios;
8
9    #include <iomanip>
10
11   using std::setprecision;
12   using std::setiosflags;
13   using std::resetiosflags;
14
15   // initialize static data member
16   double SavingsAccount::annualInterestRate = 0.0;
17
18   void SavingsAccount::calculateMonthlyInterest( void )
19      { savingsBalance += savingsBalance * ( annualInterestRate / 12.0 ); }
20
21   void SavingsAccount::modifyInterestRate( double i )
22      { annualInterestRate = ( i >= 0 && i <= 1.0 ) ? i : 0.03; }
23
24   void SavingsAccount::printBalance( void ) const
25   {
26      cout << setiosflags( ios::fixed | ios::showpoint )
27         << '$' << setprecision( 2 ) << savingsBalance
28         << resetiosflags( ios::fixed | ios::showpoint );
29   }
```

Fig. S17.5   Solution for Exercise 17.8: P17_08M.cpp.

```cpp
1   // driver for p17_08.cpp
2   #include <iostream>
3
4   using std::cout;
5   using std::endl;
6
7   #include <iomanip>
8
9   using std::setw;
10
11  #include "p17_08.h"
12
13  int main()
14  {
15     SavingsAccount saver1( 2000.0 ), saver2( 3000.0 );
16
17     SavingsAccount::modifyInterestRate( .03 );
18
19     cout << "\nOutput monthly balances for one year at .03"
20          << "\nBalances: Saver 1 ";
21     saver1.printBalance();
22     cout << "\tSaver 2 ";
23     saver2.printBalance();
24
25     for ( int month = 1; month <= 12; ++month ) {
26        saver1.calculateMonthlyInterest();
27        saver2.calculateMonthlyInterest();
28
29        cout << "\nMonth" << setw( 3 ) << month << ": Saver 1 ";
30        saver1.printBalance();
31        cout << "\tSaver 2 ";
32        saver2.printBalance();
33     }
34
35     SavingsAccount::modifyInterestRate( .04 );
36     saver1.calculateMonthlyInterest();
37     saver2.calculateMonthlyInterest();
38     cout << "\nAfter setting interest rate to .04"
39          << "\nBalances: Saver 1 ";
40     saver1.printBalance();
41     cout << "\tSaver 2 ";
42     saver2.printBalance();
43     cout << endl;
44     return 0;
45  }
```

Fig. S17.6   Solution for Exercise 17.8: Driver for P17_08.cpp. (Part 1 of 2.)

```
Output monthly balances for one year at .03
Balances: Saver 1 $2000.00      Saver 2 $3000.00
Month  1: Saver 1 $2005.00      Saver 2 $3007.50
Month  2: Saver 1 $2010.01      Saver 2 $3015.02
Month  3: Saver 1 $2015.04      Saver 2 $3022.56
Month  4: Saver 1 $2020.08      Saver 2 $3030.11
Month  5: Saver 1 $2025.13      Saver 2 $3037.69
Month  6: Saver 1 $2030.19      Saver 2 $3045.28
Month  7: Saver 1 $2035.26      Saver 2 $3052.90
Month  8: Saver 1 $2040.35      Saver 2 $3060.53
Month  9: Saver 1 $2045.45      Saver 2 $3068.18
Month 10: Saver 1 $2050.57      Saver 2 $3075.85
Month 11: Saver 1 $2055.69      Saver 2 $3083.54
Month 12: Saver 1 $2060.83      Saver 2 $3091.25
After setting interest rate to .04
Balances: Saver 1 $2067.70      Saver 2 $3101.55
```

Fig. S17.6   Solution for Exercise 17.8: Driver for P17_08.cpp. (Part 2 of 2.)

C++ Operator Overloading

Solutions to Selected Exercises

18.6 Give as many examples as you can of operator overloading implicit in C++. Give a reasonable example of a situation in which you might want to overload an operator explicitly in C++.

> **ANS:** *In C, the operators +, -, *, and & are overloaded. The context of these operators determines how they are used. It can be argued that the arithmetic operators are all overloaded, because they can be used to perform operations on more than one type of data. In C++, the same operators as in C are overloaded, as well as << and >>.*

18.10 Consider class `Complex` shown in Fig. 18.5. The class enables operations on so-called *complex numbers*. These are numbers of the form `realPart + imaginaryPart * i` where *i* has the value:

$$\sqrt{-1}$$

a) Modify the class to enable input and output of complex numbers through the overloaded >> and << operators, respectively (you should remove the `print` function from the class).
b) Overload the multiplication operator to enable multiplication of two complex numbers as in algebra.
c) Overload the == and != operators to allow comparisons of complex numbers.

```
1   // Fig. 18.5: complex1.h
2   // Definition of class Complex
3   #ifndef COMPLEX1_H
4   #define COMPLEX1_H
5
6   class Complex {
7   public:
8      Complex( double = 0.0, double = 0.0 );       // constructor
9      Complex operator+( const Complex & ) const;  // addition
10     Complex operator-( const Complex & ) const;  // subtraction
11     const Complex &operator=( const Complex & ); // assignment
12     void print() const;                          // output
13  private:
14     double real;        // real part
```

Fig. S18.1 A complex number class—`complex1.h`. (Part 1 of 2.)

```
15        double imaginary;  // imaginary part
16  };
17
18  #endif
```

Fig. S18.1   A complex number class—`complex1.h`.   (Part 2 of 2.)

```
1   // Fig. 18.5: complex1.cpp
2   // Member function definitions for class Complex
3   #include <iostream>
4
5   using std::cout;
6
7   #include "complex1.h"
8
9   // Constructor
10  Complex::Complex( double r, double i )
11     : real( r ), imaginary( i ) { }
12
13  // Overloaded addition operator
14  Complex Complex::operator+( const Complex &operand2 ) const
15  {
16     return Complex( real + operand2.real,
17                     imaginary + operand2.imaginary );
18  }
19
20  // Overloaded subtraction operator
21  Complex Complex::operator-( const Complex &operand2 ) const
22  {
23     return Complex( real - operand2.real,
24                     imaginary - operand2.imaginary );
25  }
26
27  // Overloaded = operator
28  const Complex& Complex::operator=( const Complex &right )
29  {
30     real = right.real;
31     imaginary = right.imaginary;
32     return *this;   // enables cascading
33  }
34
35  // Display a Complex object in the form: (a, b)
36  void Complex::print() const
37     { cout << '(' << real << ", " << imaginary << ')'; }
```

Fig. S18.2   A complex number class—`complex1.cpp`.

```
1   // Fig. 18.5: fig18_05.cpp
2   // Driver for class Complex
```

Fig. S18.3   A complex number class—`fig18_05.cpp`.   (Part 1 of 2.)

```
 3   #include <iostream>
 4
 5   using std::cout;
 6   using std::endl;
 7
 8   #include "complex1.h"
 9
10   int main()
11   {
12      Complex x, y( 4.3, 8.2 ), z( 3.3, 1.1 );
13
14      cout << "x: ";
15      x.print();
16      cout << "\ny: ";
17      y.print();
18      cout << "\nz: ";
19      z.print();
20
21      x = y + z;
22      cout << "\n\nx = y + z:\n";
23      x.print();
24      cout << " = ";
25      y.print();
26      cout << " + ";
27      z.print();
28
29      x = y - z;
30      cout << "\n\nx = y - z:\n";
31      x.print();
32      cout << " = ";
33      y.print();
34      cout << " - ";
35      z.print();
36      cout << endl;
37
38      return 0;
39   }
```

```
x: (0, 0)
y: (4.3, 8.2)
z: (3.3, 1.1)

x = y + z:
(7.6, 9.3) = (4.3, 8.2) + (3.3, 1.1)

x = y - z:
(1, 7.1) = (4.3, 8.2) - (3.3, 1.1)
```

Fig. S18.3   A complex number class—`fig18_05.cpp`.   (Part 2 of 2.)

ANS:

```
1   // P18_10.H
2   #ifndef P18_10_H
3   #define P18_10_H
4   #include <iostream>
5
6   using std::ostream;
7   using std::istream;
8
9   class Complex {
10      friend ostream &operator<<( ostream &, const Complex & );
11      friend istream &operator>>( istream &, Complex & );
12   public:
13      Complex( double = 0.0, double = 0.0 );      // constructor
14      Complex operator+( const Complex& ) const;  // addition
15      Complex operator-( const Complex& ) const;  // subtraction
16      Complex operator*( const Complex& ) const;  // multiplication
17      Complex& operator=( const Complex& );        // assignment
18      bool operator==( const Complex& ) const;
19      bool operator!=( const Complex& ) const;
20   private:
21      double real;        // real part
22      double imaginary;   // imaginary part
23   };
24
25   #endif
```

Fig. S18.4   Solution for Exercise 18.10: P18_10.H.

```
1   // P18_10M.cpp
2   // member function definitions for p18_10.cpp
3   #include "p18_10.h"
4   #include <iostream>
5
6   using std::ostream;
7   using std::istream;
8
9   // Constructor
10   Complex::Complex( double r, double i )
11   {
12      real = r;
13      imaginary = i;
14   }
15
16   // Overloaded addition operator
17   Complex Complex::operator+( const Complex &operand2 ) const
18   {
19      Complex sum;
20
```

Fig. S18.5   Solution for Exercise 18.10: P18_10M.cpp.   (Part 1 of 3.)

```
21        sum.real = real + operand2.real;
22        sum.imaginary = imaginary + operand2.imaginary;
23        return sum;
24    }
25
26    // Overloaded subtraction operator
27    Complex Complex::operator-( const Complex &operand2 ) const
28    {
29        Complex diff;
30
31        diff.real = real - operand2.real;
32        diff.imaginary = imaginary - operand2.imaginary;
33        return diff;
34    }
35
36    // Overloaded multiplication operator
37    Complex Complex::operator*( const Complex &operand2 ) const
38    {
39        Complex times;
40
41        times.real = real * operand2.real + imaginary * operand2.imaginary;
42        times.imaginary = real * operand2.imaginary +
43            imaginary * operand2.real;
44        return times;
45    }
46
47    // Overloaded = operator
48    Complex& Complex::operator=( const Complex &right )
49    {
50        real = right.real;
51        imaginary = right.imaginary;
52        return *this;   // enables concatenation
53    }
54
55    bool Complex::operator==( const Complex &right ) const
56        { return right.real == real && right.imaginary ==
57            imaginary ? true : false; }
58
59    bool Complex::operator!=( const Complex &right ) const
60        { return !( *this == right ); }
61
62    ostream& operator<<( ostream &output, const Complex &complex )
63    {
64        output << complex.real << " + " << complex.imaginary << 'i';
65        return output;
66    }
67
68    istream& operator>>( istream &input, Complex &complex )
69    {
70        input >> complex.real;
```

Fig. S18.5   Solution for Exercise 18.10: P18_10M.cpp.   (Part 2 of 3.)

```
71      input.ignore( 3 );          // skip spaces and +
72      input >> complex.imaginary;
73      input.ignore( 2 );
74
75      return input;
76   }
```

Fig. S18.5   Solution for Exercise 18.10: P18_10M.cpp.   (Part 3 of 3.)

```
1    // driver for p18_10.cpp
2    #include <iostream>
3
4    using std::cout;
5    using std::cin;
6
7    #include "p18_10.h"
8
9    int main()
10   {
11      Complex x, y( 4.3, 8.2 ), z( 3.3, 1.1 ), k;
12
13      cout << "Enter a complex number in the form: a + bi\n? ";
14      cin >> k;
15
16      cout << "x: " << x << "\ny: " << y << "\nz: " << z << "\nk: "
17         << k << '\n';
18
19      x = y + z;
20      cout << "\nx = y + z:\n" << x << " = " << y << " + " << z << '\n';
21
22      x = y - z;
23      cout << "\nx = y - z:\n" << x << " = " << y << " - " << z << '\n';
24
25      x = y * z;
26      cout << "\nx = y * z:\n" << x << " = " << y << " * " << z << "\n\n";
27
28      if ( x != k )
29         cout << x << " != " << k << '\n';
30
31      cout << '\n';
32
33      x = k;
34
35      if ( x == k )
36         cout << x << " == " << k << '\n';
37
38      return 0;
39   }
```

Fig. S18.6   Solution for Exercise 18.10: Driver for P18_10.cpp.   (Part 1 of 2.)

```
Enter a complex number in the form: a + bi
? 22 + 8i
x: 0 + 0i
y: 4.3 + 8.2i
z: 3.3 + 1.1i
k: 22 + 8i

x = y + z:
7.6 + 9.3i = 4.3 + 8.2i + 3.3 + 1.1i

x = y - z:
1 + 7.1i = 4.3 + 8.2i - 3.3 + 1.1i

x = y * z:
23.21 + 31.79i = 4.3 + 8.2i * 3.3 + 1.1i

23.21 + 31.79i != 22 + 8i

22 + 8i == 22 + 8i
```

Fig. S18.6   Solution for Exercise 18.10: Driver for P18_10.cpp.   (Part 2 of 2.)

C++ Inheritance

Solutions to Selected Exercises

19.7 Some programmers prefer not to use `protected` access because it breaks the encapsulation of the base class. Discuss the relative merits of using `protected` access vs. insisting on using `private` access in base classes.

> **ANS:** *Inherited* `private` *data is hidden in the derived class and is accessible only through the* `public` *or* `protected` *member functions of the base class. Using* `protected` *access enables the derived class to manipulate the* `protected` *members without using the base class access functions. If the base class members are* `private`*, the* `public` *or* `protected` *member functions of the base class must be used to access* `private` *members. This can result in additional function calls—which can decrease performance.*

19.11 Write an inheritance hierarchy for class `Quadrilateral`, `Trapezoid`, `Parallelogram`, `Rectangle` and `Square`. Use `Quadrilateral` as the base class of the hierarchy. Make the hierarchy as deep (i.e., as many levels) as possible. The `private` data of `Quadrilateral` should be the *(x, y)* coordinate pairs for the four endpoints of the `Quadrilateral`. Write a driver program that instantiates and displays objects of each of these classes.

> **ANS:**

```
1    // P19_11.H
2    #ifndef P19_11_H
3    #define P19_11_H
4
5    #include <iostream>
6    using std::ostream;
7
8    class Point {
9       friend ostream &operator<<( ostream&, const Point& );
10   public:
11      Point( double = 0, double = 0 );
12      void setPoint( double, double );
13      void print( void ) const;
```

Fig. S19.1 Solution for Exercise 19.11: P19_11.H. (Part 1 of 2.)

```
14      double getX( void ) const { return x; }
15      double getY( void ) const { return y; }
16  private:
17      double x, y;
18  };
19
20  #endif
```

Fig. S19.1 Solution for Exercise 19.11: P19_11.H. (Part 2 of 2.)

```
1   // P19_11PM.cpp
2   // member function defintions for class Point
3   #include <iostream>
4
5   using std::cout;
6   using std::ios;
7   using std::ostream;
8
9   #include <iomanip>
10
11  using std::setprecision;
12  using std::setiosflags;
13  using std::resetiosflags;
14
15  #include "p19_11.h"
16
17  Point::Point( double a, double b ) { setPoint( a, b ); }
18
19  void Point::setPoint( double a, double b )
20  {
21      x = a;
22      y = b;
23  }
24
25  ostream &operator<<( ostream &output, const Point &p )
26  {
27      output << "The point is: ";
28      p.print();
29      return output;
30  }
31
32  void Point::print( void ) const
33  {
34      cout << setiosflags( ios::fixed | ios::showpoint )
35           << '[' << setprecision( 2 ) << getX()
36           << ", " << setprecision( 2 ) << getY() << "]\n"
37           << resetiosflags( ios::fixed | ios::showpoint );
38  }
```

Fig. S19.2 Solution for Exercise 19.11: P19_11PM.cpp.

```
1    // P19_11Q.H
2    #ifndef P19_11Q_H
3    #define P19_11Q_H
4    #include "p19_11.h"
5
6    #include <iostream>
7    using std::ostream;
8
9    class Quadrilateral {
10      friend ostream &operator<<( ostream&, Quadrilateral& );
11   public:
12      Quadrilateral( double = 0, double = 0, double = 0, double = 0,
13                     double = 0, double = 0, double = 0, double = 0, );
14      void print( void ) const;
15   protected:
16      Point p1;
17      Point p2;
18      Point p3;
19      Point p4;
20   };
21
22   #endif
```

Fig. S19.3   Solution for Exercise 19.11: P19_11Q.H.

```
1    // P19_11QM.cpp
2    // member functions for class Quadrilateral
3    #include "p19_11q.h"
4
5    #include <iostream>
6    using std::cout;
7    using std::ostream;
8
9    Quadrilateral::Quadrilateral( double x1, double y1, double x2, double y2,
10                                  double x3, double y3, double x4, double y4 )
11      : p1( x1, y1 ), p2( x2, y2 ), p3( x3, y3 ), p4( x4, y4 )  { }
12
13   ostream &operator<<( ostream& output, Quadrilateral& q )
14   {
15      output << "Coordinates of Quadrilateral are:\n";
16      q.print();
17      output << '\n';
18      return output;
19   }
20
21   void Quadrilateral::print( void ) const
22   {
23      cout << '(' << p1.getX()
24           << ", " << p1.getY() << ") , (" << p2.getX() << ", " << p2.getY()
```

Fig. S19.4   Solution for Exercise 19.11: P19_11QM.cpp.   (Part 1 of 2.)

```
25                << ") , (" << p3.getX() << ", " << p3.getY() << ") , ("
26                << p4.getX() << ", " << p4.getY() << ")\n";
27    }
```

Fig. S19.4   Solution for Exercise 19.11: P19_11QM.cpp.   (Part 2 of 2.)

```
1     // P19_11T.H
2     #ifndef P19_11T_H
3     #define P19_11T_H
4     #include "p19_11q.h"
5
6     #include <iostream>
7     using std::ostream;
8
9     class Trapazoid : public Quadrilateral {
10       friend ostream& operator<<( ostream&, Trapazoid& );
11    public:
12       Trapazoid( double = 0, double = 0, double = 0, double = 0, double = 0,
13                  double = 0, double = 0, double = 0, double = 0 );
14       void print( void ) const;
15       void setHeight( double h ) { height = h; }
16       double getHeight( void ) const { return height; }
17    private:
18       double height;
19    };
20
21    #endif
```

Fig. S19.5   Solution for Exercise 19.11: P19_11T.H.

```
1     // P19_11TM.cpp
2     // member function definitions for class Trapazoid
3     #include "p19_11t.h"
4
5     #include <iostream>
6
7     using std::cout;
8     using std::ostream;
9
10    Trapazoid::Trapazoid( double h, double x1, double y1, double x2,
11                          double y2, double x3, double y3, double x4,
12                          double y4 )
13       : Quadrilateral( x1, y1, x2, y2, x3, y3, x4, y4 )
14    { setHeight( h ); }
15
16    ostream& operator<<( ostream& out, Trapazoid& t )
17    {
18       out << "The Coordinates of the Trapazoid are:\n";
```

Fig. S19.6   Solution for Exercise 19.11: P19_11TM.cpp.   (Part 1 of 2.)

```
19      t.print();
20      return out;
21   }
22
23   void Trapazoid::print( void ) const
24   {
25      Quadrilateral::print();
26      cout << "Height is : " << getHeight() << "\n\n";
27   }
```

Fig. S19.6   Solution for Exercise 19.11: P19_11TM.cpp.   (Part 2 of 2.)

```
1    // P19_11PA_H
2    #ifndef P19_11PA_H
3    #define P19_11PA_H
4    #include "p19_11q.h"
5
6    #include <iostream>
7    using std::ostream;
8
9    class Parallelogram : public Quadrilateral {
10      friend ostream& operator<<( ostream&, Parallelogram& );
11   public:
12      Parallelogram( double = 0, double = 0, double = 0, double = 0,
13                     double = 0, double = 0, double = 0, double = 0 );
14      void print( void ) const;
15   private:
16      // no private data members
17   };
18
19   #endif
```

Fig. S19.7   Solution for Exercise 19.11: P19_11PA.H.

```
1    // P19_11PAM.cpp
2    #include "p19_11q.h"
3    #include "p19_11pa.h"
4
5    #include <iostream>
6    using std::ostream;
7
8    Parallelogram::Parallelogram( double x1, double y1, double x2, double y2,
9                                  double x3, double y3, double x4, double y4 )
10      : Quadrilateral( x1, y1, x2, y2, x3, y3, x4, y4 ) { }
11
12   ostream& operator<<( ostream& out, Parallelogram& pa )
13   {
14      out << "The coordinates of the Parallelogram are:\n";
```

Fig. S19.8   Solution for Exercise 19.11: P19_11PAM.cpp.   (Part 1 of 2.)

```
15        pa.print();
16        return out;
17    }
18
19    void Parallelogram::print( void ) const
20        {   Quadrilateral::print();   }
```

Fig. S19.8   Solution for Exercise 19.11: P19_11PAM.cpp.   (Part 2 of 2.)

```
1    // P19_11R.H
2    #ifndef P19_11R_H
3    #define P19_11R_H
4    #include "p19_11pa.h"
5
6    #include <iostream>
7    using std::ostream;
8
9    class Rectangle : public Parallelogram {
10       friend ostream& operator<<( ostream&, Rectangle& );
11   public:
12       Rectangle( double = 0, double = 0, double = 0, double = 0,
13                  double = 0, double = 0, double = 0, double = 0 );
14       void print( void ) const;
15   private:
16       // no private data members
17   };
18
19   #endif
```

Fig. S19.9   Solution for Exercise 19.11: P19_11R.H.

```
1    // P19_11RM.cpp
2    #include "p19_11r.h"
3    #include "p19_11pa.h"
4
5    #include <iostream>
6    using std::ostream;
7
8    Rectangle::Rectangle( double x1, double y1, double x2, double y2,
9                          double x3, double y3, double x4, double y4 )
10      : Parallelogram( x1, y1, x2, y2, x3, y3, x4, y4 ) { }
11
12   ostream& operator<<( ostream& out, Rectangle& r )
13   {
14       out << "\nThe coordinates of the Rectangle are:\n";
15       r.print();
16       return out;
17   }
```

Fig. S19.10   Solution for Exercise 19.11: P19_11RM.cpp.   (Part 1 of 2.)

```
18
19    void Rectangle::print( void ) const
20       {   Parallelogram::print(); }
```

Fig. S19.10   Solution for Exercise 19.11: P19_11RM.cpp.   (Part 2 of 2.)

```
1     // P19_11RH.H
2     #ifndef P19_11RH_H
3     #define P19_11RH_H
4     #include "p19_11pa.h"
5
6     #include <iostream>
7     using std::ostream;
8
9     class Rhombus : public Parallelogram {
10       friend ostream& operator<<(ostream&, Rhombus&);
11    public:
12       Rhombus( double = 0, double = 0, double = 0, double = 0, double = 0,
13                double = 0, double = 0, double = 0 );
14       void print( void ) const { Parallelogram::print(); }
15    private:
16       // no private data members
17    };
18
19    #endif
```

Fig. S19.11   Solution for Exercise 19.11: P19_11RH.H.

```
1     //P19_11HM.cpp
2     #include "p19_11rh.h"
3     #include "p19_11pa.h"
4
5     #include <iostream>
6     using std::ostream;
7
8     Rhombus::Rhombus( double x1, double y1, double x2, double y2,
9                      double x3, double y3, double x4, double y4 )
10       : Parallelogram( x1, y1, x2, y2, x3, y3, x4, y4 ) { }
11
12    ostream& operator<<( ostream& out, Rhombus& r )
13    {
14       out << "\nThe coordinates of the Rhombus are:\n";
15       r.print();
16       return out;
17    }
```

Fig. S19.12   Solution for Exercise 19.11: P19_11HM.cpp.

```
1   // P19_11S.H
2   #ifndef P19_11S_H
3   #define P19_11S_H
4   #include "p19_11pa.h"
5
6   #include <iostream>
7   using std::ostream;
8
9   class Square : public Parallelogram {
10     friend ostream& operator<<( ostream&, Square& );
11  public:
12     Square( double = 0, double = 0, double = 0, double = 0,
13             double = 0, double = 0, double = 0, double = 0 );
14     void print( void ) const { Parallelogram::print(); }
15  private:
16     // no private data members
17  };
18
19  #endif
```

Fig. S19.13   Solution for Exercise 19.11: P19_11S.H.

```
1   // P19_11SM.cpp
2   #include "p19_11s.h"
3   #include "p19_11pa.h"
4
5   #include <iostream>
6   using std::ostream;
7
8   Square::Square( double x1, double y1, double x2, double y2,
9                   double x3, double y3, double x4, double y4 )
10     : Parallelogram( x1, y1, x2, y2, x3, y3, x4, y4 ) { }
11
12  ostream& operator<<( ostream& out, Square& s )
13  {
14     out << "\nThe coordinates of the Square are:\n";
15     s.print();
16     return out;
17  }
```

Fig. S19.14   Solution for Exercise 19.11: P19_11SM.cpp.

```
1   // P19_11.cpp
2   #include "p19_11.h"
3   #include "p19_11q.h"
4   #include "p19_11t.h"
5   #include "p19_11pa.h"
6   #include "p19_11rh.h"
```

Fig. S19.15   Solution for Exercise 19.11: P19_11.cpp.   (Part 1 of 2.)

```
7   #include "p19_11r.h"
8   #include "p19_11s.h"
9
10  #include <iostream>
11  using std::cout;
12  using std::endl;
13
14  int main()
15  {
16      // NOTE: All coordinates are assumed to form the proper shapes
17
18      // A quadrilateral is a four-sided polygon
19      Quadrilateral q( 1.1, 1.2, 6.6, 2.8, 6.2, 9.9, 2.2, 7.4 );
20      // A trapezoid is a quadrilateral having only two parallel sides
21      Trapezoid t( 5.0, 0.0, 0.0, 10.0, 0.0, 8.0, 5.0, 3.3, 5.0 );
22      // A parallelogram is a quadrilateral whose opposite sides are parallel
23      Parallelogram p( 5.0, 5.0, 11.0, 5.0, 12.0, 20.0, 6.0, 20.0 );
24      // A rhombus is an equilateral parallelogram
25      Rhombus rh( 0.0, 0.0, 5.0, 0.0, 8.5, 3.5, 3.5, 3.5 );
26      // A rectangle is an equiangular parallelogram
27      Rectangle r( 17.0, 14.0, 30.0, 14.0, 30.0, 28.0, 17.0, 28.0 );
28      // A square is an equiangular and equilateral parallelogram
29      Square s( 4.0, 0.0, 8.0, 0.0, 8.0, 4.0, 4.0, 4.0 );
30
31      cout << q << t << p << rh << r << s << endl;
32
33      return 0;
34  }
```

```
Coordinates of Quadrilateral are:
(1.1, 1.2) , (6.6, 2.8) , (6.2, 9.9) , (2.2, 7.4)

The Coordinates of the Trapezoid are:
(0, 0) , (10, 0) , (8, 5) , (3.3, 5)
Height is : 5

The coordinates of the Parallelogram are:
(5, 5) , (11, 5) , (12, 20) , (6, 20)

The coordinates of the Rhombus are:
(0, 0) , (5, 0) , (8.5, 3.5) , (3.5, 3.5)

The coordinates of the Rectangle are:
(17, 14) , (30, 14) , (30, 28) , (17, 28)

The coordinates of the Square are:
(4, 0) , (8, 0) , (8, 4) , (4, 4)
```

Fig. S19.15 Solution for Exercise 19.11: P19_11.cpp.   (Part 2 of 2.)

C++ Virtual Functions and Polymorphism

Solutions to Selected Exercises

20.4 How is it that polymorphism enables you to program "in the general" rather than "in the specific." Discuss the key advantages of programming "in the general."

> **ANS:** *Polymorphism enables the programmer to concentrate on the processing of common operations that are applied to all data types in the system without going into the individual details of each data type. The general processing capabilities are separated from the internal details of each type.*

20.6 Distinguish between static binding and dynamic binding. Explain the use of `virtual` functions and the *vtable* in dynamic binding.

> **ANS:** *Static binding is performed at compile-time when a function is called via a specific object or via a pointer to an object. Dynamic binding is performed at run-time when a* `virtual` *function is called via a base class pointer to a derived class object (the object can be of any derived class). The* `virtual` *functions table (vtable) is used at run-time to enable the proper function to be called for the object to which the base class pointer "points". Each class containing* `virtual` *functions has its own vtable that specifies where the* `virtual` *functions for that class are located. Every object of a class with* `virtual` *functions contains a hidden pointer to the class's vtable. When a* `virtual` *function is called via a base class pointer, the hidden pointer is dereferenced to locate the vtable, then the vtable is searched for the proper function call.*

20.7 Distinguish between inheriting interface and inheriting implementation. How do inheritance hierarchies designed for inheriting interface differ from those designed for inheriting implementation?

> **ANS:** *When a class inherits implementation, it inherits previously defined functionality from another class. When a class inherits interface, it inherits the definition of what the interface to the new class type should be. The implementation is then provided by the programmer defining the new class type. Inheritance hierarchies designed for inheriting implementation are used to reduce the amount of new code that is being written. Such hierarchies are used to facilitate software reusability. Inheritance hierarchies designed for inheriting interface are used to write programs that perform generic processing of many class types. Such hierarchies are commonly used to facilitate software extensibility (i.e., new types can be added to the hierarchy without changing the generic processing capabilities of the program).*

20.11 How does polymorphism promote extensibility?

ANS: *Polymorphism makes programs more extensible by making all function calls generic. When a new class type with the appropriate* virtual *functions is added to the hierarchy, no changes need to be made to the generic function calls.*

C++ Stream
Input/Output

Solutions to Selected Exercises

21.7 Write a program to test inputting integer values in decimal, octal and hexadecimal format. Output each integer read by the program in all three formats. Test the program with the following input data: 10, 010, 0x10.

ANS:

```
1   // Exercise 21.7 Solution
2   #include <iostream>
3
4   using std::cout;
5   using std::endl;
6   using std::cin;
7   using std::ios;
8
9   #include <iomanip>
10
11  using std::setiosflags;
12  using std::hex;
13  using std::oct;
14  using std::dec;
15
16  int main()
17  {
18     int integer;
19
20     cout << "Enter an integer: ";
21     cin >> integer;
22
23     cout << setiosflags( ios::showbase ) << "As a decimal number "  << dec
24          << integer << "\nAs an octal number " << oct << integer
25          << "\nAs a hexadecimal number " << hex << integer << endl;
26
27     cout << "\nEnter an integer in octal format\n";
```

Fig. S21.1 Solution for Exercise 21.7. (Part 1 of 2.)

```
28      cin >> setiosflags( ios::showbase ) >> oct >> integer;
29
30      cout << setiosflags( ios::showbase ) << "As a decimal number "  << dec
31          << integer << "\nAs an octal number " << oct << integer
32          << "\nAs a hexadecimal number " << hex << integer << endl;
33
34      cout << "\nEnter an integer in hexadecimal format\n";
35      cin >> setiosflags( ios::showbase ) >> hex >> integer;
36
37      cout << setiosflags( ios::showbase ) << "As a decimal number "  << dec
38          << integer << "\nAs an octal number " << oct << integer
39          << "\nAs a hexadecimal number " << hex << integer << endl;
40
41      return 0;
42   }
```

```
Enter an integer: 10
As a decimal number 10
As an octal number 012
As a hexadecimal number 0xa

Enter an integer in octal format
010
As a decimal number 8
As an octal number 010
As a hexadecimal number 0x8

Enter an integer in hexadecimal format
0x10
As a decimal number 16
As an octal number 020
As a hexadecimal number 0x10
```

Fig. S21.1   Solution for Exercise 21.7.   (Part 2 of 2.)

21.9   Write a program to test the results of printing the integer value 12345 and the floating-point value 1.2345 in various-size fields. What happens when the values are printed in fields containing fewer digits than the values?

ANS:

```
1   // Exercise 21.9 Solution
2   #include <iostream>
3
4   using std::cout;
5
6   #include <iomanip>
7
8   using std::setw;
```

Fig. S21.2   Solution for Exercise 21.9.   (Part 1 of 2.)

```
9
10   int main()
11   {
12      int x = 12345;
13      double y = 1.2345;
14
15      for ( int loop = 0; loop <= 10; ++loop )
16         cout << x << "  printed in a field of size " << loop << " is "
17               << setw( loop ) << x << '\n' << y << " printed in a field "
18               << "of size " << loop << " is " << setw( loop ) << y << '\n';
19
20      return 0;
21   }
```

```
12345  printed in a field of size 0 is 12345
1.2345 printed in a field of size 0 is 1.2345
12345  printed in a field of size 1 is 12345
1.2345 printed in a field of size 1 is 1.2345
12345  printed in a field of size 2 is 12345
1.2345 printed in a field of size 2 is 1.2345
12345  printed in a field of size 3 is 12345
1.2345 printed in a field of size 3 is 1.2345
12345  printed in a field of size 4 is 12345
1.2345 printed in a field of size 4 is 1.2345
12345  printed in a field of size 5 is 12345
1.2345 printed in a field of size 5 is 1.2345
12345  printed in a field of size 6 is   12345
1.2345 printed in a field of size 6 is 1.2345
12345  printed in a field of size 7 is     12345
1.2345 printed in a field of size 7 is  1.2345
12345  printed in a field of size 8 is      12345
1.2345 printed in a field of size 8 is  1.2345
12345  printed in a field of size 9 is       12345
1.2345 printed in a field of size 9 is   1.2345
12345  printed in a field of size 10 is       12345
1.2345 printed in a field of size 10 is    1.2345
```

Fig. S21.2   Solution for Exercise 21.9.   (Part 2 of 2.)

21.10   Write a program that prints the value 100.453627 rounded to the nearest digit, tenth, hundredth, thousandth and ten thousandth.

> ANS:

```
1   // Exercise 21.10 Solution
2   #include <iostream>
3
4   using std::cout;
5   using std::endl;
```

Fig. S21.3   Solution for Exercise 21.10.   (Part 1 of 2.)

```
 6    using std::ios;
 7
 8    #include <iomanip>
 9
10    using std::setw;
11    using std::setprecision;
12    using std::setiosflags;
13
14    int main()
15    {
16       double x = 100.453627;
17
18       cout << setiosflags( ios::fixed );
19       for ( int loop = 0; loop <= 5; ++loop )
20          cout << setprecision( loop ) << "Rounded to " << loop
21                << " digit(s) is " << x << endl;
22
23       return 0;
24    }
```

```
Rounded to 0 digit(s) is 100
Rounded to 1 digit(s) is 100.5
Rounded to 2 digit(s) is 100.45
Rounded to 3 digit(s) is 100.454
Rounded to 4 digit(s) is 100.4536
Rounded to 5 digit(s) is 100.45363
```

Fig. S21.3   Solution for Exercise 21.10. (Part 2 of 2.)

21.12 Write a program that converts integer Fahrenheit temperatures from 0 to 212 degrees to floating-point Celsius temperatures with 3 digits of precision. Use the formula

```
celsius = 5.0 / 9.0 * ( fahrenheit - 32 );
```

to perform the calculation. The output should be printed in two right-justified columns and the Celsius temperatures should be preceded by a sign for both positive and negative values.

ANS:

```
 1    // Exercise 21.12 Solution
 2    #include <iostream>
 3
 4    using std::cout;
 5    using std::ios;
 6
 7    #include <iomanip>
 8
 9    using std::setw;
10    using std::setprecision;
```

Fig. S21.4   Solution for Exercise 21.12. (Part 1 of 2.)

```
11    using std::setiosflags;
12    using std::resetiosflags;
13
14    int main()
15    {
16       double celsius;
17
18       cout << setw( 20 ) << "Fahrenheit " << setw( 20 ) << "Celsius\n"
19          << setiosflags( ios::fixed | ios::showpoint );
20
21       for ( int fahrenheit = 0; fahrenheit <= 212; ++fahrenheit ) {
22          celsius = 5.0 / 9.0 * ( fahrenheit - 32 );
23          cout << setw( 15 ) << resetiosflags( ios::showpos ) << fahrenheit
24             << setw( 23 ) << setprecision( 3 )
25             << setiosflags( ios::showpos ) << celsius << '\n';
26       }
27
28       return 0;
29    }
```

```
          Fahrenheit                 Celsius
                   0                 -17.778
                   1                 -17.222
                   2                 -16.667
                   3                 -16.111
                   4                 -15.556
                   5                 -15.000
  ...
                 206                 +96.667
                 207                 +97.222
                 208                 +97.778
                 209                 +98.333
                 210                 +98.889
                 211                 +99.444
                 212                +100.000
```

Fig. S21.4　Solution for Exercise 21.12.　(Part 2 of 2.)

21.15　Write a program that accomplishes each of the following:

　　a)　Create the user-defined class Point that contains the private integer data members xCoordinate and yCoordinate and declares stream-insertion and stream-extraction overloaded operator functions as friends of the class.

　　b)　Define the stream-insertion and stream-extraction operator functions. The stream-extraction operator function should determine if the data entered are valid data, and if not, it should set the ios::failbit to indicate improper input. The stream-insertion operator should not be able to display the point after an input error occurred.

　　c)　Write a main function that tests input and output of user-defined class Point using the overloaded stream-extraction and stream-insertion operators.

ANS:

```
1   // P21_15.H
2   #ifndef P21_15_H
3   #define P21_15_H
4   #include <iostream.h>
5
6   class Point {
7      friend ostream &operator<<( ostream&, Point& );
8      friend istream &operator>>( istream&, Point& );
9   private:
10     int xCoordinate;
11     int yCoordinate;
12  };
13
14  #endif
```

Fig. S21.5   Solution for Exercise 21.15: P21_15.H.

```
1   // P21_15M.cpp
2   // member function definitions for p21_15.cpp
3   #include "p21_15.h"
4
5   ostream& operator<<( ostream& out, Point& p )
6   {
7      if ( !cin.fail() )
8         cout << "(" << p.xCoordinate << ", " << p.yCoordinate << ")"
9            << '\n';
10     else
11        cout << "\nInvalid data\n";
12
13     return out;
14  }
15
16  istream& operator>>( istream& i, Point& p )
17  {
18     if ( cin.peek() != '(' )
19        cin.clear( ios::failbit );
20     else
21        i.ignore();  // skip (
22
23     cin >> p.xCoordinate;
24
25     if ( cin.peek() != ',' )
26        cin.clear( ios::failbit );
27     else {
28        i.ignore(); // skip ,
29
30        if ( cin.peek() == ' ' )
31           i.ignore(); // skip space
```

Fig. S21.6   Solution for Exercise 21.15: P21_15M.cpp.   (Part 1 of 2.)

```
32              else
33                  cin.clear( ios::failbit );
34          }
35
36          cin >> p.yCoordinate;
37
38          if ( cin.peek() == ')' )
39                  i.ignore();   // skip )
40              else
41                  cin.clear( ios::failbit );
42
43          return i;
44      }
```

Fig. S21.6   Solution for Exercise 21.15: P21_15M.cpp.   (Part 2 of 2.)

```
1   // driver for p21_15.cpp
2   #include "p21_15.h"
3
4   int main()
5   {
6       Point pt;
7
8       cout << "Enter a point in the form (x, y):\n";
9       cin >> pt;
10
11       cout << "Point entered was: " << pt << endl;
12       return 0;
13   }
```

```
Enter a point in the form (x, y):
(7, 8)
Point entered was: (7, 8)
```

Fig. S21.7   Solution for Exercise 21.15: Driver for P21_15.cpp.

21.18   Write a program to show that the getline and three-argument get istream member functions each end the input string with a string-terminating null character. Also, show that get leaves the delimiter character on the input stream while getline extracts the delimiter character and discards it. What happens to the unread characters in the stream?

     ANS:

```
1   // Exercise 21.18 Solution
2   #include <iostream>
3
4   using std::cout;
5   using std::endl;
```

Fig. S21.8   Solution for Exercise 21.18.   (Part 1 of 2.)

```
 6   using std::cin;
 7   using std::ios;
 8
 9   #include <cctype>
10
11   const int SIZE = 80;
12
13   int main()
14   {
15      char array[ SIZE ], array2[ SIZE ], c;
16
17      cout << "Enter a sentence to test getline() and get():\n";
18      cin.getline( array, SIZE, '*' );
19      cout << array << '\n';
20
21      cin >> c;  // read next character in input
22      cout << "The next character in the input is: " << c << '\n';
23
24      cin.get( array2, SIZE, '*' );
25      cout << array2 << '\n';
26
27      cin >> c;  // read next character in input
28      cout << "The next character in the input is: " << c << '\n';
29
30      return 0;
31   }
```

```
Enter a sentence to test getline() and get():
wishing*on*a*star
wishing
The next character in the input is: o
n
The next character in the input is: *
```

Fig. S21.8   Solution for Exercise 21.18.   (Part 2 of 2.)

C++ Templates

Solutions to Selected Exercises

22.3 Use a nontype parameter `numberOfElements` and a type parameter `elementType` to help create a template for the `Array` class we developed in Chapter 18, C++ Operator Overloading. This template will enable `Array` objects to be instantiated with a specified number of elements of a specified element type at compile time.

ANS:

```
1   #ifndef ARRAY1_H
2   #define ARRAY1_H
3
4   #include <iostream>
5
6   using std::cout;
7   using std::endl;
8   using std::cin;
9
10  #include <cstdlib>
11  #include <cassert>
12
13  template < class elementType, int numberOfElements >
14  class Array {
15  public:
16     Array();                               // default constructor
17     ~Array();                              // destructor
18     int getSize() const;                   // return size
19     bool operator==( const Array & ) const; // compare equal
20     bool operator!=( const Array & ) const; // compare !equal
21     elementType &operator[]( int );        // subscript operator
22     static int getArrayCount();            // Return count of
23                                            // arrays instantiated.
24     void inputArray();                     // input the array elements
25     void outputArray() const;              // output the array elements
```

Fig. S22.1   `#ifndef` ARRAY1_H. (Part 1 of 4.)

```
26  private:
27     elementType ptr[ numberOfElements ]; // pointer to first element
28     int size; // size of the array
29     static int arrayCount;  // # of Arrays instantiated
30  };
31
32  // Initialize static data member at file scope
33  template < class elementType, int numberOfElements >
34  int Array< elementType, numberOfElements >::arrayCount = 0; // no objects
35
36  // Default constructor for class Array
37  template < class elementType, int numberOfElements >
38  Array< elementType, numberOfElements >::Array()
39  {
40     ++arrayCount;                    // count one more object
41     size = numberOfElements;
42
43     for ( int i = 0; i < size; ++i )
44        ptr[ i ] = 0;                 // initialize array
45  }
46
47  // Destructor for class Array
48  template < class elementType, int numberOfElements >
49  Array< elementType, numberOfElements >::~Array() { --arrayCount; }
50
51  // Get the size of the array
52  template < class elementType, int numberOfElements >
53  int Array< elementType, numberOfElements >::getSize() const
54     { return size; }
55
56  // Determine if two arrays are equal and
57  // return true or false.
58  template < class elementType, int numberOfElements >
59  bool Array< elementType, numberOfElements >::
60             operator==( const Array &right ) const
61  {
62     if ( size != right.size )
63        return false;    // arrays of different sizes
64
65     for ( int i = 0; i < size; ++i )
66        if ( ptr[ i ] != right.ptr[ i ] )
67           return false; // arrays are not equal
68
69     return true;        // arrays are equal
70  }
71
72  // Determine if two arrays are not equal and
73  // return true or false.
74  template < class elementType, int numberOfElements >
75  bool Array< elementType, numberOfElements >::
```

Fig. S22.1   #ifndef ARRAY1_H. (Part 2 of 4.)

```
76                 operator!=( const Array &right ) const
77   {
78      if ( size != right.size )
79         return true;          // arrays of different sizes
80
81      for ( int i = 0; i < size; ++i )
82         if ( ptr[ i ] != right.ptr[ i ] )
83            return true;        // arrays are not equal
84
85      return false;            // arrays are equal
86   }
87
88   // Overloaded subscript operator
89   template < class elementType, int numberOfElements >
90   elementType &Array< elementType, numberOfElements >::
91                      operator[]( int subscript )
92   {
93      // check for subscript out of range error
94      assert( 0 <= subscript && subscript < size );
95
96      return ptr[ subscript ];   // reference return creates lvalue
97   }
98
99   // Return the number of Array objects instantiated
100  template < class elementType, int numberOfElements >
101  int Array< elementType, numberOfElements >::getArrayCount()
102     { return arrayCount; }
103
104  // Input values for entire array.
105  template < class elementType, int numberOfElements >
106  void Array< elementType, numberOfElements >::inputArray()
107  {
108     for ( int i = 0; i < size; ++i )
109        cin >> ptr[ i ];
110  }
111
112  // Output the array values
113  template < class elementType, int numberOfElements >
114  void Array< elementType, numberOfElements >::outputArray() const
115  {
116     int i = 0;
117     for ( ; i < size; ++i ) {
118        cout << ptr[ i ] << ' ';
119
120        if ( ( i + 1 ) % 10 == 0 )
121           cout << '\n';
122     }
123
124     if ( i % 10 != 0 )
125        cout << '\n';
```

Fig. S22.1   #ifndef ARRAY1_H. (Part 3 of 4.)

```
126  }
127
128  #endif
```

Fig. S22.1   **#ifndef** ARRAY1_H. (Part 4 of 4.)

```
1    // Exercise 22.3 solution
2    #include <iostream>
3
4    using std::cout;
5
6    #include "arraytmp.h"
7
8    int main()
9    {
10      Array< int, 5 > intArray;
11
12      cout << "Enter " << intArray.getSize() << " integer values:\n";
13      intArray.inputArray();
14
15      cout << "\nThe values in intArray are:\n";
16      intArray.outputArray();
17
18      Array< float, 5 > floatArray;
19
20      cout << "\nEnter " << floatArray.getSize()
21          << " floating point values:\n";
22      floatArray.inputArray();
23
24      cout << "\nThe values in the doubleArray are:\n";
25      floatArray.outputArray();
26
27      return 0;
28   }
```

```
Enter 5 integer values:
99 98 97 96 95

The values in intArray are:
99 98 97 96 95

Enter 5 floating point values:
1.12 1.13 1.14 1.22 9.11

The values in the doubleArray are:
1.12 1.13 1.14 1.22 9.11
```

Fig. S22.2   Solution for Exercise 22.3.

22.7   Why is it appropriate to call a class template a parameterized type?

        ANS: *When creating template classes from a class template, it is necessary to provide a type (or possibly several types) to complete the definition of the new type being declared. For example, when creating an "array of integers" from an* Array *class template, the type* int *is provided to the class template to complete the definition of an array of integers.*

22.11   Why might you typically use a nontype parameter with a class template for a container such as an array or stack?

        ANS: *To specify at compile time the size of the container class object being declared.*

C++ Exception Handling

Solutions to Selected Exercises

23.20 Under what circumstances would the programmer not provide a parameter name when defining the type of the object that will be caught by a handler?

ANS: *If there is no information in the object that is required in the handler, a parameter name is not required in the handler.*

23.25 Use inheritance to create a base exception class and various derived exception classes. Then show that a `catch` handler specifying the base class can `catch` derived-class exceptions.

ANS:

```
1    // Exercise 23.25 Solution
2    #include <iostream>
3
4    using std::cout;
5
6    #include <cstdlib>
7    #include <ctime>
8
9    class BaseException {
10   public:
11      BaseException( char *mPtr ) : message( mPtr ) {}
12      void print() const { cout << message << '\n'; }
13   private:
14      char *message;
15   };
16
17   class DerivedException : public BaseException {
18   public:
19      DerivedException( char *mPtr ) : BaseException( mPtr ) {}
20   };
21
22   class DerivedException2 : public DerivedException {
```

Fig. S23.1 Solution for Exercise 23.25. (Part 1 of 2.)

```
23   public:
24      DerivedException2( char *mPtr ) : DerivedException( mPtr ) {}
25   };
26
27   int main()
28   {
29      srand( time( 0 ) );
30
31      try {
32         throw ( rand() % 2 ? DerivedException( "DerivedException" ) :
33                             DerivedException2( "DerivedException2" ) );
34      }
35      catch ( BaseException &b ) {
36         b.print();
37      }
38
39      return 0;
40   }
```

```
DerivedException
```

Fig. S23.1   Solution for Exercise 23.25.   (Part 2 of 2.)

Introduction to Java Applications and Applets

Solutions to Selected Exercises

24.8   Fill in the blanks in each of the following:
a) _____ are used to document a program and improve its readability.
ANS: *Comments.*

b) An input dialog capable of receiving input from the user is displayed with method of class _____.
ANS: `showInputDialog, JOptionPane.`

24.10   What displays in the message dialog when each of the following Java statements is performed? Assume x = 2 and y = 3.
a) `JOptionPane.showMessageDialog( null, "x = " + x );`
ANS: `x = 2`

b) `JOptionPane.showMessageDialog( null, "The value of x + x is " + ( x + x ) );`
ANS: `The value of x + x is 4`

c) `JOptionPane.showMessageDialog( null, "x =" );`
ANS: `x =`

d) `JOptionPane.showMessageDialog(null, ( x + y ) + " = " + ( y + x ) );`
ANS: `5 = 5`

24.12   Write an application that asks the user to enter two integers, obtains the numbers from the user and displays the larger number followed by the words "`is larger`" in an information message dialog. If the numbers are equal, print the message "`These numbers are equal.`" Use the techniques shown in Fig. 24.6.

```
1   // Exercise 24.12 Solution
2   // Larger.java
3   // Program determines the larger of two numbers
```

Fig. S24.1   Solution for Exercise 24.12.   (Part 1 of 2.)

```
4   import javax.swing.JOptionPane;
5
6   public class Larger {
7     public static void main( String args[] )
8     {
9        String firstNumber,      // first string entered by user
10              secondNumber;      // second string entered by user
11        int number1,             // first number to compare
12            number2;             // second number to compare
13
14        // read first number from user as a string
15        firstNumber =
16           JOptionPane.showInputDialog( "Enter first integer:" );
17
18        // read second number from user as a string
19        secondNumber =
20           JOptionPane.showInputDialog( "Enter second integer:" );
21
22        // convert numbers from type String to type int
23        number1 = Integer.parseInt( firstNumber );
24        number2 = Integer.parseInt( secondNumber );
25
26        String result;           // a string containing the output
27        if ( number1 > number2 )
28           result = number1 + " is larger.";
29        else if ( number1 < number2 )
30           result = number2 + " is larger.";
31        else
32           result = "These numbers are equal.";
33
34        // Display results
35        JOptionPane.showMessageDialog(
36           null, result, "Comparison Results",
37           JOptionPane.INFORMATION_MESSAGE );
38
39        System.exit( 0 );
40     }
41  }
```

Fig. S24.1   Solution for Exercise 24.12.   (Part 2 of 2.)

24.14 Write an application that inputs from the user the radius of a circle and prints the circle's diameter, circumference and area. Use the constant value 3.14159 for π. Use the GUI techniques shown in Fig. 24.6. [*Note:* You may also use the predefined constant Math.PI for the value of π. This constant is more precise than the value 3.14159. Class Math is defined in the java.lang package, so you do not need to import it.] Use the following formulas (r is the radius): *diameter = 2r, circumference = 2πr, area = πr^2.*

   ANS:

```
1   // Exercise 24.14 Solution
2   // Circle.java
3   // Program calculate the area, circumference, and diameter for a circle
4   import javax.swing.JOptionPane;
5
6   public class Circle {
7     public static void main( String args[] )
8     {
9        String input,       // string entered by user
10              result;       // output display string
11       int radius;         // radius of circle
12
13       // read from user as a string
14       input =
15          JOptionPane.showInputDialog( "Enter radius:" );
16
17       // convert number from type String to type int
18       radius = Integer.parseInt( input );
19
20       result = "Diameter is " + ( 2 * radius ) +
21               "\nArea is " + ( Math.PI * radius * radius ) +
22               "\nCircumference is " + ( 2 * Math.PI * radius );
23
24       // Display results
25       JOptionPane.showMessageDialog(
26          null, result, "Calculation Results",
27          JOptionPane.INFORMATION_MESSAGE );
28
29       System.exit( 0 );
30    }
31  }
```

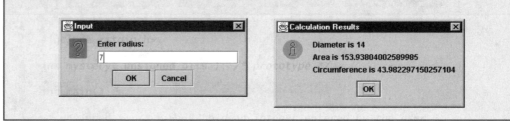

Fig. S24.2   Solution for Exercise 24.14.

Beyond C & C++: Operators, Methods & Arrays in Java

Solutions to Selected Exercises

25.6 Write statements that assign random integers to the variable *n* in the following ranges:
a) $1 \le n \le 2$
ANS: n = (**int**) (1 + Math.random() * 2);

b) $1 \le n \le 100$
ANS: n = (**int**) (1 + Math.random() * 100);

c) $0 \le n \le 9$
ANS: n = (**int**) (Math.random() * 10);

d) $1000 \le n \le 1112$
ANS: n = (**int**) (1000 + Math.random() * 113);

e) $-1 \le n \le 1$
ANS: n = (**int**) (-1 + Math.random() * 3);

f) $-3 \le n \le 11$
ANS: n = (**int**) (-3 + Math.random() * 15);

25.8 Define a method hypotenuse that calculates the length of the hypotenuse of a right triangle when the other two sides are given. The method should take two arguments of type double and return the hypotenuse as a double. Incorporate this method into an applet that reads integer values for side1 and side2 from JTextFields and performs the calculation with the hypotenuse method. Determine the length of the hypotenuse for each of the following triangles. [*Note*: Register for event handling on only the second JTextField. The user should interact with the program by typing numbers in both JTextFields and pressing *Enter* in the second JTextField.]

Triangle	Side 1	Side 2
1	3.0	4.0
2	5.0	12.0
3	8.0	15.0

ANS:

```
1   // Exercise 25.8 Solution
2   // Triangle.java
3   // Program calculates the hypotenuse of
4   // a right triangle.
5   import javax.swing.*;
6   import java.awt.event.*;
7   import java.awt.*;
8
9   public class Triangle extends JApplet
10     implements ActionListener {
11     JTextField sideInput, side2Input;
12     JLabel sidePrompt, sidePrompt2;
13
14     public void init()
15     {
16        sideInput = new JTextField( 4 );
17        side2Input = new JTextField( 4 );
18        side2Input.addActionListener( this );
19        sidePrompt = new JLabel( "Enter side 1: " );
20        sidePrompt2 = new JLabel( "Enter side 2: " );
21        Container c = getContentPane();
22        c.setLayout( new FlowLayout() );
23        c.add( sidePrompt );
24        c.add( sideInput );
25        c.add( sidePrompt2 );
26        c.add( side2Input );
27     }
28
29     public void actionPerformed( ActionEvent e )
30     {
31        double side1, side2;
32
33        side1 = Double.parseDouble( side2Input.getText() );
34        side2 = Double.parseDouble( sideInput.getText() );
35
36        double h = hypotenuse( side1, side2 );
37        showStatus( "Hypotenuse is : " + h );
38     }
39
40     public double hypotenuse( double s1, double s2 )
41     {
42        double hypotSquared = Math.pow( s1, 2 ) + Math.pow( s2, 2 );
43
44        return Math.sqrt( hypotSquared );
45     }
46  }
```

Fig. S25.1   Solution for Exercise 25.8.   (Part 1 of 2.)

Fig. S25.1   Solution for Exercise 25.8.   (Part 2 of 2.)   .

25.10   Write an applet that inputs integers (one at a time) and passes them one at a time to method isEven, which uses the modulus operator to determine if an integer is even. The method should take an integer argument and return `true` if the integer is even and `false` otherwise. Use an input dialog to obtain the data from the user.

          ANS:

```
1   // Exercise 25.10 Solution
2   // EvenOdd.java
3   // Determines if a number is odd or even
4   import javax.swing.*;
5   import java.awt.*;
6   import java.awt.event.*;
7
8   public class EvenOdd extends JApplet implements ActionListener {
9      JTextField input;
10     JLabel prompt;
11
12     public void init()
13     {
14        input = new JTextField( 4 );
15        input.addActionListener( this );
16        prompt = new JLabel( "Enter number: " );
17        Container c = getContentPane();
18        c.setLayout( new FlowLayout() );
19        c.add( prompt );
20        c.add( input );
21     }
22
23     public void actionPerformed( ActionEvent e )
24     {
25        int number = Integer.parseInt( input.getText() );
26        String result = "";
27
28        if ( isEven( number ) == true )
29           result = number + " is even";
30        else
31           result = number + " is odd ";
32
```

Fig. S25.2   Solution for Exercise 25.10.   (Part 1 of 2.)

```
33          showStatus( result );
34      }
35
36      public boolean isEven( int num )
37      {
38          if ( num % 2 == 0 )
39              return true;
40
41          return false;
42      }
43  }
```

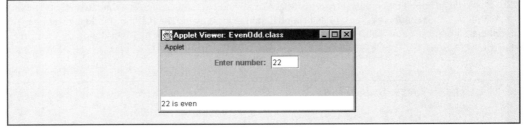

Fig. S25.2   Solution for Exercise 25.10.   (Part 2 of 2.)

25.11   Write a method `squareOfAsterisks` that displays a solid square of asterisks whose side is specified in integer parameter `side`. For example, if `side` is 4, the method displays

```
****
****
****
****
```

Incorporate this method into an applet that reads an integer value for `side` from the user at the keyboard and performs the drawing with the `squareOfAsterisks` method. Note that this method should be called from the applet's `paint` method and should be passed the `Graphics` object from `paint`.

ANS:

```
1   // Exercise 25.11 Solution
2   // Square.java
3   // Program draws a square of asterisks
4   import javax.swing.*;
5   import java.awt.*;
6
7   public class Square extends JApplet {
8      int size;
9
10     public void init()
11     {
12         String input = JOptionPane.showInputDialog(
13             "Enter square size:" );
```

Fig. S25.3   Solution for Exercise 25.11.   (Part 1 of 2.)

```
14
15        size = Integer.parseInt( input );
16    }
17
18    public void squareOfAsterisks( Graphics g )
19    {
20        int y = 50, x = 5;
21
22        for ( int a = 1; a <= size * size; a++ ) {
23            g.drawString( "*", x += 5, y );
24
25            if ( a % size == 0 ) {
26                y += 10;
27                x = 5;
28            }
29        }
30    }
31
32    public void paint( Graphics g )
33    {
34        squareOfAsterisks( g );
35    }
36 }
```

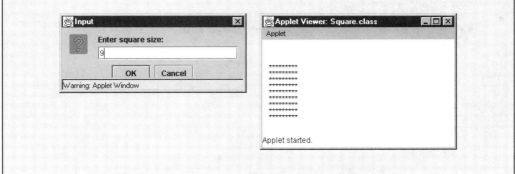

Fig. S25.3   Solution for Exercise 25.11.   (Part 2 of 2.)

25.12 Implement the following integer methods:

a) Method `celsius` returns the Celsius equivalent of a Fahrenheit temperature using the calculation

```
C = 5.0 / 9.0 * ( F - 32 );
```

b) Method `fahrenheit` returns the Fahrenheit equivalent of a Celsius temperature.

```
F = 9.0 / 5.0 * C + 32;
```

c) Use these methods to write an applet that enables the user to enter either a Fahrenheit temperature and display the Celsius equivalent or enter a Celsius temperature and display the Fahrenheit equivalent.

[*Note:* This applet will require that two JTextField objects that have registered action events. When actionPerformed is invoked, the ActionEvent parameter has method getSource() to determine the GUI component with which the user interacted. Your actionPerformed method should contain an if/else structure of the following form:

```
if ( e.getSource() == input1 ) {
    // process input1 interaction here
}
else {  // e.getSource() == input2
    // process input2 interaction here
}
```

where input1 and input2 are JTextField references.]

ANS:

```
1   // Exercise 25.12 Solution
2   // Convert.java
3   // Program converts Fahrenheit to Celcius
4   // and vice versa.
5   import javax.swing.*;
6   import java.awt.*;
7   import java.awt.event.*;
8
9   public class Convert extends JApplet implements ActionListener {
10      JTextField cInput, fInput;
11      JLabel cLabel, fLabel;
12
13      public void init()
14      {
15          cInput = new JTextField( 4 );
16          fInput = new JTextField( 4 );
17          cInput.addActionListener( this );
18          fInput.addActionListener( this );
19          cLabel = new JLabel( "Celcius:" );
20          fLabel = new JLabel( "Fahrenheit:" );
21          Container c = getContentPane();
22          c.setLayout( new FlowLayout() );
23          c.add( cLabel );
24          c.add( cInput );
25          c.add( fLabel );
26          c.add( fInput );
27      }
28
29      public void actionPerformed( ActionEvent e )
30      {
31          if ( e.getSource() == cInput ) {
32              int c = Integer.parseInt( cInput.getText() );
```

Fig. S25.4   Solution for Exercise 25.12.   (Part 1 of 2.)

```
33
34            fInput.setText( String.valueOf( celcius( c ) ) );
35            showStatus( "Celcius to Fahrenheit" );
36         }
37         else if ( e.getSource() == fInput ) {
38            int f = Integer.parseInt( fInput.getText() );
39
40            cInput.setText( String.valueOf( fahrenheit( f ) ) );
41            showStatus( "Fahrenheit to Celcius" );
42         }
43      }
44
45      public int celcius( int cTemp )
46      {
47         return ( ( int ) ( 9.0 / 5.0 * cTemp + 32 ) );
48      }
49
50      public int fahrenheit( int fTemp )
51      {
52         return ( ( int ) ( 5.0 / 9.0 * ( fTemp - 32 ) ) );
53      }
54   }
```

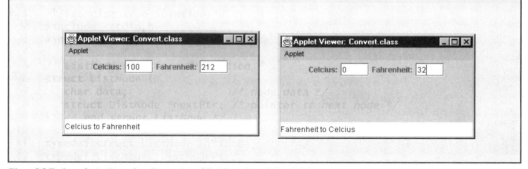

Fig. S25.4   Solution for Exercise 25.12.   (Part 2 of 2.)

25.14   Write a method that takes an integer value and returns the number with its digits reversed. For example, given the number 7631, the method should return 1367. Incorporate the method into an applet that reads a value from the user. Display the result of the method in the status bar.

　　　　ANS:

```
1   // Exercise 25.14 Solution
2   // Reverse.java
3   // Program takes a four digit number
4   // and prints out its digits reversed
5   import javax.swing.*;
6   import java.awt.*;
```

Fig. S25.5   Solution for Exercise 25.14.   (Part 1 of 3.)

```
7    import java.awt.event.*;
8
9    public class Reverse extends JApplet implements ActionListener {
10       JTextField input;
11       JLabel prompt;
12       int number;
13
14       public void init()
15       {
16          input = new JTextField( 6 );
17          input.addActionListener( this );
18          prompt = new JLabel( "Enter a four digit number: " );
19          Container c = getContentPane();
20          c.setLayout( new FlowLayout() );
21          c.add( prompt );
22          c.add( input );
23       }
24
25       public void actionPerformed( ActionEvent e )
26       {
27          number = Integer.parseInt( input.getText() );
28          reverseDigits();
29       }
30
31       public void reverseDigits()
32       {
33          int digit1 = 0, digit2 = 0, digit3 = 0,
34             digit4 = 0, factor = 1000, value = 0;
35
36          while ( factor >= 1 ) {
37             int temp = number / factor;
38
39             switch ( factor ) {
40                case 1000:
41                   digit4 = temp;
42                   break;
43                case 100:
44                   digit3 = temp * 10;
45                   break;
46                case 10:
47                   digit2 = temp * 100;
48                   break;
49                case 1:
50                   digit1 = temp * 1000;
51                   break;
52             }
53
54             number %= factor;
55             factor /= 10;
56          }
```

Fig. S25.5   Solution for Exercise 25.14.   (Part 2 of 3.)

```
57
58        if ( digit1 == 0 )   // special case when last digit initially is 0
59           showStatus( String.valueOf( 0 ) + String.valueOf( digit2 / 100 )
60              + String.valueOf( digit3 / 10 ) +
61              String.valueOf( digit4 ) );
62        else
63           showStatus( String.valueOf(digit1 + digit2 + digit3 + digit4) );
64     }
65  }
```

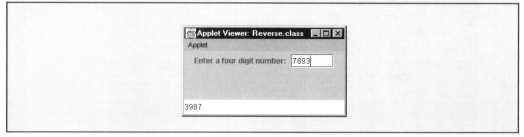

Fig. S25.5   Solution for Exercise 25.14.   (Part 3 of 3.)

25.16   Write a method `qualityPoints` that inputs a student's average and returns 4 if a student's average is 90–100, 3 if the average is 80–89, 2 if the average is 70–79, 1 if the average is 60–69 and 0 if the average is lower than 60. Incorporate the method into an applet that reads a value from the user. Display the result of the method in the status bar.

   ANS:

```
1   // Exercise 25.16 Solution
2   // Average.java
3   // Program displays a number
4   // representing the student's average
5   import javax.swing.*;
6   import java.awt.*;
7   import java.awt.event.*;
8
9   public class Average extends JApplet
10     implements ActionListener {
11     JTextField input;
12     JLabel prompt;
13
14     public void init()
15     {
16        input = new JTextField( 4 );
17        input.addActionListener( this );
18        prompt = new JLabel( "Enter average:" );
19        Container c = getContentPane();
20        c.setLayout( new FlowLayout() );
21        c.add( prompt );
```

Fig. S25.6   Solution for Exercise 25.16.   (Part 1 of 2.)

```
22          c.add( input );
23       }
24
25       public void actionPerformed( ActionEvent e )
26       {
27          int number = Integer.parseInt( input.getText() );
28
29          if ( number >= 0 && number <= 100 )
30             showStatus( "Point is: " + qualityPoints( number ) );
31          else
32             showStatus( "Invalid input." );
33       }
34
35       public int qualityPoints( int grade )
36       {
37          if ( grade >= 90 )
38             return 4;
39          else if ( grade >= 80 )
40             return 3;
41          else if ( grade >= 70 )
42             return 2;
43          else if ( grade >= 60 )
44             return 1;
45          else
46             return 0;
47       }
48    }
```

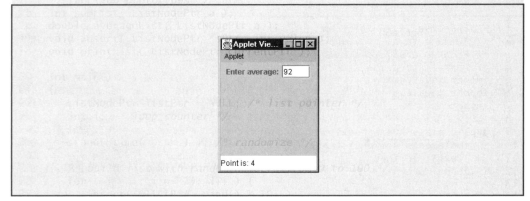

Fig. S25.6   Solution for Exercise 25.16.   (Part 2 of 2.)

25.17   Write an applet that simulates coin tossing. Let the program toss the coin each time the user presses the "Toss" button. Count the number of times each side of the coin appears. Display the results. The
program should call a separate method `flip` that takes no arguments and returns `false` for tails and `true`
for heads. [*Note:* If the program realistically simulates the coin tossing, each side of the coin should appear
approximately half the time.]

ANS:

```
1   // Exercise 25.17 Solution
2   // Coin.java
3   // Program simulates tossing a coin.
4   import javax.swing.*;
5   import java.awt.event.*;
6
7   public class Coin extends JApplet
8      implements ActionListener {
9      int heads, tails;
10     JButton b;
11
12     public void init()
13     {
14        b = new JButton( "Toss" );
15        b.addActionListener( this );
16        getContentPane().add( b );
17     }
18
19     public void actionPerformed( ActionEvent e )
20     {
21        if ( flip() == true )
22           ++heads;
23        else
24           ++tails;
25
26        showStatus( "Heads: " + heads + "    Tails: " + tails );
27     }
28
29     public boolean flip()
30     {
31        if ( ( int ) ( Math.random() * 2 ) == 1 )
32           return true;
33        else
34           return false;
35     }
36  }
```

Fig. S25.7   Solution for Exercise 25.17.

25.20 The greatest common divisor of integers x and y is the largest integer that evenly divides both x and y. Write a recursive method gcd that returns the greatest common divisor of x and y. The gcd of x and y is defined recursively as follows: If y is equal to 0, then gcd(x, y) is x; otherwise, gcd(x, y) is gcd(y, x % y), where % is the modulus operator. Use this method to replace the one you wrote in the applet of Exercise 25.15.

ANS:

```
1   // Exercise 25.20 Solution
2   // Divisor.java
3   // Program recursively finds the greatest
4   // common divisor of two numbers.
5   import javax.swing.*;
6   import java.awt.*;
7   import java.awt.event.*;
8
9   public class Divisor extends JApplet implements ActionListener {
10     JTextField input1, input2;
11     JLabel label1, label2;
12
13     public void init()
14     {
15        input1 = new JTextField( 4 );
16        input2 = new JTextField( 4 );
17        input2.addActionListener( this );
18        label1 = new JLabel( "Enter first number:" );
19        label2 = new JLabel( "Enter second number:" );
20        Container c = getContentPane();
21        c.setLayout( new FlowLayout() );
22        c.add( label1 );
23        c.add( input1 );
24        c.add( label2 );
25        c.add( input2 );
26     }
27
28     public void actionPerformed( ActionEvent e )
29     {
30        int num1, num2;
31
32        num1 = Integer.parseInt( input1.getText() );
33        num2 = Integer.parseInt( input2.getText() );
34        showStatus( "GCD is: " + gcd( num1, num2 ) );
35     }
36
37     public int gcd( int x, int y )
38     {
39        if ( y == 0 )
40           return x;
41        else
42           return gcd( y, x % y );
43     }
44  }
```

Fig. S25.8   Solution for Exercise 25.20.   (Part 1 of 2.)

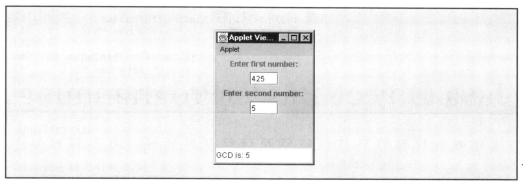

Fig. S25.8   Solution for Exercise 25.20.   (Part 2 of 2.)

Java Object-Based Programming

Solutions to Selected Exercises

26.2 Create a class called Rational for performing arithmetic with fractions. Write a driver program to test your class.

Use integer variables to represent the private instance variables of the class—the numerator and the denominator. Provide a constructor method that enables an object of this class to be initialized when it is declared. The constructor should store the fraction in reduced form (i.e., the fraction

2/4

would be stored in the object as 1 in the numerator and 2 in the denominator). Provide a no-argument constructor that sets default values in case no initializers are provided. Provide public methods for each of the following:

    a) Addition of two Rational numbers. The result of the addition should be stored in reduced form.

    b) Subtraction of two Rational numbers. The result of the subtraction should be stored in reduced form.

    c) Multiplication of two Rational numbers. The result of the multiplication should be stored in reduced form.

    d) Division of two Rational numbers. The result of the division should be stored in reduced form.

    e) Printing Rational numbers in the form a/b, where a is the numerator and b is the denominator.

    f) Printing Rational numbers in floating-point format. (Consider providing formatting capabilities that enable the user of the class to specify the number of digits of precision to the right of the decimal point.)

    ANS:

```
1   // Exercise 26.2 Solution
2   // Rational.java
3   // Definition of class Rational
4
```

Fig. S26.1 Solution for Exercise 26.2: Rational.java. (Part 1 of 3.)

```
5    public class Rational {
6        private int numerator;
7        private int denominator;
8
9        // Initialize numerator to 0 and denominator to 1
10       public Rational() { this( 0, 1 ); }
11
12       // Initialize numerator part to n and denominator part to 1
13       public Rational( int n ) { this( n, 1 ); }
14
15       // Initialize numerator part to n and denominator part to d
16       public Rational( int n, int d )
17       {
18           numerator = n;
19           denominator = d;
20           reduce();
21       }
22
23       // Add two Rational numbers
24       public Rational sum( Rational right )
25       {
26           int cd = denominator * right.denominator;
27           int numer = numerator * right.denominator +
28                       right.numerator * denominator;
29
30           return new Rational( numer, cd );
31       }
32
33       // Subtract two Rational numbers
34       public Rational subtract( Rational right )
35       {
36           int cd = denominator * right.denominator;
37           int numer = numerator * right.denominator -
38                       right.numerator * denominator;
39
40           return new Rational( numer, cd );
41       }
42
43       // Multiply two Rational numbers
44       public Rational multiply( Rational right )
45       {
46           return new Rational( numerator * right.numerator,
47                                denominator * right.denominator );
48       }
49
50       // Divide two Rational numbers
51       public Rational divide( Rational right )
52       {
53           return new Rational( numerator * right.denominator,
54                                denominator * right.numerator );
```

Fig. S26.1   Solution for Exercise 26.2: Rational.java.   (Part 2 of 3.)

```
55        }
56
57        // Reduce the fraction
58        private void reduce()
59        {
60           int gcd = 0;
61           int smaller = Math.min( numerator, denominator );
62
63           for ( int x = 2; x <= smaller; x++ )
64              if ( numerator % x == 0 && denominator % x == 0 )
65                 gcd = x;
66
67           if ( gcd != 0 ) {
68              numerator /= gcd;
69              denominator /= gcd;
70           }
71        }
72
73        // Return String representation of a Rational number
74        public String toString()
75           { return numerator + "/" + denominator; }
76
77        // Return floating-point String representation of
78        // a Rational number
79        public String toFloatString()
80        {
81           return Double.toString(
82                   ( double ) numerator / denominator );
83        }
84     }
```

Fig. S26.1   Solution for Exercise 26.2: Rational.java.   (Part 3 of 3.)

```
1     // Exercise 26.2: RationalTest.java
2     // Test the Rational number class
3     import java.awt.*;
4     import javax.swing.*;
5     import java.awt.event.*;
6
7     public class RationalTest extends JApplet implements ActionListener {
8        private Rational a, b;
9        private JLabel nlabel1, nlabel2, dlabel1, dlabel2;
10       private JTextField numer1, numer2, denom1, denom2;
11       private JButton addit, subtract, multiply, divide;
12
13       public void init()
14       {
15          nlabel1 = new JLabel( "Enter numerator 1:" );
16          nlabel2 = new JLabel( "Enter numerator 2:" );
```

Fig. S26.2   Solution for Exercise 26.2: RationalTest.java.   (Part 1 of 3.)

```
17          dlabel1 = new JLabel( "Enter denominator 1:" );
18          dlabel2 = new JLabel( "Enter denominator 2:" );
19
20          numer1 = new JTextField( 5 );
21          numer2 = new JTextField( 5 );
22          denom1 = new JTextField( 5 );
23          denom2 = new JTextField( 5 );
24
25          addit    = new JButton( "Add" );
26          subtract = new JButton( "Subtract" );
27          multiply = new JButton( "Multiply" );
28          divide   = new JButton( "Divide" );
29
30          addit.addActionListener( this );
31          subtract.addActionListener( this );
32          multiply.addActionListener( this );
33          divide.addActionListener( this );
34
35          Container c = getContentPane();
36          c.setLayout(new FlowLayout());
37
38          c.add( nlabel1 );
39          c.add( numer1 );
40          c.add( dlabel1 );
41          c.add( denom1 );
42          c.add( nlabel2 );
43          c.add( numer2 );
44          c.add( dlabel2 );
45          c.add( denom2 );
46          c.add( addit );
47          c.add( subtract );
48          c.add( multiply );
49          c.add( divide );
50      }
51
52      public void actionPerformed( ActionEvent e )
53      {
54          Rational r;
55          a = new Rational( Integer.parseInt( numer1.getText() ),
56                            Integer.parseInt( denom1.getText() ) );
57          b = new Rational( Integer.parseInt( numer2.getText() ),
58                            Integer.parseInt( denom2.getText() ) );
59
60          if ( e.getSource() == addit ) {
61             r = a.sum( b );
62             showStatus( "a + b = " + r + " = " + r.toFloatString() );
63          }
64          else if ( e.getSource() == subtract ) {
65             r = a.subtract( b );
66             showStatus( "a - b = " + r + " = " + r.toFloatString() );
```

Fig. S26.2   Solution for Exercise 26.2: RationalTest.java.   (Part 2 of 3.)

```
67          }
68          else if ( e.getSource() == multiply ) {
69             r = a.multiply( b );
70             showStatus( "a * b = " + r + " = " + r.toFloatString() );
71          }
72          else if ( e.getSource() == divide ) {
73             r = a.divide( b );
74             showStatus( "a / b = " + r + " = " + r.toFloatString() );
75          }
76       }
77    }
```

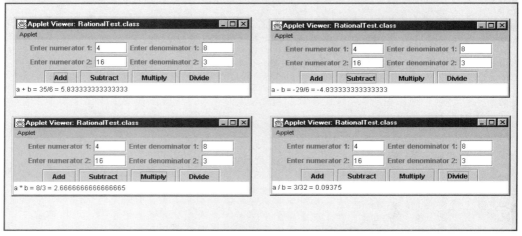

Fig. S26.2   Solution for Exercise 26.2: RationalTest.java.   (Part 3 of 3.)

26.3   Modify the Time2 class of Fig. 26.3 to include the tick method that increments the time stored in a Time2 object by one second. Also provide method incrementMinute to increment the minute and method incrementHour to increment the hour. The Time2 object should always remain in a consistent state. Write a driver program that tests the tick method, the incrementMinute method and the incrementHour method to ensure that they work correctly. Be sure to test the following cases:

a) Incrementing into the next minute.
b) Incrementing into the next hour.
c) Incrementing into the next day (i.e., 11:59:59 PM to 12:00:00 AM).

ANS:

```
1    // Exercise 26.3 Solution
2    // Time3.java
3    // Time3 class definition
4    public class Time3 {
5       private int hour;      // 0 - 23
6       private int minute;    // 0 - 59
```

Fig. S26.3   Solution for Exercise 26.3: Time3.java.   (Part 1 of 3.)

```
 7      private int second;    // 0 - 59
 8
 9      // Time constructor initializes each instance variable
10      // to zero. Ensures that Time3 object starts in a
11      // consistent state.
12      public Time3() { setTime( 0, 0, 0 ); }
13
14      // Time3 constructor: hour supplied, minute and second
15      // defaulted to 0.
16      public Time3( int h ) { setTime( h, 0, 0 ); }
17
18      // Time3 constructor: hour and minute supplied, second
19      // defaulted to 0.
20      public Time3( int h, int m ) { setTime( h, m, 0 ); }
21
22      // Time3 constructor: hour, minute and second supplied.
23      public Time3( int h, int m, int s ) { setTime( h, m, s ); }
24
25      // Set Methods
26      // Set a new Time3 value using military time. Perform
27      // validity checks on the data. Set invalid values
28      // to zero.
29      public void setTime( int h, int m, int s )
30      {
31         setHour( h );    // set the hour
32         setMinute( m );  // set the minute
33         setSecond( s );  // set the second
34      }
35
36      // set the hour
37      public void setHour( int h )
38         { hour = ( ( h >= 0 && h < 24 ) ? h : 0 ); }
39
40      // set the minute
41      public void setMinute( int m )
42         { minute = ( ( m >= 0 && m < 60 ) ? m : 0 ); }
43
44      // set the second
45      public void setSecond( int s )
46         { second = ( ( s >= 0 && s < 60 ) ? s : 0 ); }
47
48      // Get Methods
49      // get the hour
50      public int getHour() { return hour; }
51
52      // get the minute
53      public int getMinute() { return minute; }
54
55      // get the second
56      public int getSecond() { return second; }
```

Fig. S26.3   Solution for Exercise 26.3: Time3.java.   (Part 2 of 3.)

```
57
58        // Convert to String in military-time format
59        public String toMilitaryString()
60        {
61           return ( hour < 10 ? "0" : "" ) + hour +
62                  ( minute < 10 ? "0" : "" ) + minute;
63        }
64
65        // Convert to String in standard-time format
66        public String toString()
67        {
68           return ( ( hour == 12 || hour == 0 ) ? 12 : hour % 12 ) +
69                  ":" + ( minute < 10 ? "0" : "" ) + minute +
70                  ":" + ( second < 10 ? "0" : "" ) + second +
71                  ( hour < 12 ? " AM" : " PM" );
72        }
73
74        // Tick the time by one second
75        public void tick()
76        {
77           setSecond( second + 1 );
78
79           if ( second == 0 )
80              incrementMinute();
81        }
82
83        // Increment the minute
84        public void incrementMinute()
85        {
86           setMinute( minute + 1 );
87
88           if ( minute == 0 )
89              incrementHour();
90        }
91
92        // Increment the hour
93        public void incrementHour()
94        {
95           setHour( hour + 1 );
96        }
97     }
```

Fig. S26.3   Solution for Exercise 26.3: Time3.java.   (Part 3 of 3.)

```
98     // Exercise 26.3 Solution
99     // TimeTest.java
100    // Demonstrating the Time class set and get methods
101    import java.awt.*;
102    import javax.swing.*;
```

Fig. S26.4   Solution for Exercise 26.3: TimeTest.java.   (Part 1 of 3.)

```
103   import java.awt.event.*;
104
105   public class TimeTest extends JApplet implements ActionListener {
106       private Time3 t;
107       private JLabel hrLabel, minLabel, secLabel;
108       private JTextField hrField, minField, secField, display;
109       private JButton tickButton;
110
111       public void init()
112       {
113           t = new Time3();
114
115           hrLabel = new JLabel( "Set Hour" );
116           hrField = new JTextField( 10 );
117           hrField.addActionListener( this );
118           minLabel = new JLabel( "Set Minute" );
119           minField = new JTextField( 10 );
120           minField.addActionListener( this );
121           secLabel = new JLabel( "Set Second" );
122           secField = new JTextField( 10 );
123           secField.addActionListener( this );
124           display = new JTextField( 30 );
125           display.setEditable( false );
126           tickButton = new JButton( "Add 1 to Second" );
127           tickButton.addActionListener( this );
128
129           Container c = getContentPane();
130           c.setLayout( new FlowLayout() );
131           c.add( hrLabel );
132           c.add( hrField );
133           c.add( minLabel );
134           c.add( minField );
135           c.add( secLabel );
136           c.add( secField );
137           c.add( display );
138           c.add( tickButton );
139           updateDisplay();
140       }
141
142       public void actionPerformed( ActionEvent e )
143       {
144           if ( e.getSource() == tickButton )
145               t.tick();
146           else if ( e.getSource() == hrField ) {
147               t.setHour( Integer.parseInt( e.getActionCommand().toString() ) );
148               hrField.setText( "" );
149           }
150           else if ( e.getSource() == minField ) {
151               t.setMinute( Integer.parseInt(
152                   e.getActionCommand().toString() ) );
```

Fig. S26.4   Solution for Exercise 26.3: TimeTest.java.   (Part 2 of 3.)

```
153          minField.setText( "" );
154       }
155       else if ( e.getSource() == secField ) {
156          t.setSecond( Integer.parseInt(
157             e.getActionCommand().toString() ) );
158          secField.setText( "" );
159       }
160
161       updateDisplay();
162    }
163
164    public void updateDisplay()
165    {
166       display.setText( "Hour: " + t.getHour() +
167          "; Minute: " + t.getMinute() +
168          "; Second: " + t.getSecond() );
169       showStatus( "Standard time is: " + t.toString()+
170          "; Military time is: " + t.toMilitaryString() );
171    }
172 }
```

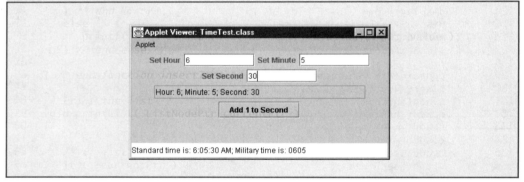

Fig. S26.4   Solution for Exercise 26.3: TimeTest.java.   (Part 3 of 3.)

26.4   Create a class Rectangle. The class has attributes length and width, each of which defaults to 1. It has methods that calculate the perimeter and the area of the rectangle. It has *set* and *get* methods for both length and width. The *set* methods should verify that length and width are each floating-point numbers larger than 0.0 and less than 20.0.

    ANS:

```
1  // Exercise 26.4 Solution
2  // MyRectangle.java
3  // Definition of class MyRectangle
4
5  public class MyRectangle {
6     private double length, width;
```

Fig. S26.5   Solution for Exercise 26.4: MyRectangle.java.   (Part 1 of 2.)

```
7
8      public MyRectangle()  { this( 1.0, 1.0 ); }
9
10     public MyRectangle( double l, double w )
11     {
12        setLength( l );
13        setWidth( w );
14     }
15
16     public void setLength( double len )
17     { length = ( len >= 0.0 && len <= 20.0 ? len : 1.0 ); }
18
19     public void setWidth( double w )
20     { width = ( w >= 0 && w <= 20.0 ? w : 1.0 ); }
21
22     public double getLength() { return length; }
23
24     public double getWidth() { return width; }
25
26     public double perimeter() { return 2 * length + 2 * width; }
27
28     public double area() { return length * width; }
29
30     public String toString (){
31        return ("Length: " + length + "\n" +
32        " Width: " + width  + "\n" +
33        " Perimeter: " + perimeter() + "\n" +
34        " Area: " + area() );
35     }
36  }
```

Fig. S26.5   Solution for Exercise 26.4: MyRectangle.java.   (Part 2 of 2.)

```
1   // Exercise 26.4 Solution
2   // Definition of class RectangleTest
3   import java.awt.*;
4   import javax.swing.*;
5   import java.awt.event.*;
6
7   public class RectangleTest extends JApplet implements ActionListener {
8       private JLabel prompt1, prompt2;
9       private JTextField input1, input2;
10      private JLabel outputLabel;
11      private JTextArea output;
12      private MyRectangle r;
13
14      public void init()
15      {
16          prompt1 = new JLabel( "Length:" );
```

Fig. S26.6   Solution for Exercise 26.4: RectangleTest.java.   (Part 1 of 2.)

```
17        prompt2 = new JLabel( "Width:" );
18        input1 = new JTextField( 10 );
19        input2 = new JTextField( 10 );
20        input2.addActionListener( this );
21
22        outputLabel = new JLabel( "Test Output" );
23        output = new JTextArea( 4, 10 );
24
25        Container c = getContentPane();
26        c.setLayout( new FlowLayout() );
27        c.add( prompt1 );
28        c.add( input1 );
29        c.add( prompt2 );
30        c.add( input2 );
31        c.add( outputLabel);
32        c.add( output);
33        r = new MyRectangle();
34     }
35
36     public void actionPerformed( ActionEvent e )
37     {
38        double d1, d2;
39
40        d1 = Double.parseDouble( input1.getText() );
41        d2 = Double.parseDouble( input2.getText() );
42
43        r.setLength( d1 );
44        r.setWidth( d2 );
45
46        output.setText( r.toString() );
47     }
48  }
```

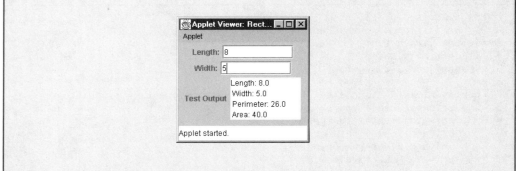

Fig. S26.6   Solution for Exercise 26.4: RectangleTest.java.   (Part 2 of 2.)

26.10 It would be perfectly reasonable for the Time1 class of Fig. 26.1 to represent the time internally as the number of seconds since midnight rather than the three integer values hour, minute and second. Clients could use the same public methods and get the same results. Modify the Time1 class of Fig. 26.1 to implement the Time1 as the number of seconds since midnight and show that there is no visible change to the clients of the class.

ANS:

```
1   // Exercise 26.10 Solution
2   // Time1 class definition
3
4   public class Time1 {
5      private int totalSeconds;
6
7      public Time1() { setTime( 0, 0, 0 ); }
8
9      public void setTime( int h, int m, int s )
10     {
11        int hour, minute, second;
12
13        hour   = ( ( h >= 0 && h < 24 ) ? h : 0 );
14        minute = ( ( m >= 0 && m < 60 ) ? m : 0 );
15        second = ( ( s >= 0 && s < 60 ) ? s : 0 );
16
17        totalSeconds = hour * 3600 + minute * 60 + second;
18     }
19
20     public String toMilitaryString()
21     {
22        int hour, minute, temp;
23
24        hour = totalSeconds / 3600;
25        temp = totalSeconds % 3600;
26        minute = temp / 60;
27
28        return ( hour < 10 ? "0" : "" ) + hour +
29               ( minute < 10 ? "0" : "" ) + minute;
30     }
31
32     public String toString()
33     {
34        int hour, minute, second, temp;
35
36        hour = totalSeconds / 3600;
37        temp = totalSeconds % 3600;
38        minute = temp / 60;
39        second = temp % 60;
40
41        return ( ( hour == 12 || hour == 0 ) ? 12 : hour % 12 ) +
42               ":" + ( minute < 10 ? "0" : "" ) + minute +
43               ":" + ( second < 10 ? "0" : "" ) + second +
44               ( hour < 12 ? " AM" : " PM" );
```

Fig. S26.7   Solution for Exercise 26.10: Time1.java.   (Part 1 of 2.)

```
45        }
46    }
```

Fig. S26.7   Solution for Exercise 26.10: Time1.java.   (Part 2 of 2.)

```
1   // Exercise 26.10 Solution
2   // TimeTest.java
3   // Class TimeTest to exercise class Time
4   import javax.swing.*;
5
6   public class TimeTest {
7      public static void main( String args[] )
8      {
9         Time1 t = new Time1();
10        String result = "";
11
12        result += "The initial military time is: " +
13                    t.toMilitaryString();
14        result += "\nThe initial standard time is: " +
15                    t.toString();
16
17        t.setTime( 13, 27, 6 );
18        result += "\nMilitary time after setTime is: " +
19                    t.toMilitaryString();
20        result += "\nStandard time after setTime is: " +
21                    t.toString();
22
23        t.setTime( 99, 99, 99 );
24        result += "\nAfter attempting invalid settings:";
25        result += "\nMilitary time: " + t.toMilitaryString();
26        result += "\nStandard time: " + t.toString();
27
28        JOptionPane.showMessageDialog(
29              null, result, "Time1Test",
30              JOptionPane.INFORMATION_MESSAGE );
31        System.exit( 0 );
32     }
33  }
```

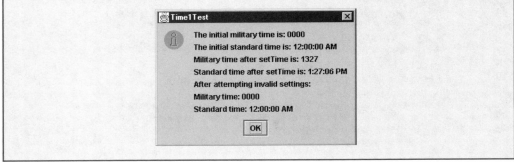

Fig. S26.8   Solution for Exercise 26.10: TimeTest.java.

26.11 *(Drawing Program)* Create a drawing applet that randomly draws lines, rectangles and ovals. For this purpose, create a set of "smart" shape classes where objects of these classes know how to draw themselves if provided with a Graphics object that tells them where to draw (i.e., the applet's Graphics object allows a shape to draw on the applet's background). The class names should be MyLine, MyRect and MyOval.

The data for class MyLine should include *x1*, *y1*, *x2* and *y2* coordinates. Method drawLine method of class Graphics will connect the two points supplied with a line. The data for classes MyRect and MyOval should include an upper-left *x*-coordinate value, an upper-left *y*-coordinate value, a *width* (must be nonnegative) and a *height* (must be nonnegative). All data in each class must be private.

In addition to the data, each class should define at least the following public methods:
   a) A constructor with no arguments that sets the coordinates to 0.
   b) A constructor with arguments that sets the coordinates to the supplied values.
   c) *Set* methods for each individual piece of data that allow the programmer to independently set any piece of data in a shape (e.g., if you have an instance variable x1, you should have a method setX1).
   d) *Get* methods for each individual piece of data that allow the programmer to independently retrieve any piece of data in a shape (e.g., if you have an instance variable x1, you should have a method getX1).
   e) A draw method with the first line

public void draw(Graphics g)

   f) will be called from the applet's paint method to draw a shape onto the screen.
The preceding methods are required. If you would like to provide more methods for flexibility, please do so.

Begin by defining class MyLine and an applet to test your classes. The applet should have a MyLine instance variable line that can refer to one MyLine object (created in the applet's init method with random coordinates). The applet's paint method should draw the shape with a statement like

    line.draw(g);

where line is the MyLine reference and g is the Graphics object that the shape will use to draw itself on the applet.

Next, change the single MyLine reference into an array of MyLine references and hard code several MyLine objects into the program for drawing. The applet's paint method should walk through the array of MyLine objects and draw every one.

After the preceding part is working, you should define the MyOval and MyRect classes and add objects of these classes into the MyRect and MyOval arrays. The applet's paint method should walk through each array and draw every shape. Create five shapes of each type.

Once the applet is running, select Reload from the appletviewer's Applet menu to reload the applet. This will cause the applet to choose new random numbers for the shapes and draw the shapes again.

In Chapter 27, we will modify this exercise to take advantage of the similarities between the classes and to avoid reinventing the wheel.

ANS:

```
1   // Exercise 26.11 Solution
2   // MyLine.java
3   // Definition of class MyLine
4   import java.awt.Graphics;
5
6   public class MyLine {
7      private int x1, x2;
8      private int y1, y2;
9
10     public MyLine()
11     {
12        x1 = 0;
13        y1 = 0;
14        x2 = 0;
15        y2 = 0;
16     }
17
18     public MyLine( int x1, int y1, int x2, int y2 )
19     {
20        setX1( x1 );
21        setX2( x2 );
22        setY1( y1 );
23        setY2( y2 );
24     }
25
26     public void setX1( int x1 )
27     { this.x1 = ( x1 >= 0 ? x1 : 0 ); }
28
29     public void setX2( int x2 )
30     { this.x2 = ( x2 >= 0 ? x2 : 0 ); }
31
32     public void setY1( int y1 )
33     { this.y1 = ( y1 >= 0 ? y1 : 0 ); }
34
35     public void setY2( int x2 )
36     { this.y2 = ( y2 >= 0 ? y2 : 0 ); }
37
38     public int getX1() { return x1; }
39     public int getX2() { return x2; }
40     public int getY1() { return y1; }
41     public int getY2() { return y2; }
42
43     public void draw( Graphics g )
44     {
45        g.drawLine( x1, y1, x2, y2 );
46     }
47  }
```

Fig. S26.9   Solution for Exercise 26.11: MyLine.java.

```
 1   // Exercise 26.11 Solution
 2   // MyOval.java
 3   // Definition of class MyRect
 4   import java.awt.Graphics;
 5
 6   public class MyOval {
 7      private int length, width;
 8      private int upperLeftX, upperLeftY;
 9
10      public MyOval()
11      {
12         length =  0;
13         width = 0;
14         upperLeftX = 0;
15         upperLeftY = 0;
16      }
17
18      public MyOval( int x, int y, int l, int w )
19      {
20         setUpperLeftX( x );
21         setUpperLeftY( y );
22         setLength( l );
23         setWidth( w );
24      }
25
26      public void setLength( int len )
27      { length = ( len >= 0 ? len : 0 ); }
28
29      public void setUpperLeftX( int x )
30      { upperLeftX =( x >= 0 ? x : 0 ); }
31
32      public void setUpperLeftY( int y )
33      { upperLeftX =( y >= 0 ? y : 0 ); }
34
35      public void setWidth( int w )
36      { width = ( w >= 0 ? w : 0 ); }
37
38      public int getLength() { return length; }
39
40      public int getWidth() { return width; }
41
42      public int getUpperLeftX() { return upperLeftX; }
43
44      public int getUpperLeftY() { return upperLeftY; }
45
46      public void draw( Graphics g )
47      {
48         g.drawOval( upperLeftX, upperLeftY, length, width );
49      }
50   }
```

Fig. S26.10   Solution for Exercise 26.11: MyOval.java.

```java
1    // Exercise 26.11 Solution
2    // MyRect.java
3    // Definition of class MyRect
4    import java.awt.Graphics;
5
6    public class MyRect {
7       private int length, width;
8       private int upperLeftX, upperLeftY;
9
10      public MyRect()
11      {
12         length =  0;
13         width = 0;
14         upperLeftX = 0;
15         upperLeftY = 0;
16      }
17
18      public MyRect( int x, int y, int l, int w )
19      {
20         setUpperLeftX( x );
21         setUpperLeftY( y );
22         setLength( l );
23         setWidth( w );
24      }
25
26      public void setLength( int len )
27      { length = ( len >= 0.0 ? len : 1 ); }
28
29      public void setUpperLeftX( int x )
30      { upperLeftX =( x >= 0 ? x : 0 ); }
31
32      public void setUpperLeftY( int y )
33      { upperLeftX =( y >= 0  ? y : 0 ); }
34
35      public void setWidth( int w )
36      { width = ( w >= 0 ? w : 1 ); }
37
38      public int getLength() { return length; }
39
40      public int getWidth() { return width; }
41
42      public int getUpperLeftX() { return upperLeftX; }
43
44      public int getUpperLeftY() { return upperLeftY; }
45
46      public void draw( Graphics g )
47      {
48         g.drawRect( upperLeftX, upperLeftY, length, width );
49      }
50   }
```

Fig. S26.11   Solution for Exercise 26.11: MyRect.java.

```
1   // Exercise 26.11 Solution
2   // Definition of class RectangleTest
3   import java.awt.*;
4   import javax.swing.*;
5
6   public class TestDraw extends JApplet {
7      private MyLine line[];
8      private MyOval oval[];
9      private MyRect rect[];
10
11     public void initDraw()
12     {
13        line = new MyLine[ 5 ];
14        line[ 0 ] = new MyLine( 100, 100, 200, 200 );
15        line[ 1 ] = new MyLine( 200, 200, 100, 100 );
16        line[ 2 ] = new MyLine( 300, 300, 100, 100 );
17        line[ 3 ] = new MyLine( 400, 400, 0, 0 );
18        line[ 4 ] = new MyLine( 100, 100, 300, 300 );
19
20        oval = new MyOval[ 5 ];
21        oval[ 0 ] = new MyOval( 100, 100, 200, 200 );
22        oval[ 1 ] = new MyOval( 200, 200, 100, 100 );
23        oval[ 2 ] = new MyOval( 300, 300, 100, 100 );
24        oval[ 3 ] = new MyOval( 400, 400, 30, 200 );
25        oval[ 4 ] = new MyOval( 100, 100, 300, 300 );
26
27        rect = new MyRect[ 5 ];
28        rect[ 0 ] = new MyRect( 100, 100, 200, 200 );
29        rect[ 1 ] = new MyRect( 200, 200, 100, 100 );
30        rect[ 2 ] = new MyRect( 300, 300, 100, 100 );
31        rect[ 3 ] = new MyRect( 400, 400, 30, 200 );
32        rect[ 4 ] = new MyRect( 100, 100, 300, 300 );
33     }
34
35     public void paint( Graphics g )
36     {
37        initDraw();
38
39        for ( int i = 0; i < line.length; i++ )
40   line[ i ].draw( g );
41
42        for ( int i = 0; i < oval.length; i++ )
43   oval[ i ].draw( g );
44
45        for ( int i = 0; i < rect.length; i++ )
46   rect[ i ].draw( g );
47     }
48  }
```

Fig. S26.12 Solution for Exercise 26.11: TestDraw.java.   (Part 1 of 2.)

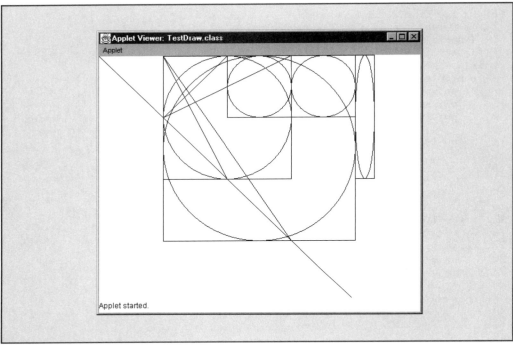

Fig. S26.12 Solution for Exercise 26.11: TestDraw.java.   (Part 2 of 2.)

Java Object-Oriented Programming

Solutions to Selected Exercises

27.3 Consider the class Bicycle. Given your knowledge of some common components of bicycles, show a class hierarchy in which the class Bicycle inherits from other classes, which, in turn, inherit from yet other classes. Discuss the instantiation of various objects of class Bicycle. Discuss inheritance from class Bicycle for other closely related subclasses.

>   **ANS:** *Possible classes are displayed in bold.*
>   Bicycle *composed of:*
>   Handle bars
>   Seat
>   Frame
>   Wheels *composed of:*
>   Tires
>   Rims
>   Spokes
>   Pedals
>   Chain *composed of:*
>   Links
>   Brakes *composed of:*
>   Wires
>   Brake *Pads*
>   Brake Handles

27.4 Define each of the following terms: single inheritance, multiple inheritance, interface, superclass and subclass.

>   ANS:

a) Single inheritance is the process by which a class incorporates the attributes and behaviors of a previously defined class.

b) Multiple inheritance is the process by which a class incorporates the attributes and behaviors of two or more previously defined classes.

c) An interface is a collection of abstract methods that can be implemented to simulate multiple inheritance.

d) A superclass is a class from which other classes inherit attributes and behaviors.

e) A subclass is a class that has inherited attributes and behaviors from a superclass.

27.5   Discuss why casting a superclass reference to a subclass reference is potentially dangerous.

ANS: *The reference must refer to an object of the subclass, before being used. When the compiler looks at an object through a subclass reference, it expects to see all the pieces of the subclass. However, if the superclass reference originally referred to a superclass object, the additional pieces added by the subclass do not exist. For this reason, an attempt to cast a subclass reference, that refers to a subclass object, into a superclass reference results in a ClassCastException at execution time.*

27.6   Distinguish between single inheritance and multiple inheritance. Why does Java not support multiple inheritance? What feature of Java helps realize the benefits of multiple inheritance?

ANS: *Single inheritance inherits from one class only. Multiple inheritance inherits from two or more classes. Java does not support multiple inheritance because of the problems that can be encountered with multiple inheritance. However, Java does support interfaces which provide the benefits of multiple inheritance without the potential problems.*

27.7   (*True/False*) A subclass is generally smaller than its superclass.

ANS: *False. A subclass is usually larger because it normally adds more data and more functionality.*

27.8   (*True/False*) A subclass object is also an object of that subclass's superclass.

ANS: *True.*

27.9   Rewrite the Point, Circle, Cylinder program of Fig. 27.4 as a Point, Square, Cube program. Do this two ways—once with inheritance and once with composition.

ANS:

```
1    // Exercise 27.9 -- Composition
2    // Point.java
3    // Definition of class Point
4
5    public class Point {
6        private double x, y; // coordinates of the Point
7
8        public Point( double a, double b ) { setPoint( a, b ); }
9
10       public void setPoint( double a, double b )
11       {
12           x = a;
13           y = b;
14       }
15
16       public double getX() { return x; }
17
18       public double getY() { return y; }
19
20       public String toString()
21           { return "[" + x + ", " + y + "]"; }
22
23       public String getName() { return "Point"; }
24   }
```

Fig. S27.1   Solution for Exercise 27.9: Point.java.

```
1   // Exercise 27.9 -- Composition
2   // Square.java
3   // Definition of class Square
4
5   public class Square {
6      private double side;
7      private Point p;        // composition
8
9      public Square()  {  this( 0.0, 0.0, 0.0 );  }
10
11     public Square( double s, double a, double b )
12     {
13        p = new Point( a, b );   // instantiate point object
14        setSide( s );
15     }
16
17     public void setSide( double s )
18        { side = ( s >= 0 ? s : 0 ); }
19
20     public double getSide() { return side; }
21
22     public double area() { return Math.pow( side, 2 ); }
23
24     public String toString()
25        { return "Corner = " + p.toString() + "; Side = " + side; }
26
27     public String getName() { return "Square"; }
28
29     public String getPointName() { return p.getName(); }
30
31     public String getPointString() { return p.toString(); }
32  }
```

Fig. S27.2   Solution for Exercise 27.9: Square.java.

```
1   // Exercise 27.9 -- Composition
2   // Cube.java
3   // Definition of class Cube
4
5   public class Cube {
6      private double depth;
7      private Square s;        // composition
8
9      public Cube( double m, double a, double b )
10     {
11        s = new Square( m, a, b );
12        depth = m;
13     }
14
15     public double getDepth() { return depth; }
```

Fig. S27.3   Solution for Exercise 27.9: Cube.java.   (Part 1 of 2.)

```
16
17    .    public double area() { return s.area() * 6; }
18
19         public double volume() { return s.area() * depth; }
20
21         public String toString()
22            { return s.toString() + "; Depth = " + depth; }
23
24         public String getName() { return "Cube"; }
25
26         public double getSquareArea() { return s.area(); }
27
28         public String getSquareName() { return s.getName(); }
29
30         public String getSquareString() { return s.toString(); }
31
32         public String getSPointString() { return s.getPointString(); }
33
34         public String getSPointName() { return s.getPointName(); }
35    }
```

Fig. S27.3   Solution for Exercise 27.9: Cube.java.   (Part 2 of 2.)

```
1     // Exercise 27.9 -- Composition
2     // Test.java
3     // Driver for point, square, cube composition program
4     import javax.swing.*;
5
6     public class Test {
7        public static void main( String args[] )
8        {
9           Cube cube = new Cube( 3.3, 10, 10 );
10          String result = "";
11
12          result += cube.getSPointName() + ": " +
13                       cube.getSPointString();
14
15          result += "\n" + cube.getSquareName() + ": " +
16                       cube.getSquareString();
17
18          result += "\n" + cube.getName() + ": " +
19                       cube.toString();
20
21          result += "\n" + cube.getSPointName() +
22                       ": " + cube.getSPointString();
23
24          result += "\n" + cube.getSquareName() +
25                       ": " + cube.getSquareString();
26          result += "\n" + "Area = " + cube.getSquareArea();
27
```

Fig. S27.4   Solution for Exercise 27.9: Test.java.   (Part 1 of 2.)

```
28          result += "\n" + cube.getName() +
29                     ": " + cube.toString();
30          result += "\n" + "Area = " + cube.area();
31          result += "\n" + "Volume = " + cube.volume();
32
33          JOptionPane.showMessageDialog(
34             null, result, "Shapes",
35             JOptionPane.INFORMATION_MESSAGE );
36          System.exit( 0 );
37       }
38   }
```

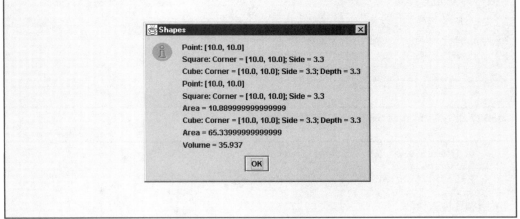

Fig. S27.4   Solution for Exercise 27.9: Test.java.   (Part 2 of 2.)

ANS:

```
1   // Exercise 27.9 -- Inheritance
2   // Point.java
3   // Definition of class Point
4
5   public class Point extends Shape {
6      protected double x, y;
7
8      public Point( double a, double b ) { setPoint( a, b ); }
9
10     public void setPoint( double a, double b )
11     {
12        x = a;
13        y = b;
14     }
15
16     public double getX() { return x; }
17
```

Fig. S27.5   Solution for Exercise 27.9: Point.java.   (Part 1 of 2.)

```
18      public double getY() { return y; }
19
20      public String toString()
21        { return "[" + x + ", " + y + "]"; }
22
23      public String getName() { return "Point"; }
24   }
```

Fig. S27.5   Solution for Exercise 27.9: Point.java.   (Part 2 of 2.)

```
1   // Exercise 27.9 -- Inheritance
2   // Shape.java
3   // Definition of abstract base class Shape
4
5   public abstract class Shape {
6      public double area() { return 0.0; }
7      public double volume() { return 0.0; }
8      public abstract String getName();
9   }
```

Fig. S27.6   Solution for Exercise 27.9: Shape.java.

```
1   // Exercise 27.9 -- Inheritance
2   // Square.java
3   // Definition of class Square
4
5   public class Square extends Point {
6      protected double side;
7
8      public Square()
9        { this( 0.0, 0.0, 0.0 ); }
10
11     public Square( double s, double a, double b )
12     {
13        super( a, b );
14        setSide( s );
15     }
16
17     public void setSide( double s )
18       { side = ( s >= 0 ? s : 0 ); }
19
20     public double getSide() { return side; }
21
22     public double area() { return Math.pow( side, 2 ); }
23
24     public String toString()
25       { return "Corner = " + super.toString() +
26               "; side = " + side; }
27
```

Fig. S27.7   Solution for Exercise 27.9: Square.java.   (Part 1 of 2.)

```
28      public String getName() { return "Square"; }
29  }
```

Fig. S27.7   Solution for Exercise 27.9: Square.java.   (Part 2 of 2.)

```
1   // Exercise 27.9 -- Inheritance
2   // Cube.java
3   // Definition of class Cylinder
4
5   public class Cube extends Square {
6      private double depth;
7
8      public Cube( double s, double a, double b )
9      {
10        super( s, a, b );
11        depth = s;
12     }
13
14     public double area() { return super.area() * 6; }
15
16     public double volume() { return super.area() * depth; }
17
18     public String toString()
19        { return super.toString() + "; depth = " + depth; }
20
21     public String getName() { return "Cube"; }
22  }
```

Fig. S27.8   Solution for Exercise 27.9: Cube.java.

```
1   // Exercise 27.9 -- Inheritance
2   // Test.java
3   // Driver for point, square, cube hierarchy
4   import javax.swing.*;
5
6   public class Test {
7      public static void main( String args[] )
8      {
9         Point point = new Point( 7, 11 );
10        Square square = new Square( 3.5, 22, 8 );
11        Cube cube = new Cube( 3.3, 10, 10 );
12
13        Shape[] arrayOfShapes = new Shape[ 3 ];
14        String result = "";
15
16        arrayOfShapes[ 0 ] = point;
17        arrayOfShapes[ 1 ] = square;
18        arrayOfShapes[ 2 ] = cube;
19
```

Fig. S27.9   Solution for Exercise 27.9: Test.java.   (Part 1 of 2.)

```
20          result += point.getName() + ": " +
21                      point.toString();
22
23          result += "\n" + square.getName() + ": " +
24                      square.toString();
25
26          result += "\n" + cube.getName() + ": " +
27                      cube.toString();
28
29          for ( int i = 0; i < 3; i++ ) {
30             result += "\n" + arrayOfShapes[ i ].getName() +
31                ": " + arrayOfShapes[ i ].toString();
32             result += "\n" + "Area = " +
33                arrayOfShapes[ i ].area();
34             result += "\n" + "Volume = " +
35                arrayOfShapes[ i ].volume();
36          }
37
38          JOptionPane.showMessageDialog(
39                null, result, "Shapes",
40                JOptionPane.INFORMATION_MESSAGE );
41          System.exit( 0 );
42       }
43    }
```

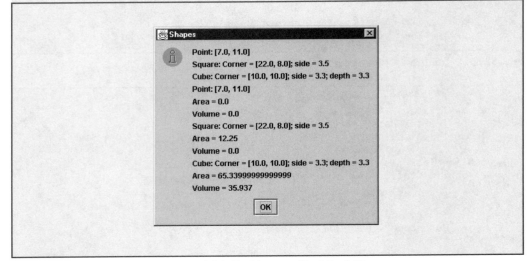

Fig. S27.9 Solution for Exercise 27.9: Test.java. (Part 2 of 2.)

27.10 In the chapter, we stated, "When a superclass method is inappropriate for a subclass, that method can be overridden in the subclass with an appropriate implementation." If this is done, does the subclass-is-a-superclass-object relationship still hold? Explain your answer.

ANS: *Yes, the subclass-is-a-superclass-object relationship still holds. In Java, it is not possible to break this relationship.*

27.12 Discuss the problems of programming with `switch` logic. Explain why polymorphism is an effective alternative to using `switch` logic.

ANS: *The main problem with programming using the* `switch` *structure is the extensibility and maintainability of the program. A program containing many* `switch` *structures is difficult to modify. All the structures must be modified to handle the processing of an additional type or of one less type. Polymorphism determines the type of an object automatically, so it is not necessary to determine the type of an object to process the object in a generic manner.*

27.14 Distinguish between non-`abstract` methods and `abstract` methods.

ANS: *A non-*`abstract` *method provides implementation. An* `abstract` *method does not provide any implementation.*

27.15 (*True/False*) All methods in an `abstract` superclass must be declared `abstract`.

ANS: *False. An* `abstract` *class must have at least one* `abstract` *method. Any number of methods in the class can be non-*`abstract`*.*

Java Graphics and Java2D

Solutions to Selected Exercises

28.4 Fill in the blanks in each of the following:
   a) Class _____ of the Java2D API is used to define ovals.
   ANS: `Ellipse2D`

   b) Methods `draw` and `fill` of class `Graphics2D` require an object of type _____ as their argument.
   ANS: `Shape`

   c) The three constants that specify font style are _____, _____ and _____.
   ANS: `Font.PLAIN`, `Font.BOLD` *and* `Font.ITALIC`

   d) `Graphics2D` method _____ sets the painting color for Java2D shapes.
   ANS: `setColor`

28.5 State whether each of the following is *true* or *false*. If *false*, explain why.
   a) The `drawPolygon` method automatically connects the endpoints of the polygon.
   ANS: *True.*

   b) The `drawLine` method draws a line between two points.
   ANS: *True.*

   c) The `fillArc` method uses degrees to specify the angle.
   ANS: *True.*

   d) In the Java coordinate system, *y* values increase from top to bottom.
   ANS: *True.*

   e) The `Graphics` class inherits directly from class `Object`.
   ANS: *True.*

   f) The `Graphics` class is an `abstract` class.
   ANS: *True.*

   g) The `Font` class inherits directly from class `Graphics`.

ANS: *False. Class* Font *inherits directly from class* Object.

28.6   Write a program that draws a series of eight concentric circles. The circles should be separated by
10 pixels. Use the drawOval method of class Graphics.

ANS:

```
1   // Exercise 28.6 Solution
2   // Concentric.java
3   // This program draws concentric circles
4   import javax.swing.*;
5   import java.awt.*;
6   import java.awt.event.*;
7
8   public class Concentric extends JFrame {
9
10      public Concentric()
11      {
12         super( "Concentric" );
13         setSize( 300, 300 );
14         show();
15      }
16
17      public void paint( Graphics g )
18      {
19         for ( int x = 0; x <= 160; x += 10 ) {
20            int y = 160 - ( x * 2 );
21            g.drawOval( x + 30, x + 30, y, y );
22         }
23      }
24
25      public static void main( String args[] )
26      {
27         Concentric app = new Concentric();
28
29         app.addWindowListener(
30            new WindowAdapter() {
31               public void windowClosing( WindowEvent e )
32               {
33                  System.exit( 0 );
34               }
35            }
36         );
37      }
38   }
```

Fig. S28.1   Solution for Exercise 28.6: Concentric.java.   (Part 1 of 2.)

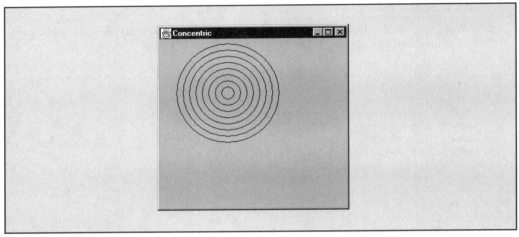

Fig. S28.1   Solution for Exercise 28.6: Concentric.java.   (Part 2 of 2.)

28.12 Write a program that randomly draws characters in different font sizes and colors.

ANS:

```
 1   // Exercise 28.12 Solution
 2   // Draw.java
 3   // This program randomly draws characters
 4   // Note: cover, resize, or restart the program
 5   // repeatedly to see multiple characters drawn
 6   import javax.swing.*;
 7   import java.awt.*;
 8   import java.awt.event.*;
 9
10   public class Draw extends JFrame {
11      private final int DELAY = 4000000;
12
13      public Draw()
14      {
15         super( "Drawing Characters" );
16         setSize( 380, 150 );
17         show();
18      }
19
20      public void paint( Graphics g )
21      {
22         int fontSize = ( int ) ( 10 + Math.random() * 63 );
23         int x = ( int ) ( 30 + Math.random() * 341 );
24         int y = ( int ) ( 50 + Math.random() * 95 );
25         char letters[] = { 'V', 'O', 'L', 'S', '8', '7' };
26         Font f = new Font( "Monospaced", Font.BOLD, fontSize );
27
```

Fig. S28.2   Solution for Exercise 28.12: Draw.java.   (Part 1 of 2.)

```
28      g.setColor( new Color( ( float ) Math.random(),
29                             ( float ) Math.random(),
30                             ( float ) Math.random() ) );
31      g.setFont( f );
32      g.drawChars( letters, ( int ) ( Math.random() * 6 ), 1, x, y );
33
34      for ( int h = 1; h < DELAY; h++ ) ;  // slow things down
35      repaint();
36   }
37
38   public static void main( String args[] )
39   {
40      Draw app = new Draw();
41
42      app.addWindowListener(
43         new WindowAdapter() {
44            public void windowClosing( WindowEvent e )
45            {
46               System.exit( 0 );
47            }
48         }
49      );
50   }
51 }
```

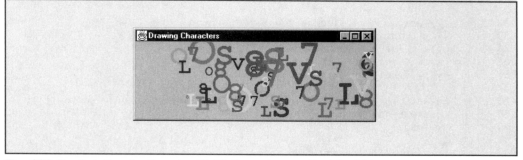

Fig. S28.2   Solution for Exercise 28.12: Draw.java.   (Part 2 of 2.)

28.19 Write an application that simulates a screen saver. The application should randomly draw lines using method `drawLine` of class `Graphics`. After drawing 100 lines, the application should clear itself and start drawing lines again. To allow the program to draw continuously, place a call to `repaint` as the last line in method `paint`. Do you notice any problems with this on your system?

　　　ANS:

```
1   // Exercise 28.19 Solution
2   // Saver1.java
3   // Program simulates a simple screen saver
4   import javax.swing.*;
5   import java.awt.*;
```

Fig. S28.3   Solution for Exercise 28.19: Saver1.java.   (Part 1 of 3.)

```
 6    import java.awt.event.*;
 7    import java.awt.geom.*;
 8
 9    public class Saver1 extends JFrame {
10       private final int DELAY = 4000000;
11       private final int XDIM = 300;
12       private final int YDIM = 300;
13       private int count;
14
15       public Saver1()
16       {
17          super( "Saver1" );
18          setSize( 300, 300 );
19          count = 0;
20          show();
21       }
22
23       public void paint( Graphics g )
24       {
25          int x, y, x1, y1;
26          Color colors[] = { Color.green, Color.cyan,
27                             Color.black, Color.yellow,
28                             Color.darkGray, Color.red,
29                             Color.orange, Color.gray,
30                             Color.pink, Color.magenta };
31
32          // assume html size is 200 x 200
33          x = ( int ) ( Math.random() * XDIM );
34          y = ( int ) ( Math.random() * YDIM );
35          x1 = ( int ) ( Math.random() * XDIM );
36          y1 = ( int ) ( Math.random() * YDIM );
37
38          g.setColor( colors[( int ) ( Math.random() * colors.length )] );
39          g.drawLine( x, y, x1, y1 );
40          ++count;
41
42          // slow the drawing down
43          for ( int q = 1; q < DELAY; q++ )
44             ;  // do nothing
45
46          if ( count == 100 ) {
47             g.setColor( Color.white );
48             g.fillRect( 0, 0, XDIM, YDIM );
49             count = 0;
50          }
51
52          repaint();
53       }
54
55       public static void main( String args[] )
```

Fig. S28.3   Solution for Exercise 28.19: Saver1.java.   (Part 2 of 3.)

```
56      {
57          Saver1 app = new Saver1();
58
59          app.addWindowListener(
60              new WindowAdapter() {
61                  public void windowClosing( WindowEvent e )
62                  {
63                      System.exit( 0 );
64                  }
65              }
66          );
67      }
68  }
```

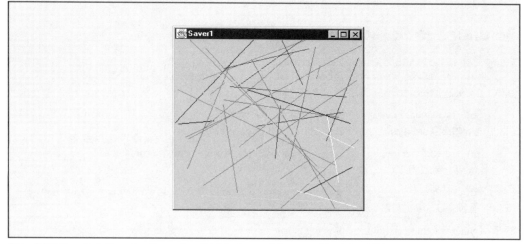

Fig. S28.3   Solution for Exercise 28.19: Saver1.java.   (Part 3 of 3.)

Java Graphical User Interface Components

Solutions to Selected Exercises

29.4   Fill in the blanks in each of the following:
a) The `JTextField` class inherits directly from _____.
ANS: `JTextComponent`.

b) The layout managers discussed in this chapter are _____, _____ and _____.
ANS: `FlowLayout`, `BorderLayout` *and* `GridLayout`.

c) `Container` method _____ attaches a GUI component to a container.
ANS: `add`.

d) Method _____ is called when a mouse button is released (without moving the mouse).
ANS: `mouseClicked`.

29.5   State whether each of the following is *true* or *false*. If *false*, explain why.
a) Only one layout manager can be used per `Container`.
ANS: *True.*

b) GUI components can be added to a `Container` in any order in a `BorderLayout`.
ANS: *True.*

c) `Graphics` method `setFont` is used to set the font for text fields.
ANS: *False.* `Component` *method* `setFont` *is used.*

d) A `Mouse` object contains a method called `mouseDragged`.
ANS: *False. A* `Mouse` *object is not provided by Java.*

29.8   Create the following GUI. You do not have to provide any functionality.

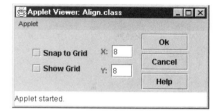

ANS:

```
1   // Exercise 29.8 Solution
2   // Align.java
3   // This program creates a simple GUI
4   import javax.swing.*;
5   import java.awt.*;
6
7   public class Align extends JApplet {
8      private JButton ok, cancel, help;
9      private JTextField xValue, yValue;
10     private JCheckBox snap, show;
11     private JLabel xLabel, yLabel;
12     private JPanel checkPanel, buttonPanel,
13                    fieldPanel1, fieldPanel2,
14                    fieldPanel;
15
16     public void init()
17     {
18        // build checkPanel
19        snap = new JCheckBox( "Snap to Grid" );
20        show = new JCheckBox( "Show Grid" );
21        checkPanel = new JPanel();
22        checkPanel.setLayout( new GridLayout( 2 , 1 ) );
23        checkPanel.add( snap );
24        checkPanel.add( show );
25
26        // build field panel1
27        xLabel = new JLabel( "X: " );
28        xValue = new JTextField( "8", 3 );
29        fieldPanel1 = new JPanel();
30        fieldPanel1.setLayout( new FlowLayout( FlowLayout.CENTER, 3, 5 ) );
31        fieldPanel1.add( xLabel );
32        fieldPanel1.add( xValue );
33
34        yLabel = new JLabel( "Y: " );
35        yValue = new JTextField( "8", 3 );
36        fieldPanel2 = new JPanel();
37        fieldPanel2.setLayout( new FlowLayout( FlowLayout.CENTER, 3, 5 ) );
38        fieldPanel2.add( yLabel );
39        fieldPanel2.add( yValue );
40
```

Fig. S29.1   Solution for Exercise 29.8: Align.java.   (Part 1 of 2.)

```
41          fieldPanel = new JPanel();
42          fieldPanel.setLayout( new BorderLayout() );
43          fieldPanel.add( fieldPanel1, BorderLayout.NORTH );
44          fieldPanel.add( fieldPanel2, BorderLayout.SOUTH );
45
46          // build button panel
47          ok = new JButton( "Ok" );
48          cancel = new JButton( "Cancel" );
49          help = new JButton( "Help" );
50          buttonPanel = new JPanel();
51          buttonPanel.setLayout( new GridLayout( 3, 1, 10, 5 ) );
52          buttonPanel.add( ok );
53          buttonPanel.add( cancel );
54          buttonPanel.add( help );
55
56          // set layout for applet
57          getContentPane().setLayout(
58              new FlowLayout( FlowLayout.CENTER, 10, 5 ) );
59          getContentPane().add( checkPanel );
60          getContentPane().add( fieldPanel );
61          getContentPane().add( buttonPanel );
62      }
63  }
```

Fig. S29.1   Solution for Exercise 29.8: Align.java.   (Part 2 of 2.)

29.9   Create the following GUI. You do not have to provide any functionality.

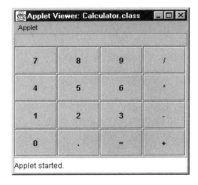

ANS:

```
1   // Solution exercise 29.9
2   // Calculator.java
3   // This program creates a simple GUI
4   // html: width = 270 height = 200
5   import javax.swing.*;
6   import java.awt.*;
7
```

Fig. S29.2   Solution for Exercise 29.9: Calculator.java.   (Part 1 of 2.)

```
 8  public class Calculator extends JApplet {
 9     private JButton keys[];
10     private JPanel keyPad;
11     private JTextField lcd;
12
13     public void init()
14     {
15        lcd     = new JTextField( 20 );
16        keyPad = new JPanel();
17        keys    = new JButton[ 16 ];
18
19        lcd.setEditable( false );
20
21        for ( int i = 0; i <= 9; i++ )
22           keys[ i ] = new JButton( String.valueOf( i ) );
23
24        keys[ 10 ] = new JButton( "/" );
25        keys[ 11 ] = new JButton( "*" );
26        keys[ 12 ] = new JButton( "-" );
27        keys[ 13 ] = new JButton( "+" );
28        keys[ 14 ] = new JButton( "=" );
29        keys[ 15 ] = new JButton( "." );
30
31        // set keyPad layout to grid layout
32        keyPad.setLayout( new GridLayout( 4, 4 ) );
33
34        for ( int i = 7; i <= 10; i++ ) // 7, 8, 9, 10
35           keyPad.add( keys[ i ] );       // divide
36
37        for ( int i = 4; i <= 6; i++ )  // 4, 5, 6
38           keyPad.add( keys[ i ] );
39
40        keyPad.add( keys[ 11 ] );          // multiply
41
42        for ( int i = 1; i <= 3; i++ )  // 1, 2, 3
43           keyPad.add( keys[ i ] );
44
45        keyPad.add( keys[ 12 ] );          // subtract
46
47        keyPad.add( keys[ 0 ] );           // 0
48
49        for ( int i = 15; i >= 13; i-- )
50           keyPad.add( keys[ i ] );        // ., =, add
51
52        // set applet layout to border layout
53        getContentPane().setLayout( new BorderLayout() );
54        getContentPane().add( lcd, BorderLayout.NORTH );
55        getContentPane().add( keyPad, BorderLayout.CENTER );
56     }
57  }
```

Fig. S29.2 Solution for Exercise 29.9: Calculator.java. (Part 2 of 2.)

29.10   Create the following GUI. You do not have to provide any functionality.

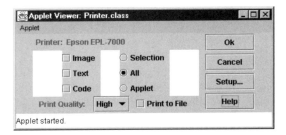

ANS:

```
1   // Exercise 29.10 Solution
2   // Printer.java
3   // This program creates a simple GUI
4   // html: width = 400 height = 130
5   import javax.swing.*;
6   import java.awt.*;
7
8   public class Printer extends JApplet {
9      private JButton b1, b2, b3, b4;
10     private JCheckBox c1, c2, c3, c4;
11     private JRadioButton rb1, rb2, rb3;
12     private ButtonGroup radioGroup;
13     private JComboBox q;
14     private JLabel label1, label2;
15     private JPanel p1, p2, p3, p4, p5, p6, p7, p8;
16
17     public void init()
18     {
19        // build left north panel
20        label1 = new JLabel( "Printer:  Epson EPL-7000" );
21        p1 = new JPanel();
22        p1.setLayout( new FlowLayout( FlowLayout.LEFT ) );
23        p1.add( label1 );
24
25        // build right east panel
26        b1 = new JButton( "Ok" );
27        b2 = new JButton( "Cancel" );
28        b3 = new JButton( "Setup..." );
29        b4 = new JButton( "Help" );
30        p2 = new JPanel();
31        p2.setLayout( new GridLayout( 4, 1, 5, 5 ) );
32        p2.add( b1 );
33        p2.add( b2 );
34        p2.add( b3 );
35        p2.add( b4 );
36
```

Fig. S29.3   Solution for Exercise 29.10: Printer.java.   (Part 1 of 3.)

```
37          // build left south panel
38          label2 = new JLabel( "Print Quality: " );
39          q = new JComboBox();
40          q.addItem( "High" );
41          c1 = new JCheckBox( "Print to File" );
42          p3 = new JPanel();
43          p3.setLayout( new FlowLayout( FlowLayout.CENTER, 10, 0 ) );
44          p3.add( label2 );
45          p3.add( q );
46          p3.add( c1 );
47
48          // build left east panel
49          c2 = new JCheckBox( "Image" );
50          c3 = new JCheckBox( "Text" );
51          c4 = new JCheckBox( "Code" );
52          p4 = new JPanel();
53          p4.setLayout( new BorderLayout( ) );
54          p4.add( c2, BorderLayout.NORTH );
55          p4.add( c3, BorderLayout.CENTER );
56          p4.add( c4, BorderLayout.SOUTH );
57
58          // build left west panel
59          p5 = new JPanel();
60          p5.setLayout( new BorderLayout() );
61          p5.add( rb1 = new JRadioButton( "Selection", false ),
62                  BorderLayout.NORTH );
63          p5.add( rb2 = new JRadioButton( "All", true ),
64                  BorderLayout.CENTER );
65          p5.add( rb3 = new JRadioButton( "Applet", false ),
66                  BorderLayout.SOUTH );
67          // Group the radio buttons
68          radioGroup=new ButtonGroup();
69          radioGroup.add( rb1 );
70          radioGroup.add( rb2 );
71          radioGroup.add( rb3 );
72
73          // build left center
74          p8 = new JPanel();
75          p8.setLayout( new FlowLayout( FlowLayout.CENTER, 30, 0 ) );
76          p8.setBackground( Color.white );
77          p8.add( p4 );
78          p8.add( p5 );
79
80          // setup left panel
81          p6 = new JPanel();
82          p6.setLayout( new BorderLayout() );
83          p6.add( p1, BorderLayout.NORTH );
84          p6.add( p8, BorderLayout.CENTER );
85          p6.add( p3, BorderLayout.SOUTH );
86
```

Fig. S29.3   Solution for Exercise 29.10: Printer.java.   (Part 2 of 3.)

```
87              // setup applet layout
88              p7 = new JPanel();
89              p7.setLayout( new FlowLayout( FlowLayout.CENTER, 10, 0 ) );
90              p7.add( p6 );
91              p7.add( p2 );
92
93              getContentPane().add( p7 );
94          }
95      }
```

Fig. S29.3   Solution for Exercise 29.10: Printer.java.   (Part 3 of 3.)

29.12   Write an application that allows the user to draw a rectangle by dragging the mouse on the application window. The upper-left coordinate should be the location where the user presses the mouse button, and the lower-right coordinate should be the location where the user releases the mouse button. Also display the area of the rectangle in a JLabel in the SOUTH region of a BorderLayout. All drawing should be done on a subclass of JPanel. Use the following formula for the area:

    area = width ∞ height

    ANS:

```
1    // Exercise 29.12 Solution
2    // Draw.java
3    // Program draws a rectangle with the mouse
4    import javax.swing.*;
5    import java.awt.*;
6    import java.awt.event.*;
7
8    public class Draw extends JFrame {
9        private int topX, topY;
10       private int width, height;
11       private int bottomX, bottomY;
12       protected JLabel status;
13
14       public Draw()
15       {
16           super( "Draw" );
17           topX = topY = 0;
18           addMouseListener( new MouseHandler( this ) );
19
20           status = new JLabel();
21           getContentPane().add( status, BorderLayout.SOUTH );
22           setSize( 300, 150 );
23           show();
24       }
25
26       public int getTopX() { return topX; }
27       public int getTopY() { return topY; }
28       public int getWidth() { return width; }
```

Fig. S29.4   Solution for Exercise 29.12: Draw.java.   (Part 1 of 3.)

```
29     public int getHeight() { return height; }
30     public int getBottomX() { return bottomX; }
31     public int getBottomY() { return bottomY; }
32     public void setTopX( int x ) { topX = x; }
33     public void setTopY( int y ) { topY = y; }
34     public void setBottomX( int x ) { bottomX = x; }
35     public void setBottomY( int y ) { bottomY = y; }
36     public void setWidth( int w ) { width = w; }
37     public void setHeight( int h ) { height = h; }
38
39     public void paint( Graphics g )
40     {
41        super.paint( g );
42
43        g.drawRect( topX, topY, width, height );
44     }
45
46     public static void main( String args[] )
47     {
48        Draw app = new Draw();
49
50        app.addWindowListener(
51           new WindowAdapter() {
52              public void windowClosing( WindowEvent e )
53              {
54                 System.exit( 0 );
55              }
56           }
57        );
58     }
59  }
60
61  class MouseHandler extends MouseAdapter {
62     private Draw draw;
63
64     public MouseHandler( Draw d ) { draw = d; }
65
66     public void mouseReleased( MouseEvent e )
67     {
68        draw.setBottomX( e.getX() );
69        draw.setBottomY( e.getY() );
70        draw.setWidth( Math.abs( draw.getTopX() - draw.getBottomX() ) );
71        draw.setHeight( Math.abs( draw.getTopY() - draw.getBottomY() ) );
72        draw.setTopX( Math.min( draw.getTopX(), draw.getBottomX() ) );
73        draw.setTopY( Math.min( draw.getTopY(), draw.getBottomY() ) );
74        draw.status.setText( "Area is " + ( draw.getWidth() * draw.getHeight() ) );
75        draw.repaint();
76     }
77
78     public void mousePressed( MouseEvent e )
```

Fig. S29.4   Solution for Exercise 29.12: Draw.java.   (Part 2 of 3.)

```
79      {
80          draw.setTopX( e.getX() );
81          draw.setTopY( e.getY() );
82      }
83  }
```

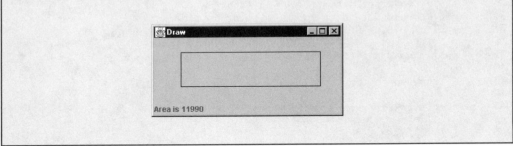

Fig. S29.4   Solution for Exercise 29.12: Draw.java.   (Part 3 of 3.)

29.13 Write a program that displays a circle of random size and calculates and displays the area, radius, diameter and circumference. Use the following equations: *diameter = 2 ∞ radius, area = π ∞ radius²*, *circumference = 2 ∞ π ∞ radius*. Use the constant Math.PI for pi (π). All drawing should be done on a subclass of JPanel and the results of the calculations should be displayed in a read-only JTextArea.

   ANS:

```
1   // Exercise 29.13 Solution
2   // Circle1.java
3   // Program draws a circle of a random
4   // diameter and displays the area, diameter,
5   // and circumference.
6   import javax.swing.*;
7   import java.awt.*;
8   import java.awt.event.*;
9
10  public class Circle1 extends JFrame {
11      private CircleCanvas theCanvas;
12      private JTextArea display;
13
14      public Circle1()
15      {
16          super( "Circle1" );
17          theCanvas = new CircleCanvas();
18          display = new JTextArea( 5, 30 );
19
20          display.setText( "The Radius is: " + theCanvas.getRadius() +
21                          "\nThe Diameter is: " + theCanvas.getDiameter()
22                          + "\nThe Area is: " + theCanvas.getArea() +
23                          "\nThe Circumference is: " +
24                          theCanvas.getCircumference() );
```

Fig. S29.5   Solution for Exercise 29.13: Circle1.java.   (Part 1 of 3.)

```
25
26              getContentPane().add( theCanvas, BorderLayout.CENTER );
27              getContentPane().add( display, BorderLayout.SOUTH );
28              setSize( 200, 200 );
29              show();
30          }
31
32      public static void main( String args[] )
33      {
34          Circle1 app = new Circle1();
35
36          app.addWindowListener(
37             new WindowAdapter() {
38                public void windowClosing( WindowEvent e )
39                {
40                   System.exit( 0 );
41                }
42             }
43          );
44      }
45   }
46
47   class CircleCanvas extends JPanel {
48      private int radius;
49
50      public CircleCanvas()
51      {
52          radius = ( int )( 1 + Math.random() * 100 );
53          setSize( 100, 100 );
54      }
55
56      public void paintComponent( Graphics g )
57      {  g.drawOval( 0, 0, radius, radius );  }
58
59      public int getDiameter()  {  return ( 2 * radius );  }
60
61      public int getCircumference()
62      {  return ( int )( 2 * Math.PI * radius );  }
63
64      public int getArea()
65      {  return ( int )( radius * radius * Math.PI );  }
66
67      public int getRadius()  {  return radius;  }
68   }
```

Fig. S29.5   Solution for Exercise 29.13: Circle1.java.   (Part 2 of 3.)

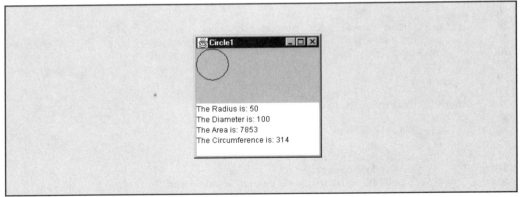

Fig. S29.5   Solution for Exercise 29.13: Circle1.java. (Part 3 of 3.)

29.15 Write a program using methods from interface MouseListener that allows the user to press the mouse button, drag the mouse and release the mouse button. When the mouse is released, draw a rectangle with the appropriate upper-left corner, width and height. (*Hint*: The mousePressed method should capture the set of coordinates at which the user presses and holds the mouse button initially, and the mouseReleased method should capture the set of coordinates at which the user releases the mouse button. Both methods should store the appropriate coordinate values. All drawing should be done on a subclass of JPanel and all calculations of the width, height and upper-left corner should be performed by the paintComponent method before the shape is drawn).

  ANS:

```
1    // Exercise 29.15 Solution
2    // Draw.java
3    // Program draws a rectangle with the mouse
4    import javax.swing.*;
5    import java.awt.*;
6    import java.awt.event.*;
7
8    public class Draw extends JFrame {
9       private int topX, topY;
10      private int width, height, upperX, upperY;
11      private int bottomX, bottomY;
12
13      public Draw()
14      {
15         super( "Draw" );
16         addMouseListener( new MouseHandler() );
17         setSize( 300, 200 );
18         show();
19      }
20
21      public void setTopX( int x ) { topX = x; }
22      public void setTopY( int y ) { topY = y; }
```

Fig. S29.6   Solution for Exercise 29.15: Draw.java. (Part 1 of 3.)

```
23      public void setBottomX( int x ) { bottomX = x; }
24      public void setBottomY( int y ) { bottomY = y; }
25
26      public void paint( Graphics g )
27      {
28         super.paint( g );
29
30         width = Math.abs( topX - bottomX );
31         height = Math.abs( topY - bottomY );
32         upperX = Math.min( topX, bottomX );
33         upperY = Math.min( topY, bottomY );
34
35         g.drawRect( upperX, upperY, width, height );
36      }
37
38      public static void main( String args[] )
39      {
40         Draw app = new Draw();
41
42         app.addWindowListener(
43            new WindowAdapter() {
44               public void windowClosing( WindowEvent e )
45               {
46                  System.exit( 0 );
47               }
48            }
49         );
50      }
51
52      private class MouseHandler extends MouseAdapter {
53         public void mouseReleased( MouseEvent e )
54         {
55            setBottomX( e.getX() );
56            setBottomY( e.getY() );
57            repaint();
58         }
59
60         public void mousePressed( MouseEvent e )
61         {
62            setTopX( e.getX() );
63            setTopY( e.getY() );
64         }
65      }
66   }
```

Fig. S29.6   Solution for Exercise 29.15: Draw.java.   (Part 2 of 3.)

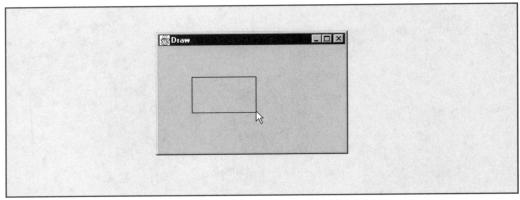

Fig. S29.6   Solution for Exercise 29.15: Draw.java.   (Part 3 of 3.)

29.16   Modify Exercise 29.15 to provided a "rubber-banding" effect. As the user drags the mouse, the user should be able to see the current size of the rectangle to know exactly what the rectangle will look like when the mouse button is released. (*Hint*: Method `mouseDragged` should perform the same tasks as `mouseReleased`).

    ANS:

```
1    // Exercise 29.16 Solution
2    // Draw3.java
3    // Program draws a rectangle with the mouse
4    import javax.swing.*;
5    import java.awt.*;
6    import java.awt.event.*;
7
8    public class Draw3 extends JFrame {
9       private int topX, topY;
10      private int width, height, upperX, upperY;
11      private int bottomX, bottomY;
12
13      public Draw3()
14      {
15         super( "Draw3" );
16         addMouseListener( new MouseHandler() );
17         addMouseMotionListener( new MouseMotionHandler() );
18         setSize( 300, 200 );
19         show();
20      }
21
22      public void setTopX( int x ) { topX = x; }
23      public void setTopY( int y ) { topY = y; }
24      public void setBottomX( int x ) { bottomX = x; }
25      public void setBottomY( int y ) { bottomY = y; }
26
27      public void paint( Graphics g )
```

Fig. S29.7   Solution for Exercise 29.16: Draw3.java.   (Part 1 of 3.)

```
28        {
29            super.paint( g );
30
31            width = Math.abs( topX - bottomX );
32            height = Math.abs( topY - bottomY );
33            upperX = Math.min( topX, bottomX );
34            upperY = Math.min( topY, bottomY );
35
36            g.drawRect( upperX, upperY, width, height );
37        }
38
39        public static void main( String args[] )
40        {
41            Draw3 app = new Draw3();
42
43            app.addWindowListener(
44                new WindowAdapter() {
45                    public void windowClosing( WindowEvent e )
46                    {
47                        System.exit( 0 );
48                    }
49                }
50            );
51        }
52
53        private class MouseHandler extends MouseAdapter {
54            public void mouseReleased( MouseEvent e )
55            {
56                setBottomX( e.getX() );
57                setBottomY( e.getY() );
58                repaint();
59            }
60
61            public void mousePressed( MouseEvent e )
62            {
63                setTopX( e.getX() );
64                setTopY( e.getY() );
65            }
66        }
67
68        private class MouseMotionHandler extends MouseMotionAdapter {
69            public void mouseDragged( MouseEvent e )
70            {
71                setBottomX( e.getX() );
72                setBottomY( e.getY() );
73                repaint();
74            }
75        }
76    }
```

Fig. S29.7   Solution for Exercise 29.16: Draw3.java.   (Part 2 of 3.)

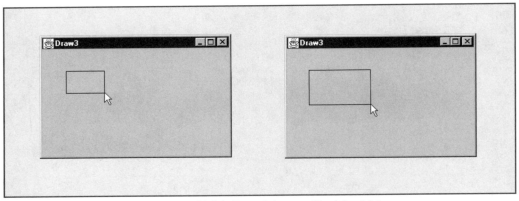

Fig. S29.7   Solution for Exercise 29.16: Draw3.java.   (Part 3 of 3.)

Java Multimedia:
Images, Animation, and Audio

Solutions to Selected Exercises

30.5 Explain the technique of graphics double buffering.

> **ANS:** *Method* createImage *is used to create an empty image. The graphics context of the empty image is retrieved with a call to* getGraphics. *The empty image can then be used to store pixels drawn on the image with the* Graphics *object that was obtained via* getGraphics. *When the image is complete, it can be displayed using method* drawImage. *Swing components such as* JPanel *have built-in double buffering.*

30.6 Describe the Java methods for playing and manipulating audio clips.

> **ANS:** *The applet* play *method. The* AudioClip *interface methods:* play, loop *and* stop.

30.9 *(Randomly Erasing an Image)* Suppose an image is displayed in a rectangular screen area. One way to erase the image is simply to set every pixel to the same color immediately, but this is a dull visual effect. Write a Java program that displays an image then erases it by using random-number generation to select individual pixels to erase. After most of the image is erased, erase all of the remaining pixels at once. You can refer to individual pixels by having a line that starts and ends at the same point. You might try several variants of this problem. For example, you might display lines randomly or you might display shapes randomly to erase regions of the screen.

> **ANS:**

```
1   // Exercise 30.9 Solution
2   // Eraser.java
3   // Program randomly covers up an image.
4   import javax.swing.*;
5   import java.awt.*;
6   import java.awt.event.*;
7
8   public class Eraser extends JApplet implements ActionListener {
9       private ImageIcon image;
10      private int imageWidth, imageHeight, count;
11      private int numberOfTimes;
12      private boolean showImage = true;
```

Fig. S30.1   Solution for Exercise 30.9: Eraser.java.   (Part 1 of 2.)

```
13      private Timer t;
14
15      public void init()
16      {
17         image = new ImageIcon( "icons2.gif" );
18         t = new Timer( 10, this );
19         t.start();
20
21         imageWidth = image.getIconWidth();
22         imageHeight = image.getIconHeight();
23         numberOfTimes = imageWidth * imageHeight / 8;
24      }
25
26      public void paint( Graphics g )
27      {
28         if ( showImage == true ) {
29            image.paintIcon( this, getGraphics(), 0, 0 );
30            showImage = false;
31         }
32
33         g.setColor( getBackground() );
34         g.fillRect( ( int ) ( Math.random() * imageWidth ),
35                     ( int ) ( Math.random() * imageHeight ), 4, 4 );
36      }
37
38      public void actionPerformed( ActionEvent e )
39      {
40         repaint();
41
42         if ( count == numberOfTimes ) {
43            showImage = true;
44            count = 0;
45         }
46
47         ++count;
48      }
49   }
```

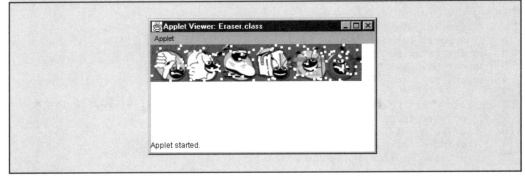

Fig. S30.1   Solution for Exercise 30.9: Eraser.java.   (Part 2 of 2.)

30.11 *(Image Flasher)* Create a Java program that repeatedly flashes an image on the screen. Do this by interspersing the image with a plain background color image.

ANS:

```
1   // Exercise 30.11 Solution
2   // Flash2.java
3   // Program flashes text.
4   import javax.swing.*;
5   import java.awt.*;
6   import java.awt.event.*;
7
8   public class Flash2 extends JApplet
9           implements ActionListener, ItemListener {
10     private MyCanvas theCanvas;
11     private JComboBox colorSelect;
12     private JLabel prompt;
13     private JTextField input;
14
15     public void init()
16     {
17        prompt = new JLabel( "Enter rate ( 50 - 1000 ):" );
18        input = new JTextField( 5 );
19        input.addActionListener( this );
20        theCanvas = new MyCanvas();
21        String items[] = { "Black", "Red", "Blue", "Green" };
22        colorSelect = new JComboBox( items );
23        colorSelect.addItemListener( this );
24        Container c = getContentPane();
25        c.setLayout( new FlowLayout() );
26        c.add( theCanvas );
27        c.add( colorSelect );
28        c.add( prompt );
29        c.add( input );
30     }
31
32     public void itemStateChanged( ItemEvent e )
33     {
34        Color c;
35
36        if ( e.getItem().equals( "Black" ) )
37           c = Color.black;
38        else if ( e.getItem().equals( "Red" ) )
39           c = Color.red;
40        else if ( e.getItem().equals( "Blue" ) )
41           c = Color.blue;
42        else
43           c = Color.green;
44
45        theCanvas.setBackground( c );
46     }
```

Fig. S30.2   Solution for Exercise 30.11: Flash2.java.   (Part 1 of 3.)

```
47
48      public void actionPerformed( ActionEvent e )
49      {
50         theCanvas.setSleepTime( Integer.parseInt( input.getText() ) );
51         showStatus( "current blink rate: " + theCanvas.getSleepTime() );
52      }
53   }
54
55   class MyCanvas extends JPanel implements ActionListener {
56      private ImageIcon image;
57      private Timer t;
58      boolean flash = true;
59
60      public MyCanvas()
61      {
62         setBackground( Color.black );
63         image = new ImageIcon( "icons2.gif" );
64         t = new Timer( 500, this );
65         t.start();
66      }
67
68      public synchronized void paintComponent( Graphics g )
69      {
70         super.paintComponent( g );
71
72         if ( flash )
73            g.drawImage( image.getImage(), 0, 0, this );
74      }
75
76      public synchronized void actionPerformed( ActionEvent e )
77      {
78         flash = !flash;
79         repaint();
80      }
81
82      public void setSleepTime( int time )
83         { t.setDelay( time >= 50 && time <= 1000 ? time : 500 ); }
84
85      public int getSleepTime() { return t.getDelay(); }
86
87      public Dimension getPreferredSize()
88      {
89         return new Dimension( image.getIconWidth(),
90                               image.getIconHeight() );
91      }
92   }
```

Fig. S30.2   Solution for Exercise 30.11: Flash2.java.   (Part 2 of 3.)

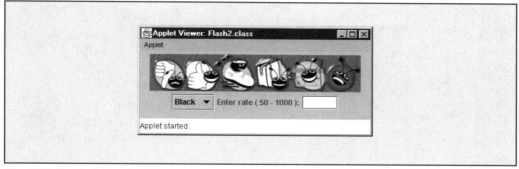

Fig. S30.2   Solution for Exercise 30.11: Flash2.java.   (Part 3 of 3.)

30.12 *(Digital Clock)* Implement a program that displays a digital clock on the screen. You might add options to scale the clock; display day, month and year; issue an alarm; play certain audios at designated times and the like.

ANS:

```
1   // Exercise 30.12 Solution
2   // DigitalClock.java
3   // Program creates a digital clock.
4   import javax.swing.*;
5   import java.awt.*;
6   import java.awt.event.*;
7   import java.util.*;
8
9   public class DigitalClock extends JApplet
10                          implements ActionListener {
11      private String theTime;
12      private Timer t;
13
14      public void init()
15      {
16         theTime = "";
17         t = new Timer( 1000, this );
18      }
19
20      public void paint( Graphics g )
21      {
22         super.paint( g );  // clears the background
23
24         g.drawString( theTime, 20, 50 );
25      }
26
27      public void start()
28      {
29         t.start();
30      }
```

Fig. S30.3   Solution for Exercise 30.12: DigitalClock.java.   (Part 1 of 2.)

```
31
32      public void stop()
33      {
34         t.stop();
35      }
36
37      public void actionPerformed( ActionEvent e )
38      {
39         theTime = new Date().toString();
40         repaint();
41      }
42   }
```

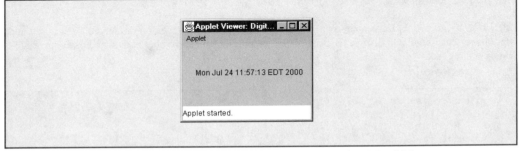

Fig. S30.3   Solution for Exercise 30.12: DigitalClock.java.   (Part 2 of 2.)

30.13 (*Calling attention to an image*) If you want to emphasize an image, you might place a row of simulated light bulbs around your image. You can let the light bulbs flash in unison or you can let them fire on and off in sequence one after the other.

ANS:

```
1    // Exercise 30.13 Solution
2    // Flash3.java
3    // Program highlights an image.
4    import javax.swing.*;
5    import java.awt.*;
6    import java.awt.event.*;
7
8    public class Flash3 extends JApplet {
9       private MyCanvas theCanvas;
10
11      public void init()
12      {
13         ImageIcon image1 = new ImageIcon( "icons2.gif" );
14
15         int width = image1.getIconWidth() + 20;
16         int height = image1.getIconHeight() + 20;
17         Image image2 = createImage( width, height );
18         Image image3 = createImage( width, height );
```

Fig. S30.4   Solution for Exercise 30.13: Flash3.java.   (Part 1 of 3.)

```
19
20          theCanvas = new MyCanvas( image1.getImage(), image2, image3,
21                           width, height );
22          getContentPane().add( theCanvas, BorderLayout.CENTER );
23       }
24    }
25
26    class MyCanvas extends JPanel implements ActionListener {
27       private Image img, img2, img3;
28       private Graphics graph2, graph3;
29       private boolean flashSwitch;
30       private Timer t;
31
32       public MyCanvas( Image i, Image i2, Image i3, int w, int h )
33       {
34          t = new Timer( 300, this );
35          t.start();
36          flashSwitch = true;
37          setSize( w, h );
38          img = i;
39          img2 = i2;
40          img3 = i3;
41          createBuffers( w, h );
42       }
43
44       public void createBuffers( int w, int h )
45       {
46          graph2 = img2.getGraphics();
47          graph3 = img3.getGraphics();
48
49          graph2.setColor( Color.black );
50          graph2.fillRect( 0, 0, w, h );
51          graph3.setColor( Color.black );
52          graph3.fillRect( 0, 0, w, h );
53
54          int count = 0;
55
56          for ( int x = 0; x < w; x += 10 ) {
57             for ( int y = 0; y < h; y += 10 ) {
58
59                // Change ++count to y to get the effect of
60                // all the lights "turning off" then "turning on"
61                // Also the line below that alternates the lights
62                // should be commented out or removed.
63                if ( ++count % 2 == 0 ) {
64                   graph2.setColor( Color.yellow );
65                   graph3.setColor( Color.white );
66                }
67                else {
68                   graph2.setColor( Color.white );
```

Fig. S30.4   Solution for Exercise 30.13: Flash3.java.   (Part 2 of 3.)

```
69                    graph3.setColor( Color.yellow );
70                }
71
72                graph2.fillOval( x, y, 10, 10 );
73                graph3.fillOval( x, y, 10, 10 );
74            }
75
76            // Allow the lights to alternate
77            count = ( count % 2 == 0 ? 1 : 0 );
78        }
79
80        graph2.drawImage( img, 10, 10, this );
81        graph3.drawImage( img, 10, 10, this );
82    }
83
84    public void paintComponent( Graphics g )
85    {
86        super.paintComponent( g );
87
88        if ( flashSwitch )
89            g.drawImage( img2, 0, 0, this );
90        else
91            g.drawImage( img3, 0, 0, this );
92    }
93
94    public void actionPerformed( ActionEvent e )
95    {
96        flashSwitch = !flashSwitch;
97        repaint();
98    }
99 }
```

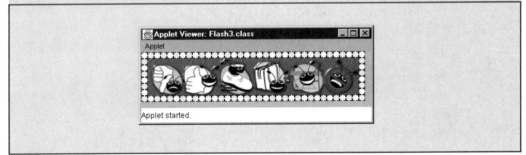

Fig. S30.4   Solution for Exercise 30.13: Flash3.java.   (Part 3 of 3.)

30.14 *Image Zooming)* Create a program that enables you to zoom in on, or away from, an image.

ANS:

```
1   // Exercise 30.14 Solution
2   // Zoom.java
3   // Program zooms an image.
4   import javax.swing.*;
5   import java.awt.*;
6   import java.awt.event.*;
7
8   public class Zoom extends JApplet
9          implements ItemListener {
10     private MyCanvas theCanvas;
11     private JPanel p;
12     private JComboBox select;
13     private int width, height;
14
15     public void init()
16     {
17        ImageIcon image1 = new ImageIcon( "icons2.gif" );
18
19        p = new JPanel();
20        String items[] = { "50%", "100%", "200%", "300%" };
21        select = new JComboBox( items );
22        select.addItemListener( this );
23        p.add( select );
24
25        width = image1.getIconWidth() / 2;
26        height = image1.getIconHeight() / 2;
27
28        theCanvas = new MyCanvas( image1.getImage(), width, height );
29        Container c = getContentPane();
30        c.add( theCanvas, BorderLayout.CENTER );
31        c.add( p, BorderLayout.SOUTH );
32     }
33
34     public void itemStateChanged( ItemEvent e )
35     {
36        if ( e.getItem().equals( "50%" ) )
37           theCanvas.setWidthHeight( ( int ) ( width * .5 ),
38              ( int ) ( height * .5 ) );
39        else if ( e.getItem().equals( "100%" ) )
40           theCanvas.setWidthHeight( width, height );
41        else if ( e.getItem().equals( "200%" ) )
42           theCanvas.setWidthHeight( width * 2, height * 2 );
43        else  // 300%
44           theCanvas.setWidthHeight( width * 3, height * 3 );
45     }
46   }
47
48   class MyCanvas extends JPanel {
49     private Image img;
```

Fig. S30.5   Solution for Exercise 30.14: Zoom.java.   (Part 1 of 2.)

```
50        private int imgWidth, imgHeight;
51
52        public MyCanvas( Image i, int w, int h )
53        {
54            setBackground( Color.green );
55            setSize( w, h );
56            img = i;
57            setWidthHeight( w, h );
58        }
59
60        public void setWidthHeight( int w, int h )
61        {
62            imgWidth = w;
63            imgHeight = h;
64            repaint();
65        }
66
67        public void paintComponent( Graphics g )
68        {
69            super.paintComponent( g );
70            g.drawImage( img, 0, 0, imgWidth, imgHeight, this );
71        }
72    }
```

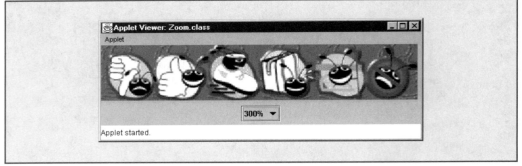

Fig. S30.5   Solution for Exercise 30.14: Zoom.java.   (Part 2 of 2.)

End User License Agreements

Prentice Hall License Agreement and Limited Warranty

READ THE FOLLOWING TERMS AND CONDITIONS CAREFULLY BEFORE OPEN-ING THIS SOFTWARE PACKAGE. THIS LEGAL DOCUMENT IS AN AGREEMENT BE-TWEEN YOU AND PRENTICE-HALL, INC. (THE "COMPANY"). BY OPENING THIS SEALED SOFTWARE PACKAGE, YOU ARE AGREEING TO BE BOUND BY THESE TERMS AND CONDITIONS. IF YOU DO NOT AGREE WITH THESE TERMS AND CON-DITIONS, DO NOT OPEN THE SOFTWARE PACKAGE. PROMPTLY RETURN THE UN-OPENED SOFTWARE PACKAGE AND ALL ACCOMPANYING ITEMS TO THE PLACE YOU OBTAINED THEM FOR A FULL REFUND OF ANY SUMS YOU HAVE PAID.

1.   GRANT OF LICENSE: In consideration of your purchase of this book, and your agreement to abide by the terms and conditions of this Agreement, the Company grants to you a nonexclusive right to use and display the copy of the enclosed software program (hereinafter the "SOFTWARE") on a single computer (i.e., with a single CPU) at a single location so long as you comply with the terms of this Agreement. The Company reserves all rights not expressly granted to you under this Agreement.

2.   OWNERSHIP OF SOFTWARE: You own only the magnetic or physical media (the enclosed media) on which the SOFTWARE is recorded or fixed, but the Company and the software developers retain all the rights, title, and ownership to the SOFTWARE recorded on the original media copy(ies) and all subsequent copies of the SOFTWARE, regardless of the form or media on which the original or other copies may exist. This license is not a sale of the original SOFTWARE or any copy to you.

3.   COPY RESTRICTIONS: This SOFTWARE and the accompanying printed materials and user manual (the "Documentation") are the subject of copyright. The individual programs on the media are copyrighted by the authors of each program. Some of the programs on the media include separate licensing agreements. If you intend to use one of these programs, you must read and follow its accompanying license agreement. You may not copy the Documentation or the SOFTWARE, except that you may make a single copy of the SOFTWARE for backup or archival purposes only. You may be held legally responsible for any copying or copyright infringement which is caused or encouraged by your failure to abide by the terms of this restriction.

4.   USE RESTRICTIONS: You may not network the SOFTWARE or otherwise use it on more than one computer or computer terminal at the same time. You may physically transfer the SOFTWARE from one computer to another provided that the SOFTWARE is used on only one computer at a time. You may not distribute copies of the SOFTWARE or Documentation to others. You may not reverse engineer, disassemble, decompile, modify, adapt, translate, or create derivative works based on the SOFTWARE or the Documentation without the prior written consent of the Company.

5.   TRANSFER RESTRICTIONS: The enclosed SOFTWARE is licensed only to you and may not be transferred to any one else without the prior written consent of the Company. Any unauthorized transfer of the SOFTWARE shall result in the immediate termination of this Agreement.

6.   TERMINATION: This license is effective until terminated. This license will terminate automatically without notice from the Company and become null and void if you fail to comply with any provisions or limitations of this license. Upon termination, you shall destroy the Documentation and all copies of the SOFTWARE. All provisions of this Agreement as to warranties, limitation of liability, remedies or damages, and our ownership rights shall survive termination.

7.   MISCELLANEOUS: This Agreement shall be construed in accordance with the laws of the United States of America and the State of New York and shall benefit the Company, its affiliates, and assignees.

8.   LIMITED WARRANTY AND DISCLAIMER OF WARRANTY: The Company warrants that the SOFTWARE, when properly used in accordance with the Documentation, will operate in substantial conformity with the description of the SOFTWARE set forth in the Documentation. The Company does not warrant that the SOFTWARE will meet your requirements or that the operation of the SOFTWARE will be uninterrupted or error-free. The Company warrants that the media on which the SOFTWARE is delivered shall be free from defects in materials and workmanship under normal use for a period of thirty (30) days from the date of your purchase. Your only remedy and the Company's only obligation under these limited warranties is, at the Company's option, return of the warranted item for a refund of any amounts paid by you or replacement of the item. Any replacement of SOFTWARE or media under the warranties shall not extend the original warranty period. The limited warranty set forth above shall not apply to any SOFTWARE which the Company determines in good faith has been subject to misuse, neglect, improper installation, repair, alteration, or damage by you. EXCEPT FOR THE EXPRESSED WARRANTIES SET FORTH ABOVE, THE COMPANY DISCLAIMS ALL WARRANTIES, EXPRESS OR IMPLIED, INCLUDING WITHOUT LIMITATION, THE IMPLIED WARRANTIES OF MERCHANTABILITY AND FITNESS FOR A PARTICULAR PURPOSE. EXCEPT FOR THE EXPRESS WARRANTY SET FORTH ABOVE, THE COMPANY DOES NOT WARRANT, GUARANTEE, OR MAKE ANY REPRESENTATION REGARDING THE USE OR THE RESULTS OF THE USE OF THE SOFTWARE IN TERMS OF ITS CORRECTNESS, ACCURACY, RELIABILITY, CURRENTNESS, OR OTHERWISE.

        IN NO EVENT, SHALL THE COMPANY OR ITS EMPLOYEES, AGENTS, SUPPLIERS, OR CONTRACTORS BE LIABLE FOR ANY INCIDENTAL, INDIRECT, SPECIAL, OR CONSEQUENTIAL DAMAGES ARISING OUT OF OR IN CONNECTION

WITH THE LICENSE GRANTED UNDER THIS AGREEMENT, OR FOR LOSS OF USE, LOSS OF DATA, LOSS OF INCOME OR PROFIT, OR OTHER LOSSES, SUSTAINED AS A RESULT OF INJURY TO ANY PERSON, OR LOSS OF OR DAMAGE TO PROPERTY, OR CLAIMS OF THIRD PARTIES, EVEN IF THE COMPANY OR AN AUTHORIZED REPRESENTATIVE OF THE COMPANY HAS BEEN ADVISED OF THE POSSIBILITY OF SUCH DAMAGES. IN NO EVENT SHALL LIABILITY OF THE COMPANY FOR DAMAGES WITH RESPECT TO THE SOFTWARE EXCEED THE AMOUNTS ACTUALLY PAID BY YOU, IF ANY, FOR THE SOFTWARE.

SOME JURISDICTIONS DO NOT ALLOW THE LIMITATION OF IMPLIED WARRANTIES OR LIABILITY FOR INCIDENTAL, INDIRECT, SPECIAL, OR CONSEQUENTIAL DAMAGES, SO THE ABOVE LIMITATIONS MAY NOT ALWAYS APPLY. THE WARRANTIES IN THIS AGREEMENT GIVE YOU SPECIFIC LEGAL RIGHTS AND YOU MAY ALSO HAVE OTHER RIGHTS WHICH VARY IN ACCORDANCE WITH LOCAL LAW.

ACKNOWLEDGMENT

YOU ACKNOWLEDGE THAT YOU HAVE READ THIS AGREEMENT, UNDERSTAND IT, AND AGREE TO BE BOUND BY ITS TERMS AND CONDITIONS. YOU ALSO AGREE THAT THIS AGREEMENT IS THE COMPLETE AND EXCLUSIVE STATEMENT OF THE AGREEMENT BETWEEN YOU AND THE COMPANY AND SUPERSEDES ALL PROPOSALS OR PRIOR AGREEMENTS, ORAL, OR WRITTEN, AND ANY OTHER COMMUNICATIONS BETWEEN YOU AND THE COMPANY OR ANY REPRESENTATIVE OF THE COMPANY RELATING TO THE SUBJECT MATTER OF THIS AGREEMENT.

Should you have any questions concerning this Agreement or if you wish to contact the Company for any reason, please contact in writing at the address below.

Robin Short
Prentice Hall PTR
One Lake Street
Upper Saddle River, New Jersey 07458